CD and DVD Recording For Dummies®

Cheat Sheet

Sizing Up Today's DVD Media

Type	DVD-ROM Compatible *	Rewritable	Capacity per Side
DVD-R	Almost always	No	4.7GB
DVD-RAM	Usually not	Yes	5.2GB
DVD-RW	Almost always	Yes	4.7GB
DVD+RW	Almost always	Yes	4.7GB

* Several generations of DVD-ROM players are on the market; generally, the newer the player, the more compatible it is with all four of these media types.

Strengths and Weaknesses of "Those Interface Things"

Type	Internal or External	Plug and Play?	High-Speed?	Maximum Number of Devices per Cable
EIDE	Internal only	N/A	Yes	4
SCSI	Both	No	Yes	14
FireWire	External only	Yes	Yes	63
USB	External only	Yes	No	127
Parallel	External only	No	No	1

Mark's Common-Sense Installation Tips

- **Read the installation instructions!** Only the manufacturer's instructions can tell you whether to cut the blue wire or the red wire!

- **Take your time:** No one's looking over your shoulder with a stopwatch, so relax and follow the steps the right way the first time.

- **Keep those parts:** You're likely to remove small parts, so keep a bowl handy that can hold everything you remove. You need some of the parts when you reassemble your computer, and anything left over should be saved as spare parts for future upgrades and repairs.

- **Prepare your work surface:** If you're installing an internal drive, prepare a flat, soft, well-lighted surface — several sheets of newspaper on a table work fine.

- **Ask for help:** Got a hardware-knowledgeable friend or family member? Put 'em to work and buy 'em a meal.

CD and DVD Recording For Dummies®

Cheat Sheet

CD-ROM File Systems

Type	Platform	Long Filenames?	Suggested Use
Joliet	Windows	Yes	Recording for Windows
HFS	Macintosh	Yes	Recording for Mac operating system
Hybrid	Windows and Mac	Yes	Recording for both Windows and Mac operating systems
ISO 9660	All	No	Recording for any platform or operating system

Smart Tips for Buying Online

- **Never buy from an online Web store that doesn't offer a secure connection.** Look for the padlock icon on your Web browser's status bar before you enter your personal information and credit card number.
- **Beware of exorbitant shipping options.** If you can wait three or four days for your drive, choose the slowest delivery method and save your cash.
- **Watch for the words *refurbished* and *factory remanufactured*.** It may be cheap, but it's also used.
- **Avoid online Web stores that charge a restocking fee for unopened merchandise you return.**

Clearing Drive Space: Unnecessary Stuff You Can Delete

- **Demos, samples, and ancient files:** Say good-bye to ten-year-old game demos, one-shot software installations you no longer need, and unnecessary documents you've created yourself.
- **Log files:** You can delete files created by programs as they're running. As long as you don't need the information, you can safely get rid of things like virus-scanning files and disk diagnostic log files.
- **The contents of your Trash or Recycle Bin:** Don't forget to toss those files that are still tenaciously hanging on for possible "undeletion."
- **Typical browser refuse:** You can toss out images, Web pages, and sound files that your browser stores in its cache to speed things up when you reload a page. Your browser should provide a method of deleting these temporary cache files.
- **Windows temporary files:** If you're running Windows 98 or later, choose Start⇨Programs⇨Accessories⇨ System Tools⇨Disk Cleanup to run the Disk Cleanup Wizard; it will take care of those tacky temporary files created by practically every Windows program ever written.

Copyright © 2002 Wiley Publishing, Inc. All rights reserved.

Item 1627-2.

For more information about Wiley Publishing, call 1-800-762-2974.

For Dummies: Bestselling Book Series for Beginners

CD and DVD
Recording

FOR

DUMMIES®

CD and DVD Recording

FOR

DUMMIES®

by Mark L. Chambers

Wiley Publishing, Inc.

CD and DVD Recording For Dummies®

Published by
Wiley Publishing, Inc.
909 Third Avenue
New York, NY 10022
www.wiley.com

Copyright © 2002 Wiley Publishing, Inc., Indianapolis, Indiana

Published simultaneously in Canada

For general information on our other products and services or to obtain technical support, please contact our Customer Care Department within the U.S. at 800-762-2974, outside the U.S. at 317-572-3993, or fax 317-572-4002.

Wiley also publishes its books in a variety of electronic formats. Some content that appears in print may not be available in electronic books.

Library of Congress Cataloging-in-Publication Data:

Library of Congress Control Number: 2001096626

ISBN: 0-7645-1627-2

Manufactured in the United States of America

10 9 8 7 6 5 4 3

About the Author

Mark L. Chambers has been an author, a computer consultant, a BBS sysop, a programmer, and a hardware technician for more than 20 years. (In other words, he's been pushing computers and their uses far beyond "normal" performance limits for decades now.) His first love affair with a computer peripheral blossomed in 1984, when he bought his lightning-fast 300 bps modem — now he spends entirely too much time on the Internet and drinks far too much caffeine-laden soda. His favorite pastimes include collecting gargoyles, watching St. Louis Cardinals baseball, playing his three pinball machines and the latest computer games, supercharging computers, and rendering 3D flights of fancy with TrueSpace — and during all that, he listens to just about every type of music imaginable. (For those of his readers who are keeping track, he now has more than 1,200 audio CDs in his collection.)

With a degree in journalism and creative writing from Louisiana State University, Mark took the logical career choice and started programming computers; however, after five years as a COBOL programmer for a hospital system, he decided that there must be a better way to earn a living, and he became the documentation manager for Datastorm Technologies, a well-known communications software developer. Somewhere in between organizing and writing software manuals, Mark began writing computer books; his first book, *Running a Perfect BBS,* was published in 1994.

Along with writing several books a year and editing whatever his publishers throw at him, Mark has recently branched out into Web-based education, designing and teaching a number of online classes, called WebClinics, for Hewlett-Packard.

Mark's rapidly expanding list of books includes *Building a PC For Dummies, Scanners For Dummies, The Hewlett-Packard Official Printer Handbook, The Hewlett-Packard Official Recordable CD Handbook, The Hewlett-Packard Official Digital Photography Handbook, Computer Gamer's Bible, Recordable CD Bible, Teach Yourself the iMac Visually, Running a Perfect BBS, Official Netscape Guide to Web Animation,* and *Windows 98 Troubleshooting and Optimizing Little Black Book.*

His books have been translated into 12 different languages — his favorites are German, Polish, Dutch, and French. Although he can't read them, he enjoys the pictures a great deal.

Mark welcomes all comments and questions about his books — you can reach him at mark@mlcbooks.com or at his Web site: MLC Books Online, at http://home.mlcbooks.com.

Acknowledgments

In this, my third book on CD and DVD recording, I find that I'm again in debt to a number of great people at Hungry Minds. I'm noticing a pattern here, and I must say I like it!

As with all my books, I'd like to first thank my wife, Anne, and my children — Erin, Chelsea, and Rose — for their support and love and for letting me follow my dream!

No book would see the light of day without the Production team, this time led by project coordinator Nancee Reeves — starting with my words and adding a tremendous amount of work, they've once again taken care of artwork, proofreading, and countless steps that I can't fathom. Thanks to each of the team members for a beautiful book.

Next, my appreciation goes to my editorial manager, Constance Carlisle, and to my technical editor, Dennis Short, who checked the technical accuracy of every word — including that baker's dozen of absurd acronyms that crops up in every computer book I've ever written. Their work ensures that my work is the best it can be!

Finally, we come to the Big Two who have worked on this project since the beginning. I promised Bob Woerner, my acquisitions editor, the fewest number of gray hairs possible: I hope that I succeeded! Despite what many folks think, *Dummies* titles don't grow on trees. He was instrumental in launching this one. And this great title is the latest of my books guided by my favorite project editor, Rebecca Whitney, who checked the grammar and clarity of every word. Becky, you are the best, and that's why our books turn out so well! My heartfelt thanks to you both for another chance to put pen to paper — well, actually, fingers to keyboard!

Publisher's Acknowledgments

We're proud of this book; please send us your comments through our Hungry Minds Online Registration Form located at www.dummies.com/register

Some of the people who helped bring this book to market include the following:

Acquisitions, Editorial, and Media Development

Project Editor: Rebecca Whitney

Acquisitions Editor: Bob Woerner

Technical Editor: Dennis R. Short

Editorial Manager: Constance Carlisle

Editorial Assistant: Amanda M. Foxworth

Production

Project Coordinator: Nancee Reeves

Layout and Graphics: LeAndra Johnson, Jill Piscitelli, Erin Zeltner

Proofreaders: Valery Bourke, TECHBOOKS Production Services

Indexer: TECHBOOKS Production Services

General and Administrative

Wiley Technology Publishing Group: Richard Swadley, Vice President and Executive Group Publisher; Bob Ipsen, Vice President and Group Publisher; Joseph Wikert, Vice President and Publisher; Barry Pruett, Vice President and Publisher; Mary Bednarek, Editorial Director; Mary C. Corder, Editorial Director; Andy Cummings, Editorial Director

Wiley Manufacturing: Carol Tobin, Director of Manufacturing

Wiley Marketing: John Helmus, Assistant Vice President, Director of Marketing

Wiley Composition Services: Gerry Fahey, Vice President, Production Services; Debbie Stailey, Director of Composition Services

Contents at a Glance

Cartoons at a Glance

By Rich Tennant

page 7

"You know kids - you can't buy them just any CD creation software."

page 83

"Do you think the 'Hidden Rhino' clip should come before or after the 'Waving Hello' video clip?"

page 131

page 183

page 263

"Room service? Please send someone up to refresh the mini bar with CD-RW discs."

page 299

Cartoon Information:
Fax: 978-546-7747
E-Mail: richtennant@the5thwave.com
World Wide Web: www.the5thwave.com

Table of Contents

Introduction

● ●

*M*y first book on CD recording was published by Hungry Minds, Inc. (then IDG Books Worldwide) in 1997 — it was called *Recordable CD Bible,* and I'm proud to say that it was one of the first consumer books on the shelves that covered all aspects of the art. Yes, in those days, CD burning was indeed an art form! Recording software was still expensive and hard to handle, with no wizards to guide you. Drives were three or four times as expensive as they are now. It was all too easy to ruin a recording and burn a shiny, useless drink coaster. In fact, most computers literally weren't fast enough to deliver data to a recorder at the rate it demanded — I can vividly remember telling readers to drop their recording speed to 1x in many situations to avoid recording errors!

Everything has changed in the new millennium. Most PCs and Macs come with a recorder built-in, or you can practically buy one for pocket change. Recording formats, like packet-writing, and new hardware advances, like burnproofing, allow just about any PC to burn a disc without errors — not to mention that recording software has been refined to the point that it's virtually foolproof. (If all this sounds like I'm speaking in a foreign language, fear not: I cover it completely in the chapters to follow!)

So, if things are so easy and foolproof today, why did I decide to write a new *Dummies* book about CD and DVD recording? Because the challenge is still there! It has just shifted from "the art of successfully recording *anything*" to "the art of using your recorder to its full potential." Today, a CD or DVD recorder can produce everything from superb-sounding audio CDs to DVD-Video discs you can play in your home DVD player. More applications than ever are available for your recorded discs: digital photo albums, system backups, mixed data and audio CDs, and much, much more. I've written this book to introduce you to the entire range of discs you can produce and how to create each of them like an experienced expert.

Also, the road to perfect recording still isn't perfectly flat. For example, if you're buying and installing a drive, you still need all the information you can get. I still give you an entire glossary full of terms, formats, and crazy acronyms that you need to understand. (Go ahead — flip to the back of this book and check it out!) Just because your recording software doesn't display all those configuration settings on the main menu any more doesn't mean that they're not there, and sooner or later, you need to know what all those settings do.

That's the reason I wrote this book: It's for readers who want to know everything about recording, from top to bottom! As in my other *Dummies* books, I begin with the basics and lead you into advanced recording, with the tips and tricks you need added along the way. I promise to stick to the English language, so you don't need an engineer or a computer programmer handy to "decode" anything. Like any *Dummies* author, I get to be myself and use my sense of humor. This book is not your typical dry, dreary computer manual — I hope that this book is entertaining enough to read in the bathtub! (Just be careful not to drop it.)

What's Really Required

Forget the engineering degree and keep your wallet in your pocket (unless you haven't bought this book yet — if so, please proceed to the cashier and support a computer book author). I find that many folks have preconceived notions of what's needed to burn a great CD, so this gives me an opportunity to set things right. To wit, these are the requirements you *don't* need for this book:

- ✔ A decade of experience with computers, recording, hardware, or even software.

- ✔ An entire bank account to spend on expensive software. Most software I describe in this book either came with your recorder or can be bought as shareware for a few bucks — and some applications I cover are free for the asking!

- ✔ The latest drive on the market. If you've scavenged an older drive at a garage sale or on eBay, you're in good hands. I cover information, tips, and tricks that apply to older drives and their idiosyncrasies.

If you haven't bought your CD or DVD recorder yet, this book will become your trusted friend in a hurry! I cover each of the features you should consider plus how to install and configure your new toy.

About This Book

Each self-contained chapter in this book covers a specific topic relating to your recorder. Although you can begin reading anywhere or skip chapters at will (for example, if you've already installed your drive, you don't need that chapter), I think that reading from front to back makes the most sense — it's the whole linear-order thing, you know.

I've also included a glossary of all the computer and recording terms I cover in the text as well as an appendix with contact information for manufacturers of recorders and software.

Conventions Used in This Book

Like any other computer book, I have to ask that you type commands and click menu items from time to time. Luckily, *Dummies* books have a set of conventions that can help keep things clear.

Stuff you type

If you have to type a command within Windows or the Mac operating system, the text appears like this:

```
Type me
```

Press the Enter (or Return) key to process the command.

Menu commands

Menu commands you should use appear in the following format:

Edit⇨Copy

For example, this shorthand indicates that you should click the Edit menu and then choose the Copy menu item.

Display messages

Whenever I talk about messages you should see displayed onscreen, those messages look like this: `This is a message displayed by a program.`

In case you're curious about computers

I try to steer clear about much of what goes on underneath the suave exterior of your recorder — after all, computers are supposed to be getting easier to use, not harder. If you're like me, however, you sometimes like to know what makes something tick. Occasionally, you see sidebars that provide a little more technical background about what I'm discussing. Feel free to read these technical sidebars (or gleefully ignore them because I don't give you tests on this material afterward).

How This Book Is Organized

My editors demanded that I organize this book *somehow* — and because they have this contract thing I had to sign, I've divided the book into six major parts, with cross-references where appropriate. The book also has an index you can use to locate a specific topic.

The six parts are described in this section (in no particular order).

Part I: Shake Hands with Your Recorder!

This part familiarizes you with your CD or DVD recorder. You find out how both types of optical media work, what to look for (and what to avoid) when shopping for a new recorder and what you can do with DVD technology. I also have you installing your drive like a professional, even if you've never opened your computer's case before.

Part II: It's All in the Preparation

In this part, I discuss the preparations you should take before you burn your first disc. I show you how to optimize your computer's performance, how to select the right recording software for the job, and how to select the right configuration settings for the type of disc you want to record (things like the format, the organization, and the file system).

Part III: Hang On — Here We Go!

Here's where things get *really* good — we advance to recording typical audio CDs and data discs using Easy CD Creator (for the PC) and Toast (for the Mac). These discs are the "bread and butter" of most home recording projects, and you find out to use them by following step-by-step examples. I also show you how to use DirectCD, a program that can deliver effortless recording using the drag-and-drop convenience of Windows.

Part IV: So You're Ready to Tackle Tougher Stuff?

I cover the advanced ground in this part as I show you how to create video CDs, photo CDs, and DVD projects. I also demonstrate how to transfer your music from albums and cassettes to audio CDs. For that professional appearance, I show you how to print custom disc labels and box inserts, and I help you create a custom HTML menu system to spruce up your data CDs.

Part V: The Part of Tens

If you're a devoted fan of the *Dummies* series, you should immediately recognize these four chapters — they provide tips and advice on recording, including troubleshooting tips and software recommendations. Oh, and I also include my traditional chapter on Ten Things to Avoid Like the Plague — not to be missed!

Part VI: Appendixes

Here you can find a hardware and software manufacturers list and a glossary of computer terms and unwieldy acronyms.

Icons Used in This Book

Consider the icons in this book as signposts pointing at particularly important stuff.

Whenever you see the Tip icon, it's sure to be accompanied by information that saves you time, trouble, or cash.

Look to the handsome sign of the Scavenger for information on buying or using an older recorder.

Like the sidebars in this book, the Technical Stuff icon indicates material that is entirely optional: It's for folks with computer curiosity.

Like a roadside warning sign, potential trouble is up ahead. *Always* read the information next to this icon first to avoid damage to your hardware and software!

This information is the stuff you would see in the *CliffsNotes* version of this book. It's highlighter material that reminds you of something important.

Where to Go from Here

As I said earlier, I recommend that you read this book in linear order, but where you start depends on your knowledge (and whether you already have your recorder). To wit:

- ✔ If you're shopping for a recorder or you have yet to install your hardware, start with Part I. (That is also a good place to start if you're curious about how CD and DVD technology works.)

- ✔ If your recorder is already working, but you need help burning discs, start with Part II.

- ✔ In any other case, use the index, or jump straight to the chapter that holds the information you need. (Don't forget to check out the other chapters when you have time!)

I wish you the best of luck with your recording projects, and I hope that you find this book valuable. Be prepared to keep a spindle of 50 blank discs next to your computer!

Part I

Shake Hands with Your Recorder!

In this part . . .

It's always best to start at the beginning — and in this part I'll introduce you to your recorder, how stuff is saved to and read from a disc, and how DVDs and CDs are similar (and different). You'll learn about the features you need to evaluate when shopping for a new recorder, including strangeness like the speed of the drive, the type of connection it uses, and the size of the drive's recording buffer. I'll cover the latest advances in DVD recording (as well as explain all the confusing formats and technobabble). Finally, I'll close this part by showing you how to install your drive. (If that sounds rather like "And then I'll show you how to land the space shuttle," don't worry — all it takes is my tutorial and a screwdriver. In fact, you may not even need the screwdriver.)

Chapter 1

Optical Storage: It's All in the Pits

*W*hen's the last time you really looked at a CD? I mean *really* stared at it, in rapt fascination? Believe it or not, CDs used to be enthralling!

CDs are now a staple of the technical wonderland that you and I live in. Unless you're older and you were around long before 1980 — the days of disco, "Charlie's Angels," and Rubik's Cube — you won't remember the lure of the compact disc. In those dark times, before the introduction of CDs, music lived on huge, clunky vinyl albums. Computer software was loaded on floppy disks. Movies? They were kept on videotape (and still are, but not for long).

At first, this situation wasn't a bad one — at least until you kept these old-fashioned storage media for a year or two. Suddenly, you would find that those records had picked up scratches and pops. Computer programs were growing so large that they would span five or six floppies. And sooner or later, those floppy disks and movie videotapes could no longer be read reliably; after a mere 100 viewings or so, you would end up buying another copy of *Enter the Dragon*. (Okay, so I'm a big Bruce Lee fan. Substitute your favorite movie instead.)

Like a circular knight in shining armor, the arrival of the CD heralded the beginning of the digital consumer age. I'm not kidding; I can remember an entire room of technotypes jumping with excitement just to *see* their first compact disc! (None of us could afford an audio CD player, and computer CD-ROM drives hadn't arrived yet, but it was great just to see a real, live CD.)

In the beginning, audio CDs brought us crystal-clear sound and the convenience of jumping instantly from track to track. Then computer software suddenly fit on one CD, and the software could always be read reliably. Now, with the advent of DVD, movies are accompanied by luxuries like alternative soundtracks and interviews with the cast and director. Would you go back to anything less?

In this chapter, I introduce you to the basics of the compact disc: You don't have to know *all* this stuff before you jump into recording your own discs, but if you understand the basics of what's going on, you avoid mistakes. (Always be prepared.) I promise to tell you along the way about what you absolutely need to know. You find out how discs store information, video, and music as well as what's inside your CD or DVD recorder. I cover what types of media you can use and what you can store. Finally, I show you how to properly care for your optical pets. (You may not stare at CDs like I used to, but you still have to keep them clean.)

Always Begin with a Definition

In this case, let me start by defining the now-familiar term *CD-ROM* — short for *compact disc-read-only memory*. (I've shortened this to "CD" throughout this book, which will save about 200 trees by the time I've finished.) This high-tech description simply means that a CD stores information of some sort that your computer or audio CD player can read but can't write to (which makes the CD-ROM drive different from a hard drive, for example, which you can both read from and write to). In general, I use the word *disc* to describe both CD-ROM and DVD-ROM discs; both are similar, and they both look very much alike.

Keep that in mind: Whenever someone refers to just a CD-ROM or DVD-ROM drive (without using the word *recordable*), they're talking about the drives that just read discs and can't record them.

The basic specifications of both audio CDs and data CDs (those discs you use in your computer) are the same; they're 12 centimeters in diameter and a millimeter thick, and they have an opaque top and reflective bottom. Such is the Tao of the disc.

As you can see in Figure 1-1, however, the structure of a mass-produced disc isn't a single piece of plastic. It's made up of a number of layers, each of which has something special to add to the mix:

Figure 1-1:
And you
thought that
a CD was
just a piece
of plastic!

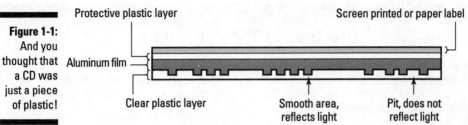

Protective plastic layer

Aluminum film

Screen printed or paper label

Clear plastic layer

Smooth area,
reflects light

Pit, does not
reflect light

✔ **A label:** Commercially manufactured discs you buy in the store have screen-printed labels; these graphics are created from layers of ink applied one on top of the other (like that Metallica T-shirt you may be wearing).

What's that, you say? You don't have $2,000 or so to spend on a special CD screen printer? (Come to think of it, neither do I!) In that case, do what I do and use your inkjet or laser printer to create a fancy paper label, complete with the graphics and text you choose (more on this topic in Chapter 14).

"Do I really need a label?" To be honest, no. A disc you've recorded works fine without one. However, if you've ever dug through a 6-inch stack of unlabeled CDs to find that *Andy Williams Greatest Hits* disc you burned a month ago for Aunt Harriet, I *guarantee* that you will understand. If you don't need a professional look and you're not into appearances, just use a CD marking pen and scribble a quick title on top. Most recordable discs have blank lines printed on them for just this purpose. You can pick up one of these handy pens at any office supply store, but make sure that you buy a pen designed especially for marking CDs.

✔ **Opaque plastic:** You need something to protect the top of the disc. I suppose that you could use steel, but then a disc would weigh two pounds and cost much more — therefore, add a layer of scratch-resistant plastic.

✔ **Aluminum film:** Mass-produced CDs use a thin layer of aluminum that's covered with microscopic indentations called *pits*. These pits are arranged in a single, tiny groove that spirals around the disc, just like the groove on one of those antique record albums. (If something works, why mess with it?) However, the groove on a CD starts at the center and spirals to the outside of the disc, so it goes in the opposite direction.

✔ **More plastic:** Again, you have to protect that shiny aluminum — however, in this case, the plastic must be crystal-clear (for reasons that soon become apparent). Here's a hint: It has to do with the passage of laser light.

Dig that crazy acronym!

I have to use a truckload of acronyms in this book — luckily, each one has only one meaning, right? Almost! One strange exception applies: You may be wondering what DVD stands for, and as the mondo author expert, I *should* be able to tell you.

When DVD-ROM technology was first introduced, everyone agreed that it stood for *digital versatile disc-read-only memory* because it could store so many types of data. Although a CD can store music and computer files, it doesn't have the room for a full-length movie at the highest-quality level. You find out later in this chapter that you can cram a huge amount of cool stuff on a DVD-ROM, so it was the first

optical media to hold all the different types of digital information we use today. Hence, the word *versatile,* and everyone seemed happy.

At some point, however, those first owners of DVD-ROM players who weren't acronym aficionados decided that DVD stood for *digital video disc* — and for a time that was true because DVDs were first used for only movies. This name situation leaves us in a quandary because more and more folks think *video* rather than *versatile.* Naturally, it doesn't matter a hoot because everyone just uses the acronym anyway, but it does make a great killer trivia question!

As I mention earlier in this chapter, this yummy sandwich is a cross-section of a commercial CD produced at a factory — the discs you record are different in one important way, which I cover in a minute.

How Is Data Recorded on CDs and DVDs?

Consider just how audio, video, and computer files are stored on CD. Although these three types of information are different, they're stored in the same way: digitally. But what does that word really mean?

Programmers, technotypes, and hardware jockeys use the word *digital* when they're talking about *binary,* the language used by computers around the world. Unlike the imprecise languages spoken and written by mere humans, binary data is built from only two values — zero and 1, which are often referred to as Off and On, as shown in Figure 1-2. (In fact, a computer is only a huge collection of switches, but that's another story.) Therefore, computer files and digital music are a long line of zeros and ones. If you sat next to a light switch for 100 years and flipped it off and on in the proper sequence, you would have the visual version of a digital song from a CD (and a bad headache along with incredibly sore fingers).

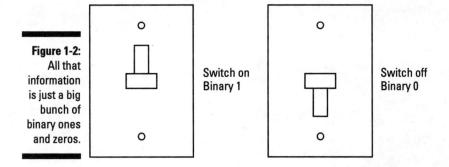

Figure 1-2:
All that information is just a big bunch of binary ones and zeros.

Switch on
Binary 1

Switch off
Binary 0

Now that you're privy to the binary master plan, you can see how the absence and presence of light perfectly represents binary data — things are either dark in a room or bright. The geniuses who developed CD technology took this concept one step further! They had the great idea of using a laser beam to read the binary data stored on a disc, and that's where those pits in the aluminum layer that I mention in the preceding section take center stage.

Figure 1-3 shows how the binary data is read: when the laser beam hits a pit on the surface of the CD, the beam scatters, so most of it isn't reflected back (hence, darkness, which in this case stands for a zero in binary data). If the laser beam hits one of the flat surfaces — they're called *lands,* by the way — the beam is reflected cleanly back, and the drive senses that reflected light. (Think of a one in binary.) And, ladies and gentlemen, that is why the bottom of a CD shines like a mirror; the rainbow effect is caused by the microscopic groove that runs across the surface. Naturally, this process happens very fast (I talk about speed in Chapter 2), but that's really all there is to it.

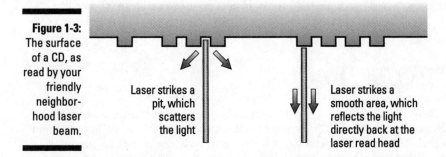

Figure 1-3:
The surface of a CD, as read by your friendly neighborhood laser beam.

Laser strikes a
pit, which
scatters
the light

Laser strikes a
smooth area, which
reflects the light
directly back at the
laser read head

Essentially, DVD technology works the same way — with a difference or two. A DVD-ROM disc can hold the approximate equivalent of seven CDs, and Figure 1-4 shows why: The pits on a DVD-ROM are much smaller and are packed closer together on the surface of the disc, and the drive uses a much more powerful laser beam to read them. DVD discs can also have multiple reflective layers, so data can be stored on both sides.

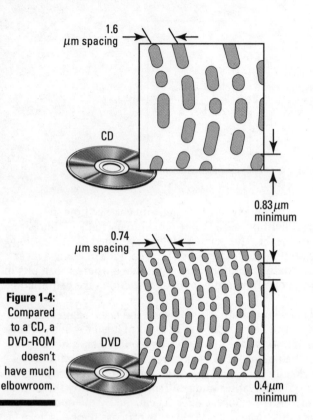

1.6
µm spacing

CD

0.83 µm
minimum

0.74
µm spacing

DVD

0.4 µm
minimum

Figure 1-4:
Compared
to a CD, a
DVD-ROM
doesn't
have much
elbowroom.

Believe it or not, the DVD specification standard provides for 2-sided DVD-ROM discs that have *two* layers on each side, for more than 27 CDs' worth of storage space on a single DVD-ROM! However, these discs are so hard to manufacture that they're on the endangered species list, and I've never seen one.

It's All in the Dye

Consider the structure of recordable discs, which includes both recordable CDs and recordable DVDs. Remember the aluminum film? Sounds permanent, doesn't it? Indeed it is, which is why you can't use commercially manufactured discs to record your own data; your recorder has to be able to create the equivalent of pits and lands in some other way. (Not even Bill Gates has a CD-R manufacturing plant in his house.)

Why all the different colors?

I get asked this question all the time. Some CD-R discs are gold with a green dye, and others are silver with a blue dye. Everything acts the same: You're just looking at two different recipes for the dye used by different manufacturers. Most drives record on either type of disc, but in rare situations an older drive seems to work better with one or the other color combination.

Personally, I think that it has something to do with the alignment of the planets and the phase of the moon, but I must report what I hear.

On the other hand, CD-RW and DVD discs all use the same type of dye, so they're all colored the same.

Figure 1-5 shows the answer as well as a really bad pun. The CD-R (short for *compact disc-recordable*) disc, which can be recorded once, uses a layer of green or blue reactive dye under a smooth reflective surface of either aluminum or gold. The groove is still there, but until the disc has been recorded, the disc is perfectly empty. This dye permanently melts or darkens when hit by a laser beam of a certain frequency, which results in a pit.

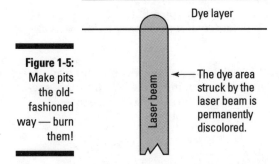

Figure 1-5:
Make pits the old-fashioned way — burn them!

"Hang on, Mark — wouldn't the beam from my regular read-only CD-ROM drive cause problems?" Good question, but the designers of recordable CD and DVD drives have you covered. The laser beam that is used to read a CD is far less powerful than the beam used to record one; therefore, when the beam from the laser in your CD-ROM drive hits one of these dark spots, the beam is swallowed like an apple pie at a state fair, so it acts just like a pit in a mass-produced CD. In fact, your CD-ROM drive can't tell the difference.

The inside of your CD or DVD recorder sounds like it's getting a little crowded with all these different laser beams, but it's really not. A recorder has a beam that can be set at two levels: a lower power setting that can read a disc and a higher setting to record it. Slick, eh?

A CD-RW disc, which is short for *compact disc-rewritable,* is another story. (Get ready: You're going to *love* this description. It honestly sounds like something out of "Star Trek" — the original series, not any of those later failures that don't have Captain Kirk.) Here goes: A CD-RW disc uses a "phase change recording process" using a "crystalline layer with amorphous properties" rather than a dye layer. Didn't I tell you? It sounds like something Spock would say! You can promptly forget that stuff because nobody cares and no one gives a test afterward.

Anyway, although the crystalline layer starts out clear, the correct type of laser beam can change it to opaque, creating — you guessed it — a pit. When you're ready to erase the disk, that same beam of laser light "resets" the crystalline layer to clear again, and you're ready to record all over again. Talk about recycling!

Behind the Curtain: Inside CD-RW and DVD Drives

Before I delve into the depths of your CD hardware, I want to make one thing perfectly clear: *You do not have to read this section!* In fact, if raising the hood on your car and just looking at the engine gives you a headache, I encourage you to skip this section entirely. It's definitely not necessary to know what makes your drive tick.

Still here? I didn't scare you away? Good! If you're like me, and cool machinery like your recorder fascinates you, stick with me and read on! In this section, I show you the interior guts of your CD-RW (or DVD) recorder.

The motor

Because pits are arranged around the entire disc, something has to turn that CD — in this case, an efficient, high-speed electric motor. (No coal or gas here, Bucko.) The motor turns a spindle, which holds the disc by the hole in the center — yet another similarity to vinyl record albums!

The laser stuff

A read-only CD-ROM or DVD-ROM drive has a laser read head, and a recorder has both a read head and a record head. When you read a disc, the laser beam is focused through a lens upward toward the surface of the disc; if the beam is reflected by a land, the light travels through a prism to an optical pickup. In turn, the pickup yells to your computer — in effect — "Hey, I just passed a land back there, so add a 1 to the file."

The record head doesn't need a prism or fancy optics; it's just there to burn, baby, burn. As I mention earlier in this chapter, a more powerful laser beam simply travels up to the surface of the disc and creates a pit by discoloring or melting the dye layer in one tiny spot.

How do these two heads get around the entire surface of the disc? They're on a moving track that can move forward and back between the center and outside edge of the disc.

The tray

The tray is self explanatory, but still pretty doggone important: You need some method of inserting and ejecting discs. Although most drives use a tray that extends to hold the disc, some integrated CD-RW and DVD drives use a slot with a motor-loading system that draws the disc inside the drive (just like a car audio CD player). Older drives used a thin plastic box called a *caddy* — you opened the caddy and stuck the disc inside. Although you would be hard pressed to find a new CD-RW recorder that uses a caddy, some high-capacity DVD-RAM recorders now use them to help protect the disc.

The controls

Your recorder is certain to have an eject button and probably also a headphone jack and volume control for listening to audio CDs. More expensive drives can go a step further with more audio CD controls, like Pause, Play, Next Track, and Previous Track.

The emergency hole

I know that it sounds weird, but every drive has an *emergency disc eject hole.* Think of it as being similar to the ejection seat in a jet fighter plane or one of those cool emergency airlock controls that crops up in every science fiction horror movie. (How many times now has Sigourney Weaver blasted something nasty into space by slapping a button?) You can use this microscopic hole on the front of your drive to forcibly eject a disc whenever your drive has locked up or if a disc is caught inside. To use the emergency eject, push the end of a paper clip or a piece of stiff wire into this hole. This technique usually works even when there's no power to the drive.

Love Those Discs: CD-R, CD-RW, DVD-R, and DVD-RAM

If you've been reading this chapter at a single sitting, you may have a media-induced headache by now. No, I'm not talking about the nightly TV news — I mean the four different kinds of discs I mention from time to time in this chapter. You may have read a little about CD-R and CD-RW in this chapter, but it's high time that I identify each of the four and fill in all the details. This section does just that.

"Hey, can't I buy just one drive?"

Ah, there's the rub: At the time this book was written, it was still hard to find just one drive that writes more than one or two of these formats. There are exceptions, like the SuperDrive, from Apple, which ships on its high-end Power Mac G4 and can record CD-R, CD-RW, and DVD-R. Other drives from Samsung and Ricoh have appeared as well. Until this technology drops significantly in price, however, you're still restricted to either recordable CD or recordable DVD — and, if you're already the proud owner of a CD-RW drive, I can assure you that it can't be upgraded to record DVDs.

First on the block: CD-R

In the beginning, there was the CD-R disc, and it's still by far the most popular media on the market. A typical CD-R disc can store anywhere from 650 to 700MB (megabytes) of computer data or 74 to 80 minutes of audio. (The higher numbers are for higher-capacity, 80-minute CD-R discs.) You can also stack more stuff on a CD-R disc using the overburning feature; read more on this rather nasty-sounding feature in Chapter 2. As I mention earlier in this chapter, after you've filled a CD-R to capacity, there's no turning back; the data is permanently recorded and can't be erased.

Other sizes of CD discs are indeed available — for example, discs with a diameter of 8 centimeters that can hold 184MB — but they're so specialized that you and I can safely ignore them.

CD-R discs are the most compatible optical media. Any CD-ROM drive — no matter how old — can read CD-R discs, and they're the only discs that play in your home or car audio CD player. In other words, use CD-R whenever

✔ You're recording a disc to send to someone else.

✔ You're recording an audio CD for playing on anything other than your recorder.

✔ You're not sure whether a drive reads a CD-RW disc.

Reusable and loving it: CD-RW

The CD-RW disc is the most common rewritable media on the market right now. It can store 650MB or 74 minutes of audio. A CD-RW must be formatted before you use it, just like a floppy disk or your hard drive; most discs come preformatted from the manufacturer. You also have to reformat the disc if you want to erase its contents.

Did you read about the amorphous crystalline stuff I mention earlier in this chapter? On the positive side, that's what allows your CD-RW drive to erase the disc and use it again. On the downside, however, most read-only CD-ROM drives that are older than three or four years old can't read a CD-RW disc, and a CD-RW disc can't be used in an audio CD player. Use CD-RW whenever

✔ You're recording a disc for use on your computer, like a backup.

✔ You're sure that another CD-ROM drive can read a CD-RW disc.

How can you tell if a CD-ROM drive can read CD-RW discs? Many manufacturers add a MultiRead symbol to their faceplates; if you're still unsure, try reading a recorded CD-RW disc in the drive (don't worry — you won't hurt the hardware). If you can load files from the CD-RW disc, you have a MultiRead drive.

Ready for stardom: DVD-R

Perhaps I shouldn't say "ready for stardom" — heck, in the video world, the DVD-ROM disc is already fast overtaking the traditional VHS tape. (I don't suppose that makes Betamax VCR owners feel any better, but every dog has his day.) DVD-ROM is also poised to take over the reign of CD as the media of choice for virtually every new computer on the planet. But what about recordable DVD?

Unfortunately, things are still a little tenuous in the world of recordable DVD standards. However, two format standards are now in use and are (in my opinion) destined to win any turf battles. Luckily, they correspond pretty closely to the world of recordable CDs.

The first of these standards is the DVD-R disc, which is short for — you guessed it — *DVD-recordable*. Like your old friend the CD-R, a DVD-R disc can be recorded only once, although it can hold either a whopping 4.7GB per side of the disc (that's gigabytes, friends and neighbors), for a total of 9.4GB of data on a double-sided disc. DVD-R is the darling of the video-editing crowd because it allows you to record a disc that can be used in a standard DVD player. Naturally, the discs you create with a DVD-R drive can't be read on a standard CD-ROM drive.

The rewritable warehouse: DVD-RAM

Along with CD-RW discs, you find DVD-RAM discs — a rewritable disc that can store as much as 9.4GB of data using both sides. (By the way, a double-sided DVD doesn't have a standard label; printing can appear only around the spindle hole. You may have already noticed it if you have a DVD player because many DVD movies have a wide-screen version of the film on one side and a standard-ratio version on the other side.)

Like DVD-R, DVD-RAM is well established. It's a great option for storing those huge digital video files, and because DVD-RAM discs are reusable, I find them the best media for backing up my hard drives. Note, however, that most DVD-ROM players can't read a DVD-RAM disc, so use DVD-R if you're recording something to distribute to others.

Clouds on the horizon: DVD-RW and DVD+RW

No, that's not a typo: Two other standards are just arriving on the DVD scene. Although DVD-RW and DVD+RW are similar standards, they're being touted by two different sets of computer hardware manufacturers. I suppose that they needed two different names — but couldn't they have chosen something easier to remember? (Whatever happened to the guy who chose the name Microsoft Bob for an operating system? I still have my copy.)

Anyway, DVD-RW and DVD+RW discs can store 4.7GB, and a DVD-ROM player can read both types of discs. However, whereas a DVD-RW disc can be rewritten only 1,000 times, a DVD+RW disc has no limit on the number of times you can reuse it.

Again, these two standards are in a state of flux, so if you're keen on using a standard that's here to stay, I recommend that you stick with DVD-R and DVD-RAM for the foreseeable future.

What's Wrong with Tape, Disks, and Removable Media?

Nothing, really! It's just that they're antique technologies compared to rewritable CDs and DVDs. In this section, I list the most important reasons that optical beats magnetic hands-down.

I strongly recommend that you *never keep any data of value stored exclusively on floppy disks!* They are the most unreliable media on the planet — they're easily demagnetized, they don't hold much, and they often can't be read by other computers.

More reliable

First (and to many folks, most important), a CD-RW or DVD-RAM disc provides permanent storage with a high degree of reliability. Unlike magnetic media — including tape cartridges, floppy disks, and even Zip disks and hard drives — a CD or DVD doesn't stretch or demagnetize. As long as you keep your discs clean, reasonably cool, and free from scratches, you should be able to read them without error for a century or more. (I don't know about you, but I don't know just how important my tax returns will be in 100 years; then again, I want my priceless family photographs to last as long as possible!) A disc has no moving parts to wear out, and they don't rust.

Higher capacity

Forget about storing 700MB of data on a floppy disk! Even Jaz and Orb drives, which can record as much as 2.2GB on a cartridge, are simply no match for the 9.4GB capacity of a double-sided DVD-RAM disc. All that room comes in handy for backing up your system's hard drive, too.

Cheaper

Have you priced a stack of 50 blank, 700MB CD-R discs these days? At the time I wrote this book, I could find that 50-pack all over the Internet at $30; a 50-pack of 650MB CD-RW discs is about $70. DVD-RAM prices are hovering around $35 to $45 for a 9.4GB disc, and 4.7GB DVD-R discs are selling for about $10.

As you can imagine, the lower the cost per megabyte for a storage method, the better, and no other type of media can beat recordable CDs and DVDs. And, if the current trend continues, prices will just drop lower. Ain't life grand?

Faster and more convenient

If you've ever waited for a tape to rewind or a floppy disk to load, you've wished for a faster method of loading your stuff — CDs and DVDs feature fast access time, and there's no rewinding. To put it another way, even if something did fit in the tight space of a floppy disk, would you want to run that program from that floppy? Unlike tape drives — which must move linearly from one section of tape to another — you can jump directly from one part of a disc to another instantly. Take my word for it, it makes restoring files from a backup *much* faster!

Compatibility

Virtually every PC that's still running these days has a CD-ROM drive, so compatibility is a big advantage to recordable CD for folks like software developers, network administrators, and your Uncle Milton. To put it another way: Ever tried to stick a Zip disk into your car audio player? 'Nuff said.

"What Do I Need in Order to Record?"

You knew that there would be a catch, didn't you? You're probably thinking, "I bet that I have to have a $1,000 software program and a cutting-edge computer to record discs." Not true, good reader, not true! It used to be that way in the ancient mid-1990s, but CD and DVD recorders are now tame and lovable creatures. They ask for only the basics — in fact, if your computer came with a CD-RW drive already installed, you can skip this section because you're likely to have everything you need.

What you need for Windows

Here's a list of the basic minimum requirements you need for recording on a PC running Windows 95, Windows 98, or Windows Me:

- ✔ **A Pentium II PC (or better):** You need at least 64MB of memory and 1GB of free hard drive space.

- ✔ **A CD or DVD recorder:** Naturally, you also need the proper connection. Internal recorders use EIDE or SCSI connections. External recorders can use SCSI, USB, or FireWire connections. If you're using an external drive, it should come with the necessary cables you need.

- ✔ **Recording software:** Most recorders come bundled with some sort of software; if your computer already has a recorder, it probably also came with the programs you need to burn your discs.

- ✔ **Blank media:** Naturally.

What you need for the Macintosh

Here's a list of the basic minimum recording requirements for a Macintosh running Mac OS 8, Mac OS 9, or Mac OS X:

- ✔ **A PowerPC Mac of any speed with at least 64MB of memory and 1GB of free hard drive space**

- ✔ **A CD or DVD recorder:** Most Macs use external recorders with SCSI, USB, or FireWire connections.

- ✔ **Recording software:** Apple makes some of the best recording software around, and other commercial recording programs are available.

- ✔ **Blank media:** Gotta have it.

If all this talk of connections is making you nervous, don't worry: It's all covered in rich detail in Chapters 2 and 3, including what you need to know before you buy and before you install a drive.

"What Kind of Discs Can I Record?"

This question is the easiest of all to answer: Everything! If you can use it on a computer, listen to it in your stereo's CD player, or watch it on your DVD player, you can record it using either a CD or DVD recorder.

Later in this book, I take you step-by-step through the creation of different types of discs; for now, this section gives you an overview.

Briefcase backup

Never heard of that term? It's my own; I always carry a Briefcase backup when I'm traveling with my laptop. Because my computer has a CD-ROM drive (and the notoriously small hard drive found on most laptops), I record on a CD-R any files that are specific to my trip. PowerPoint presentations, Word files, contracts, digital audio and video — even an offline copy of my Web site — they all fit on a Briefcase backup. Therefore, my trip-specific data doesn't take up space on my laptop's hard drive, and it's protected from damage. Plus, copying any of that data to my client's computer if necessary is a cinch: No cables, no network configuration — just pop the disc in and read files and programs directly! (My Mom always said that I had potential.)

Computer files and data of all sorts

If it can be stored on your hard drive, you can store it on CD or DVD as well. This includes

- Files and programs
- Digital images
- Sound clips
- Web sites
- Backups

Digital audio

With a CD-RW drive, you can record standard audio CDs for use in any audio CD player as well as "mixed" CDs that have both audio and computer data. Plus, you can extract, or *rip*, tracks from existing audio CDs and record them on a new disc in any order you choose.

Digital video

A CD-RW drive can create standard video CDs for your video CD player, and a DVD-R drive can create interactive DVD discs with your own digital video.

Network storage

If you have data that is accessed often but never changed on your home or office network, record that stuff to a CD-R and load it in your file server's CD-ROM drive. (Getting your network administrator's help with this process is a good idea — those folks get very nervous about such initiatives.) Now you can still access every byte of those files, but you're not using precious disk space and you don't have to worry about backing that information up.

Photo discs

You can use your CD-RW drive to create slideshow discs with images from your digital camera or with scanned photographs.

Caring for Your Optical Pets

I tell you earlier in this chapter about how CD and DVD are nearly perfect storage media — but notice the word *nearly*. You have two or three outstanding methods of ruining a disc; the trick is not to become proficient at any of them, so in this last section I cover the best ways to use, clean, and store your discs.

You gotta grip 'em by the rim!

Let me sound like your mother for a second: Take a good, close look at your hands! When was the last time you washed them? Reading data from a disc covered in fingerprints and dust is a touch-and-go process at best because the laser beam has to get through all that crud twice (especially on DVDs because the data is packed even closer together). Therefore, you must find out how to hold a disc properly.

In my travels, I've encountered two methods of comfortably holding a disc for a decent length of time. You can even jog or tap dance using these holds — whatever floats your boat. Either hold the disc by the outside edge, as shown in Figure 1-6 or — if your fingers are small enough — create your own "spindle" using a convenient finger, as shown in Figure 1-7.

The idea behind these holds is simple: Never touch the underside of a disc, and never put a disc down on any surface. Flipping a disc over and setting it label side down for a second or two is okay, but put the disc back in its case as soon as possible.

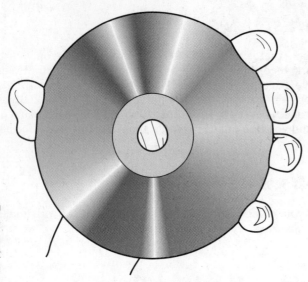

Figure 1-6:
I call this the Wilt Chamberlain hold.

Fingers grip on outside edge

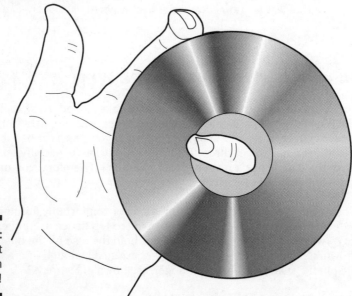

Figure 1-7:
Look, Aunt Harriet, I'm a spindle!

The deadly enemies

To keep your disks safe and avoid skips or data read errors, shelter them from these archvillains:

- **Pointed objects:** Scratches are taboo, and that goes for either side of a disc.

- **Heat:** How would you like to spend a hot summer afternoon in a closed car, baking on the seat? Underneath all that high-tech, a disc is basically a circle of plastic. Keep your discs cool and out of direct sunlight.

- **Surface crud:** This includes liquids, dust, dirt, and peanut butter.

You may have seen one or more CD laser lens cleaners at your local computer store; they usually look something like a disc with a little hairbrush mounted on it. *Never use one of these cleaners on a CD or DVD recorder — it can damage the laser!* In fact, the laser read and write heads inside a recorder need no maintenance.

The Disc Hotel

So where should you put all your recorded discs? Stacking them in a big pile in front of your monitor is one answer, but it's the *wrong* answer. Your discs must be protected from dust and scratches! Of course, storing discs in their jewel boxes is a good idea — that is, until you have an entire 200-disc stand filled up, and it takes up an entire corner of your room! Take a tip from me: You can save that space and still provide the protection your disks need with a disc binder, as shown in Figure 1-8. A binder has individual pockets for anywhere from 10 to 250 discs, so you can donate your jewel boxes to your friends.

Figure 1-8:
A true
technotype
uses a disc
binder to
save space.

Sometimes you've just gotta wipe

You may say "I've seen an entire shelf full of CD cleaning stuff. Do my discs need cleaning?" If a disc is only dusty, I recommend a lint-free photographer's lens cloth, which you can pick up at any camera shop. You can also pick up a spray bottle of disc cleaning fluid for liquid disasters, like those unavoidable soda stains. Other than a cloth and some fluid, however, you can leave all the expensive James Bond contrivances on the shelf at the department store.

To close this chapter on a high note, Figure 1-9 illustrates how to wipe a disc: Start at the center spindle hole and wipe straight toward the outside of the disc, making sure that you apply no more than fingertip pressure. Wiping harder — or wiping in a circular motion, as shown in Figure 1-10 — can scratch your disc and invite chaos into its ordered world of ones and zeros.

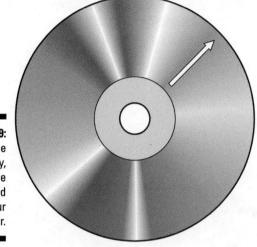

Wipe a CD from the center to the edge in a straight motion

Figure 1-9: Wipe correctly, and the digital world is your oyster.

If you wipe a disc like this, you're asking for trouble

Figure 1-10: Wipe incorrectly, and your data eventually shows you the door.

Chapter 2

Buying Your CD Recording Beast

● ●

In This Chapter

▶ Choosing an internal or external drive

▶ Selecting the right interface

▶ Understanding recorder read and write speeds

▶ Shopping for the right features

▶ Understanding CD-ROM formats

▶ Selecting the right software

▶ Choosing a used recorder

▶ Buying your recorder locally

▶ Buying your recorder online

● ●

Despite the rumors you may have heard, buying a CD recorder in the modern world is no longer a dreadful experience (at least, not with this book by your side). In days past, you would be at the mercy of that fast-moving predator of the electronics store — the computer salesperson — who would either turn on the high-pressure hose and sell you the most expensive drive on the planet or stand motionless with hands in pockets, oblivious to the answers to any of your questions. I know friends who still bear the emotional and psychological scars of such an attack.

Today, however, you may never even enter a brick-and-mortar store to buy your drive; if you're on the Web, you can choose from literally hundreds of online stores. You can shop 24 hours a day, at your leisure, and you have all the time you need to compare features and prices. It's paradise for those of us who are ready to purchase online.

If your CD or DVD recorder is already installed and comfortable, you don't need this chapter (although you still may want to read it to brush up on what's available). If your computer came with a CD-RW, DVD-R, or DVD-RAM drive, feel free to skip to Chapter 5. If, on the other hand, you're shopping for a CD or DVD recorder, you should devour every word to come.

In this chapter, I cover everything you need to know about buying a CD-RW drive, including the features you should covet, the differences between internal and external drives, what type of connection you need, and the formats your drive should record. Almost all the stuff in this chapter also applies to DVD recorders. Take copious notes or just circle the important stuff directly in this book — whatever floats your boat.

I also provide you with tips on online shopping, which has both its peaks and its pitfalls. Finally, I even cover a few pointers on how to face those salespeople sharks head-on at your local store and *win*. (As my favorite actor, Jack Nicholson, croons in the film *Batman,* "Wait 'til they get a load of me — ooooOOOOooooop.")

Enough talk. Let's go shopping.

Internal or External: Thinking Outside the Box

Your first choice to make in your trip down Hardware Boulevard is a simple one, yet it has the most effect on the price and performance of a recorder. If you've never run across these terms, an *internal* drive lives inside your computer (just like your floppy drive or your existing read-only CD-ROM drive). An *external* drive sits outside your computer, using a power cord of its own and a connection of some sort to your computer's case (like the HP external CD-RW drive shown in Figure 2-1).

Figure 2-1: The HP CD-Writer Plus 8210e external CD-RW drive is ready to go solo.

Stay inside with internal

Why not pick an internal drive? Most folks do, and here are the reasons why:

✔ **Convenient:** Your drive is built-in to your computer, without an extra power cord to mess with and some sort of connection cable to boot.

✔ **Fast:** Depending on the interface (read more about this party topic in the next section), most internal drives are faster than their external brethren.

✔ **Cheap:** Also, an internal drive is usually less expensive than an external unit because it's not carrying around its home like a digital hermit crab.

Breathe the open air with external

For some computers (for example, laptops and the stylish Apple iMac and G4 Cube), you have to pick an external drive because you have literally no room to install a recorder. (I don't recommend the hacksaw route.) However, a number of good reasons explain why an external recorder would appeal to even the stodgiest PC owner:

✔ **It saves a bay:** To explain, a *bay* is an internal space inside your PC's case where you can add devices. Most desktop PCs have several of them, but technowizards and power users can easily fill up every bay with other gadgets. Because the case has no room inside, an external drive suddenly looks sexy and attractive (at least to them).

✔ **It's easy to install:** Afraid to open your computer's case? Believe me — you are not alone, and you have no reason to be embarrassed. Adding an external drive means that you can leave your desktop alone, and it may even be easier than installing an internal drive — if you choose a USB or FireWire drive, for example, the process is as simple as plugging in a connector and the power cord. (Read more about USB and FireWire later in this chapter, in the section "'Edna, He Says We Need an Interface'.")

If you want to conquer your fear of computer hardware and delve inside your PC's case, let me recommend another of my books, conveniently titled *Building a PC For Dummies,* 3rd Edition, from Hungry Minds, Inc. In the process of showing you how to build an entire computer (yes, the whole ball of wax), I cover the complete process of adding all sorts of internal hardware, including an internal CD recorder.

✔ **It's portable:** Everyone in the building can share your recorder, perhaps as a backup device or to carry along with laptops. (By the way, you can also lock up an external drive to keep it from being carried away, if you get my drift.)

Here's the bottom line: Unless your computer simply doesn't have room or you don't want to open it, I would save money and stick with an internal recorder.

"Edna, He Says We Need an Interface"

Geez, what a word. It sounds like something you would hear from an engineer — ack! — but the word *interface* really has a simple and straightforward meaning: It's the type of connection you use to unite your computer and your recorder in everlasting friendship (at least until you unplug them).

In this section, I help you determine which of these exotic connections is for you.

EIDE

The first connection I cover is the most popular for PC owners all over the world — which, naturally, is why I want to begin with EIDE. Because it's not a freedom-loving English word, it must therefore be one of those doggone acronyms; in this case, EIDE stands for Enhanced Integrated Drive Electronics. Unfortunately, EIDE drives don't come in external form, so if you need an external drive, you can skip to the next interface.

Virtually all desktop PCs built today use EIDE hard drives and read-only CD-ROM drives. To handle the workload, your PC likely has both a primary and secondary EIDE connector; each of these connectors supports two EIDE devices, so you have the capacity for a total of four EIDE drives. If you already have one hard drive and one read-only CD-ROM drive in your computer, you're using only two of those four connections.

EIDE drives are simpler and cheaper to install than SCSI and are a good pick for most home PCs.

SCSI

This time, the evil acronym is short for Small Computer System Interface. SCSI is significantly faster and more efficient than a typical EIDE drive, and a single SCSI card can connect anywhere from 8 to 14 different devices — which is great if you plan to expand your computer to help NASA with the space shuttle. (Seriously, a real power user can add things like scanners and tape drives to a SCSI connection.) SCSI drives are available in both internal and external form. If you have an older Macintosh computer, it likely has an external SCSI port.

Unfortunately, SCSI is harder to configure than EIDE because a number of settings have to be made correctly for anything to work. Also, a SCSI recorder is usually significantly more expensive than its EIDE counterpart.

SCSI drives are a good choice for the experienced PC or Mac owner who's willing to spend a little more for better performance and all those extra connections — but be prepared to spend more time configuring and fine-tuning.

USB

At least this acronym is only three letters long. It stands for Universal Serial Bus, a connection type that's used exclusively for external drives. Let me be honest with you: USB is the best thing to happen to PC and Mac owners since the invention of canned air. Yes, believe it or not, the same USB drive can be used by both types of computers, and Figure 2-2 shows how simple it is to connect.

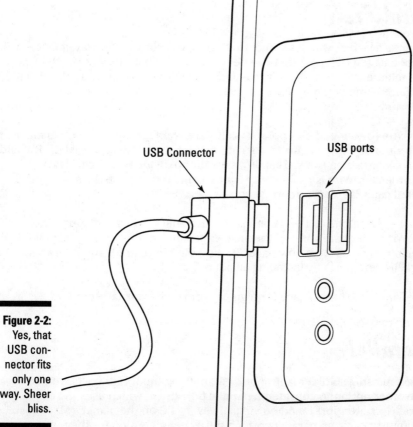

USB Connector   USB ports

Figure 2-2:
Yes, that
USB con-
nector fits
only one
way. Sheer
bliss.

USB is *Plug and Play,* which means that you don't have to reboot your computer when you connect a USB recorder. Plus, your computer automatically recognizes that USB drive, so you have nothing to fiddle with or set. Many USB drives don't even need a separate power supply.

On the downside, a USB connection is much slower than an EIDE or SCSI connection, so today's fastest recorders can't use it. USB drives tend to be somewhat more expensive — remember that USB is external only. Finally, most computers have only two USB ports, so if you're already using USB devices, you may need a USB hub; this little black box converts one of your USB ports into four ports. Cool!

I heartily recommend USB for anyone who wants a typical external CD recorder.

FireWire

Imagine a — hey, wait a second, that's not an acronym. Anyway, imagine a turbocharged USB port that can deliver an entire hard drive's worth of data in a minute or two, and you're thinking of FireWire. (Techheads also call it the IEEE-1394, and you may see it advertised as such when shopping for digital camcorders.)

FireWire (developed by Apple) has all the advantages of USB, but its much faster transfer rate means that it's perfect for the fastest external CD-RW and DVD recorders on the market. If you're shopping for an external DVD recorder, FireWire is probably a requirement. You can use the same port for digital cameras, camcorders, scanners, and the like.

What's the catch? As I mentioned, only external drives need apply, and FireWire drives are some of the most expensive on the market. Just about all Macintosh computers now have FireWire built-in (natch), and PC owners can add FireWire ports by installing an adapter card.

FireWire is the best choice for high-performance external recorders.

Parallel

If you're using an older laptop or desktop PC without USB ports, you have one other option to consider: a parallel port drive, which uses the existing parallel printer port found on virtually every PC on the planet. (Macintosh computers have no parallel port, so this is not an option for them.)

I don't talk much about this type of interface because parallel port drives are slow and more prone to errors, and they often don't work if you're already using a printer or another external device on your printer port, like a Zip drive or a backup tape drive.

Again, consider a parallel port drive only if nothing else works.

The X Factor Explained

Of all the gobbledygook associated with buying a CD recorder, nothing is as foreign to a normal human being — or affects the price of a drive as much — as the *X factor*. You encounter these X numbers in every description of every drive you see, so let's cover the X factor thing like a wet blanket (or a new coat of paint).

In plain English, the *X factor* is the speed at which a drive can read and record data. It's typically expressed as three numbers, like 12x/4x/32x. The order is always important:

 ✔ The first number indicates the CD-R recording speed.

 ✔ The second number is the CD-RW recording speed.

 ✔ The last number provides the read-only speed.

Therefore, whenever you apply these conventions to the example, you're looking at a drive that can record a CD-R at 12x and a CD-RW at 4x and can read a CD-ROM at 32x. Naturally, higher numbers are better, so follow this general rule (I really like those):

The faster the X factor, the faster the drive performs at either recording or reading data.

Most internal drives on the market these days do at least 8x CD-R recording, and most external drives record at a minimum of 4x.

If you're considering a drive that's slower than 4x, promise me that you won't pay much (if anything) when you buy it. A 2x recorder is an antique now — of course, it works fine if your Uncle Milton gives it to you for free. Scavengers forever!

For those who care about such arcane measurements, the X factor is technically a multiplier of the original read-only speed for the first drives that appeared in the early 1980s. (You can call them 1x drives.) These 1x drives could send data to a computer at 150K per second; therefore, a 2x CD-ROM drive can send data to a computer at 300K per second. Read-only drives can now reach blinding transfer rates of 52x, or 7800K per second.

The X Factor General Rule (or, in the acronym-happy world of computers, the XFGR) would seem to recommend that you shell out every possible penny for the fastest drive around. If you were Bill Gates, you would be right. However, common folk like you and me have things called *budgets,* so buying the fastest sports car of a recorder may not always be the best road to take; for example:

- If your computer already has a 40x or 48x read-only CD-ROM drive, you don't need to spend anything extra for faster read-only speeds. Play your games and video CDs in the read-only drive, and use the recorder just for burning discs.

- If you plan to use your new drive exclusively for recording audio CDs, why pay extra for a drive that records CD-RW discs faster? A faster CD-RW speed is better suited for you if you plan to use it to back up your computer's hard drive.

- If you plan to record once or twice a week and you can wait the extra four or five minutes per disc, an 8x CD-RW drive works just as well as a 16x drive that may cost twice as much.

In the end, the drive performance you should choose depends on the number of discs you record, how fast you want them, and the difference in price for a faster drive.

Features on Parade

At this point in this chapter, you may have read about the Big Three features: internal versus external, drive connections, and raw speed figures. Now consider individual features that add convenience, performance, and (coincidentally) cost to a drive. The more of these you can pack into your purchase, the happier you will be. Note that I also mention which features are especially important for certain recording tasks; believe me — it's better to discover that a drive has a tiny recording buffer before you buy it than after you buy it.

Make use of every pit: Overburning

Sounds like you're making digital toast, doesn't it? *Overburning* is a recent phenomenon in the world of CD recording; it refers to a drive that can record more than the "rated" maximum capacity of a CD-R disc. For example, a drive that can overburn to 76 minutes can record 76 minutes of music on a standard 74-minute CD-R, or you could use the same drive to store 685MB of data rather than 650MB. The amount you can overburn depends on your recorder and the specific brand of discs you're using.

Overburning is mucho grande, but you must remember two caveats:

✔ Most CD-ROM drives made in the past two or three years have no trouble with overburned discs, although some older drives spit them back out as unreadable. Therefore, if you distribute your discs, I recommend that you don't overburn them.

✔ Media manufacturers don't guarantee their discs past the 74- or 80-minute rating, so you overburn at your own risk.

How does a drive overburn? It uses the lead-out portion of the disc, which was not originally intended to store data; in fact, the lead-out area is *supposed* to indicate to your drive that it has reached the end of the disc. When you overburn, you're burning past that point. If your read-only CD-ROM doesn't care and can read an overburned CD-ROM, you're, in effect, storing more in the same space. Real "8-bit old-timers" like myself who used the early Atari and Commodore computers remember something similar: We used to flip over a 5¼-inch single-density disk and use the other side, which you weren't supposed to do. Shameful, really.

Important: Any CD recorder can use an 80-minute CD-R disc — you're not overburning when you put 80 minutes of music or 700MB of data on this kind of media. Again, however, not every recorder can use these larger-capacity discs; check the specifications of any recorder you're considering to see whether it can use 80-minute/700MB discs.

Three words: Buffer, buffer, buffer

For today's faster drives, a large data buffer (also known as an internal RAM or RAM cache) is indeed an important feature. All recorders have at least some buffer RAM. This memory stores data that your computer has retrieved from your hard drive until your recorder is ready for it. Figure 2-3 tells the tale. The larger the buffer, the more efficient this process becomes, and the less likely your drive is to return an error and ruin a disc because it ran out of data to write.

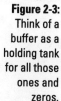
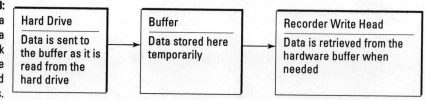

Figure 2-3: Think of a buffer as a holding tank for all those ones and zeros.

Hard Drive
Data is sent to the buffer as it is read from the hard drive

Buffer
Data stored here temporarily

Recorder Write Head
Data is retrieved from the hardware buffer when needed

Most drives made these days have at least 1MB of buffer memory, and more expensive drives can have 2MB, 4MB, or even 8MB. When comparing drives, always try to pick a model with a larger buffer.

The ultimate safety net: Burnproof recording

Consider now the hottest-burning feature (horrible pun intended) to come along in several years. Burnproof recorders effectively end any problems that folks generally had when they were

- ✔ Recording on slower PCs
- ✔ Recording in the background under Windows or the Mac operating system (for example, using Word or Internet Explorer while recording)
- ✔ Recording at high speeds (10x or faster)

Before the arrival of burnproof drives about a year ago, engaging in one of these activities was risky business indeed. As you may already know if you've been following along in this chapter, a recorder had to have a constant flow of data to prevent buffer underrun errors. Any interruption or "hiccup" in the transfer of data from the computer's hard drive to the recorder was usually disastrous. A larger buffer helped, but that still didn't solve the problem entirely, and your recorder certainly couldn't stop in the middle of a disc — it was now or never.

If your CD-RW drive doesn't support burnproof recording (and you're not alone because the vast majority of drives now on the market don't), you should be happy to know that I devote Chapter 6 to helping you optimize your computer and recorder to help prevent buffer underrun errors.

Burnproof recording changes all this by interrupting the recording process. The drive monitors the buffer, and when things look dangerous (for example, if you've run Adobe Photoshop, which is a notorious disk and memory hog), the recorder takes note of the position of the laser and stops recording. After the buffer has been refilled (which can take a few seconds), the laser write head is automatically repositioned at the point where the recording was interrupted and the recording process continues.

I can't stress just how revolutionary burnproof recording really is. If you can afford this feature (which is now available on only the highest-priced drives), by all means, get it.

DAO: Funny acronym, important feature

DAO is one acronym I don't mind mentioning. It's short for disc-at-once, and I wouldn't buy a drive that doesn't offer DAO recording. (Is that a definite enough recommendation?) Rather than record digital audio or computer data as individual tracks, DAO records the entire disc at one time (you find out all about this subject in Chapter 7). Suffice it to say that the audio CDs you record sound better on some audio CD players, and you can get more music on a single disc if you use DAO. Again, check a drive's specifications to see whether it offers DAO recording.

Sorry, but We Have to Talk CD-ROM Formats

Formats are tricky things. Any CD-RW drive can create a simple audio CD (which by definition conforms to an international set of format standards called the Red Book) or a simple data CD-ROM with files on it (which uses the Yellow and Orange Book standards). You don't have to worry about these basic functions; for a CD recorder, they're like walking and chewing gum.

However, there's no telling when you may suddenly find yourself needing a Video CD or a CD Extra disc, and if your drive doesn't support them, it can never record those discs. You can't add formats to your drive after you've bought it.

Therefore, this section has two goals: First, I introduce you to each format, and then I help you determine which of them you're likely to need later. Here's another of Mark's Patented General Rules: *Cast your purchasing eye on the drive that can write the largest number of formats.*

Packet writing

Remember my discussion of burnproof recording earlier in this chapter? No? If you skipped it, you should flip back a page or two and read it. I'll wait for you here.

Anyway, packet writing is almost as cool as burnproof recording: It allows you to write files to a CD-R or CD-RW just as you would write files to your hard drive, using Windows Explorer, the Mac OS Finder, or any of your other applications. You can add files one at a time or in groups, without having to record the entire disc at one sitting. In effect, packet writing turns your drive into a gigantic, superfast floppy that can store more than 600MB.

You can also "erase" data from a disc. Yes, I tell you in Chapter 1 that you can't erase data from a CD-R, but I'm stretching the truth a bit. Rather than be physically removed from the disc, the data you're erasing becomes unreadable, so it can't be retrieved. The data is still there — you just can't access it.

Again, it's time to be blunt: Most CD-RW drives now available support packet writing, and I wouldn't buy one if it didn't.

Video CD

Although DVD-R is the unequivocal king of digital video recording, those of you with lowly CD-RW drives can produce your own brand of visual magic: A drive that records in Video CD format can create discs for a video CD player (and many DVD players can read them, too). Most read-only CD-ROMs can now also read Video CDs — all you need is the right software. I use Windows Media Player.

With a Video CD, you have many of the same features that you would find on a DVD player, including an interactive menu for selecting video clips and freeze-frame or slow-motion effects.

CD Extra

Another format that has recently come into its own, CD Extra allows you to record a disc with a mixture of audio and data tracks. Why create a mutant disc like this? Most computers these days have high-fidelity audio systems, so many musicians are using CD Extra to add a music video, song lyrics, and other multimedia material to their audio CDs. (Remember that the disc can also be played on your computer's CD-ROM drive.) For example, two of my favorite bands — the Squirrel Nut Zippers and the Rolling Stones — have recently turned out CD Extra discs.

A CD Extra disc doesn't overlook the folks who just want to listen to the disc in an audio CD player. The audio track on a CD Extra disc is recorded first, so it's compatible with any audio CD player — in fact, the player doesn't know the difference. The only restriction, naturally, is the amount of audio you can record on a CD Extra disc; because you're adding data as well, you don't get a full 74 or 80 minutes of audio elbowroom.

Digging deep for specifications

I admit that I'm letting loose a landslide of features and formats in this chapter, but I have a reason: I can't tell how you will use your drive, so I can't tell you what features and formats are most important for *you*. Instead, I explain all the relevant stuff, and you can pick and choose what's necessary for your Dream Drive.

Unfortunately, the Feature Fairy doesn't drop in to tell you what formats and features are supported by a drive, or what software ships with it. To buy the best drive for you, you have to roll up your sleeves and do the research. First, visit the manufacturer's Web site and look for that all-important specification sheet. (This is also a good time to check on the quality of the manufacturer's support, like updated drivers, firmware upgrades, and FAQ files.) In many cases, the specification list should tell you everything you need to know.

Next, try visiting www.buy.com or www.computershopper.com, where product features can be compared side-by-side between different drives. These sites are great for asking questions like "Show me all the 12x CD-RW drives under $300 with burnproof recording."

If you have an Internet connection and you're familiar with newsgroups, I can recommend comp.publish.cdrom.hardware and alt.comp.hardware. Someone in one of these groups may know the features of a particular drive (although you may get opinions mixed in liberally with your answers).

Most computer magazines have online Web editions, and they often cover CD and DVD recorders with hardware comparisons and performance evaluations. Finally, use a search engine like www.google.com to locate information about a specific make and model of drive; you may be surprised at what turns up.

Multisession/CD-ROM XA

I can't discuss CD-ROM XA format without introducing you to the idea of a *session,* so here goes: A session is, in effect, a self-contained dataset recorded on a disc. In English, think of it as a single track on an audio CD. You can store multiple tracks on one disc and access each of them individually as you like. As an example, think of one year's tax returns recorded in one session, followed by the next year's returns in the next session; it's a way to update the existing data on a CD without losing the old data. Each of the sessions on a multisession mode CD-ROM XA disc can be read, but only one at a time. (I get into this subject more later in Chapter 8.)

CD-ROM XA isn't anywhere as popular as it once was because of three "gotchas:"

- ✔ **Not all CD-ROM drives can read CD-ROM XA:** Older, read-only CD-ROM drives may be able to read only the last session recorded or may not even be able to read the disc.

- ✔ **Software is required in order to change sessions:** Some sort of session-selection program or function is necessary; it comes with most CD recording programs, but if you're sending a disc to someone else and that person doesn't have a CD recorder, she's out of luck.

- ✔ **Packet writing is better:** The availability of packet writing on most drives has made multisession recording as outmoded as the Model T. Packet writing is far easier than recording multiple sessions.

Software You Just Gotta Have

I really shouldn't say that: of course, the software you receive with your recorder isn't as important as the hardware itself. After all, you can always add software later or upgrade what you have. Hardware is, well, *hard*. Other than a firmware upgrade, your drive's features and performance are fixed, so the software should take a back seat (not too far back, though).

Often, one drive you're considering has a much better selection of software than another. If their prices, features, and speeds are similar, a superior software selection can tip the scales. However, every CD recorder you consider should ship with basic recording software that

- ✔ Allows you to burn discs in all supported formats
- ✔ Erases and formats CD-RW discs
- ✔ Tests for proper installation and configuration of your drive

My favorite recording software is Easy CD Creator, from Roxio, and I use it throughout much of this book. I'm also fond of WinOnCD, though, also from Roxio (see Figure 2-4), and the great shareware program CDRWin, from Golden Hawk Software (see Figure 2-5). On the Macintosh, my recording program of choice is Roxio Toast (www.roxio.com), which I use later in this book.

After you've taken care of the basics, however, you find that some drives offer additional software that can save you money and — as the marketing types would say — "enhances your recording experience." (In other words, the more of this nifty software you get, the better off you are.) I cover this extra stuff you want in this section.

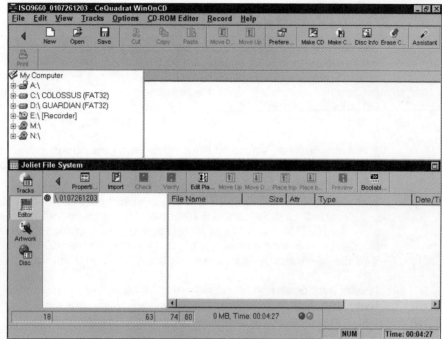

Figure 2-4:
WinOnCD —
great
recording
program,
funny name.

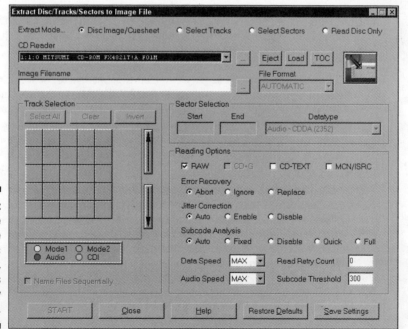

Figure 2-5:
The
shareware
classic
CDRWin,
with its
classy
icons.

A sharp-dressed disc

Can you imagine Fred Astaire in a leisure suit? No way! The tuxedo was practically made for him. Many people feel the same way about the discs they record: They want those discs to look as professional as possible. As I mention in Chapter 1, one way to do this is to spend a couple of thousand dollars on a CD label screen printer. If you would rather save the cash and put your inkjet printer to work, these programs can spruce up the appearance of a CD-ROM:

- **Label-printing software:** Print labels with everything from simple text to line art or full-color photographs. Labels are particularly nice for audio CDs.

- **Jewel box printing software:** You can print custom front and back inserts for a CD's jewel box (that plastic whatchamacallit that stores the disc) — I think that it completes the look of a recorded CD-ROM. Again, audio CDs benefit from track listings, and computer CD-ROMs can use the space for file descriptions or installation instructions.

I cover both these bad boys in Chapter 14, including a step-by-step project that shows how to create inserts and a label.

Slick recording add-ons

As I mention earlier in this chapter, any self-respecting recording program should be able to take care of basic recording tasks all by itself, although separate add-on programs can take care of specialized recording jobs:

- **Packet-writing software:** Why run that big, stodgy recording program each time you want to write a UDF disc? With this thought in mind, most software developers "spin off" packet-writing into a separate program that can run in the background under Windows or the Mac operating system. The perfect example is DirectCD, from Roxio, which runs automatically when you start your PC and doesn't require Easy CD Creator. (Read more about this program in Chapter 10.)

- **Backup and disaster-recovery software:** Call these programs digital peace of mind — use your CD-RW to back up either part or all of your system, and you can rest easy at night. I use Retrospect Express, from Dantz Development (see Figure 2-6), which can even format a CD-RW for you. I've said it before in most of my books, and I'll say it again: *If you value your data, back it up.*

Are you already using a backup program with a tape drive or Zip disks? If so, check to see whether it already supports the use of a CD-RW drive: If so, you can keep original backup sets, avoiding a "hole" in your backup schedule while you switch to CD-RW.

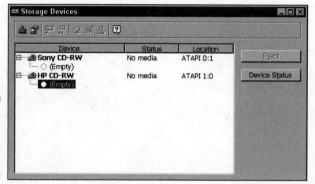

Figure 2-6:
I'm backed
up. *Are*
you?

Tools to organize and play your stuff

I go into the organization of your recording projects in complete detail in Chapter 7. For now, suffice it to say that some of these programs make finding stuff on your finished discs easier, and other software is required to play the digital video and audio you've recorded:

- ✔ **Image- and video-editing software:** Many drives are bundled with an image editor for digital photographs and a simple video editor for chopping Uncle Milton out of this year's Christmas video. This feature makes sense because the majority of recorder owners probably burn digital images and video all the time.

- ✔ **Multimedia filing software:** Think of these programs as organizers for your audio, video, and images; the programs can help you locate and retrieve a single clip or image from thousands stored on a single CD-RW for your next presentation or Office document. Plus, you can play or view those images from within the program to make sure that you've found the right one. My favorite multimedia filing program is Media Center Plus, from Jasc Software, as shown in Figure 2-7.

- ✔ **Audio CD/MP3/WAV player:** If you don't get an audio media player with your recorder, you will need one eventually. My favorite is WinAmp, from Nullsoft, Inc. (see Figure 2-8), which can probably handle anything you encounter: audio in MP3 format, audio CDs themselves, Windows WAV files, and Macintosh AIF files. Plus, it marks you as technokeen.

- ✔ **Video CD/MPEG player:** The counterpart to your audio media player, a video player is a welcome addition to any recorder's software bundle. My favorite is PowerDVD, from CyberLink, which can play Video CDs on any CD-ROM drive; if you have a DVD-ROM or DVD-R drive, it can also turn your computer into your own, personal DVD theater. Figure 2-9 shows PowerDVD playing one of my collection of "Batman" episodes: Go, Adam West!

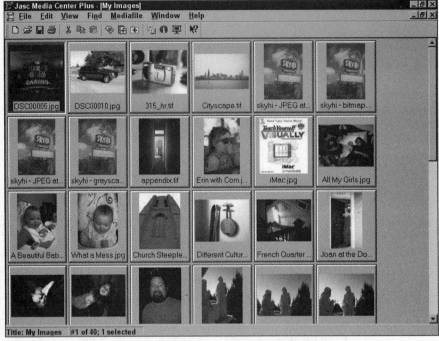

Figure 2-7:
Finding a
needle in a
haystack
(and
retrieving it)
is what
Media
Center Plus
is all about.

Figure 2-8:
WinAmp can
rock the
socks off
your llama.
(Don't ask —
private joke.)

Figure 2-9:
PowerDVD
is great for
watching
my favorite
TV series of
all time on
Video CD.
Sweet!

Scavenging a Fossilized CD-R Drive

The vulture may not be the prettiest *scavenger* on the planet, but it gets the job done. In the world of computer hardware, a scavenged component can often bring you and your computer a world of new possibilities for little or no cost. This is a good thing, and I'm proud to say that I've been scavenging for many years.

Fate can present a number of different ways to acquire a used recorder: You may inherit one from a family member or friend who's upgrading, or you may stumble across one at a garage sale. The most popular method of picking up a used drive, however, is probably one of the online auction centers; eBay is the prime location. If you're looking for a used drive, here's what I recommend:

✔ **Don't settle for less than 4x:** Unless someone flat out gives you a 2x drive for free, ignore the deal and move on. These drives are just too slow, and any drive with such poor performance probably doesn't have features like DAO recording or a decent-size buffer.

✔ **Get those drivers.** Nothing is quite as frustrating as searching the world over for CD recorder device drivers, especially when the drive is five years old or more. If you're running Windows 98 or later, the process is easier because the operating system comes with a host of drivers built-in. The moral? Whenever possible, get the original software disks and manual for a drive, and check the manufacturer's Web site to see whether you can still find software and support.

✔ **Buy from recognized sellers:** The seller feedback ratings on eBay make seeing who has a good track record easy, so use them; if a seller has a feedback rating of less than 5 or has a number of negative feedback entries, be wary. Don't be shy about asking questions through e-mail, and keep an eye out for exorbitant "handling" charges. (I do lots of selling on eBay myself, and I've never charged someone for the overwhelmingly difficult act of slipping something into an envelope or packing it in a box.)

✔ **Consider new versus used:** Finally, consider the current prices for a new drive: At the time this book was written, I could pick up a 12x4x32 CD-RW drive for less than $200. Before you spend more than $25 on a used drive, make sure that you're really getting a bargain.

Buying Your Drive at the Maze o' Wires Mall

Let's get one thing straight: You should feel no shame in buying locally. In the next section, I harp away on the advantages of buying online, and I admit that I buy most of my hardware on the Web these days; however, where you buy your drive is your business, and I don't try to push you into shoving dollars through your modem.

Besides the help from a salesperson (hopefully one who really knows all the ins and outs of recording), a local store offers three things that no Web store can ever match: immediate delivery, hands-on shopping, and a fast, friendly return policy. (No matter how good Internet Explorer becomes, you can't use your mouse to open a box that's 2,000 miles away.) No waiting is involved, either to receive your drive or to bring it back in case you find you're the proud owner of a lemon.

Watch out, however, for pressure tactics from a "sales thug." Ask plenty of questions, request a demo, and bring along a knowledgeable friend to help you shop. Check out several stores before settling on one drive.

Considering buying returned (or refurbished) hardware? Have the salesperson connect the drive and give it a thorough check before you take it home. Also, don't forget to ask what kind of warranty you receive on your purchase.

Your drive costs you more, and you pay local sales tax, but if you're nervous about buying online or you want to install that drive tonight, jump in the car and head to your local computer marketplace.

Buying Your Drive on that Web Thing

"Okay, I need to save money, and I've got a credit card — plus, it's hurricane season, I have nothing clean to wear, and my favorite episode of "My Three Sons" is starting in five minutes. Can I buy a drive online?" Indeed, you can — in fact, in a situation like that, it's sheer madness to buy locally.

It really does take only five minutes to buy your recorder on the Web (after, of course, you've done your thorough research). The Web offers the widest selection of drives at the lowest prices, and you can use sites like www.pricewatch.com to search out the best deal. Depending on the state you're in (pun not intended that time), you may be exempt from local sales taxes, too.

Why pay for next-day or second-day shipping if you're not itching for the fastest delivery? Many sites select next-day shipping as a default option, and you're stuck paying twice or three times the cost of five-day shipping. Don't fall for this old trick, and choose the shipping option that suits your pocketbook.

One final word about ordering on the Web: Most mail-order companies charge a virtual arm and a leg for "restocking" your drive if you decide to return it. Make sure that you're not charged if you have to return a defective recorder.

No lock, no sale

If you're ready to buy a recorder online and the Web store doesn't offer a secure connection, tell 'em to take a hike. A secure connection is encrypted to protect your credit card number and personal information, which makes it challenging for the online criminal element to intercept your data as it's sent to the Web site.

If you're using Internet Explorer or Netscape Navigator, look for a closed padlock icon on the status bar at the bottom of the browser's screen. If you see the lock, the connection is secure, and you can enter your information. If you don't see a locked padlock icon (or the lock is open and not closed) and you're being asked for your personal information and card number, I would immediately move on to the next online store.

Chapter 3

DVD Is Not a Bad Word

. . . .

. . . .

*T*he acceptance of CD-ROM back in the early 1980s by the general public was painfully slow — but perfectly understandable. For example, John T. Everyman had been listening to vinyl albums all his life and had just begun to mesh with the psychology of the cassette tape; along comes the audio CD, and many folks couldn't help but ask, "Is this just a flash in the pan, like my Betamax VCR?" Because only a handful of plants manufacturing CDs existed, CD-ROMs started out prohibitively expensive, and the first year or two saw only a pitiful selection.

What's worse, recording your own CD was simply science fiction for more than a decade; developing the technology took several years, and then when the first CD-R drives appeared, they were priced so high that tech-types like myself got nosebleeds just reading the advertisements. I can remember wishing that I had $6,000 — that's right — $6,000 — so that I could become an optical alchemist and "burn" like professional musicians and video editors. Only around 1995 or so did CD recorders descend from the heavens to less than $1,000, and it took three more years for the typical CD recorder to drop to less than $500. Recording software? You may as well have written it yourself because what was available was almost as expensive as the drive.

Thank goodness, we have all learned our lesson. Things have changed so dramatically that the introduction of DVD a few years ago was a complete mirror image of the early years of the compact disc. First, the CD-ROM has become so common that DVD was immediately accepted as "the next step in optical media." No uncertainty, wailing, or gnashing of teeth this time. We all want the storage space and convenience of DVD. A large number of well-established factories were already ready and waiting to produce DVDs, and the selection of films has mushroomed quickly. Prices on many popular DVD movies are already less than $10.

Finally, DVD recording is light-years ahead of where CD recording was at this stage of the game. Drives are dropping in price, and software abounds to help you produce your own interactive discs. Many computers are already shipping with DVD-R and DVD-RAM drives, and within a year or two I'm certain that prices will drop across the board for both recordable DVD drives and blank media.

Many features I cover in Chapter 2 apply in this chapter as well, such as internal versus external drives and the connections you can use. Therefore, I focus more on the important questions you need to ask before you plunk down your hard-earned greenbacks for a new DVD drive. I also include a discussion of additional hardware and software that comes in handy before you record as well as information on those pesky DVD formats.

"Do I Need DVD-R or DVD-RAM?"

Why not get both? (Oh, brother.) Unless you've been hanging out with Regis Philbin or Ed McMahon, that's probably not an option. However, I still have good news: The relative strengths of both types of recordable DVD media make it easy to decide which one you need. Check out Table 3-1 for the scoop.

Table 3-1	Will DVD-R or DVD-RAM Escort You to the Ball?	
Can Be Read in DVD Players	*Reusable/Rewritable?*	*Media Cost*
DVD-R	Almost always/No	$20 per disc (4.7GB)
DVD-RAM	Usually not/Yes	$30 per disc (5.2GB)

Remember these other two up-and-coming recordable DVD formats: DVD-RW and DVD+RW, which I mention in Chapter 2. However, only DVD-R and DVD-RAM are now standardized and generally available.

I should point out something about Table 3-1: Besides being incredibly informative, it uses the words *almost* and *usually,* which don't show up in many definitive tables. Why? The answer lies not in today's recorders, but rather in yesterday's DVD-ROM players; *four* distinct generations of DVD-ROM players have existed since their introduction in late 1997, and each succeeding generation has a better chance of reading both DVD-R and DVD-RAM discs.

The result is a big question mark. Because of the wide disparity in manufacturers, I can't tell you whether the DVD-ROM player you have now reads either type of disc. If you're using a DVD-RAM disc, you have the best chance with a DVD-ROM player manufactured since the beginning of 2001. If you're using DVD-R, you have the best chance with a DVD-ROM player made after late 1999. Thoroughly confused now? Sorry about that. This vegetable soup of different standards and rapidly evolving hardware can turn a computer book author's hair very gray very quickly.

Anyway, here are my recommendations. First, pick DVD-R if

- ✔ You're looking for the highest level of compatibility with DVD-ROM drives.
- ✔ You're distributing discs to others.
- ✔ You couldn't care less about reusing discs.

Choose DVD-RAM if

- ✔ Compatibility with DVD-ROM drives is not an issue, such as when you're creating backups or discs that you read only on your computer.
- ✔ You want to rewrite data on an existing disc.

Which one saves you more money? That's an interesting question. At first, you would think that it's the wondrous rewritable DVD-RAM (especially because it has a slightly larger capacity), but only if you keep reusing the same disc and you don't buy additional media in the future. DVD-R discs, on the other hand, are likely to drop to a rock-bottom price in the next couple of years — following the lead of CD-R discs before them. If you're going to be giving discs to others, you definitely save money with DVD-R.

Oh, and yes, Virginia: You can read a commercially manufactured DVD-ROM movie disc in either type of recorder. At least I can guarantee you the extra bonus of adding a DVD-ROM drive to your computer when you install a DVD recorder.

"Hey — I Can't Copy 'Curse of the Mollusk People'!"

Man, of all the clunkers that Hollywood has turned out, why would you possibly want to copy a movie about mobile glowing clams that enslave the minds of simple townsfolk? (I've bought titles like *Robot Monster, Nude on the Moon,* and *Blood Feast* for my collection, too; perhaps I shouldn't be too proud.)

Anyway, you can't copy a DVD-ROM movie for good reason: Lots of smart engineers, software developers, and designers worked hard to make sure that you can't. Some discs are protected by the addition of unreadable areas on the disc during manufacture, and other protection schemes involve encrypted key codes that must be present on the disc for it to be recognized by either your player or your computer's DVD-ROM drive.

Also, as you remember from my masterful Table 3-1, a typical blank DVD-R disc now costs about $20. Why go to all the trouble to copy a DVD-ROM — even if you could — to save a dollar or two? Heck, it makes better sense to order a bona fide copy from www.amazon.com.

This stuff gets really technical really quickly, so I don't go into it here in any great detail. Suffice it to say that buying a DVD-R or DVD-RAM drive is not a free ticket to a shelf of cheap movies.

(And no, I didn't think that you would do such a thing. Copyrights are important — ask any book author.)

Weird, Wild DVD Format Stuff

Close the windows, bar the door: You can't escape them. I have two more acronyms to discuss, and I do the best I can to make sure that we all make it out of this section in one piece.

DVD-V

If you've been perusing the DVD movie aisle at your local discount store, you may think that you were looking at DVD-ROM — and you would be right. However, I can be even more specific than that: A DVD-V (short for DVD-video, of all things) disc is a DVD-ROM that holds broadcast-quality digital video in a special compressed format named MPEG-2. (You find out a little more about MPEG in the next section and much more in Chapter 13.) You also get niceties like Dolby audio, Surround Sound, subtitles, and different aspect ratios with a DVD-V disc. You can even run programs from a DVD-V disc if it's being played in a computer DVD-ROM drive.

You may ask, "Can I burn a commercial-quality DVD-V disc with my new DVD recorder?" Technically, yes; however, lots of work is involved in compressing digital video, creating interactive menus, and adding a quality audio track. It's nowhere near as simple as recording something on comfortable old VHS tape, but I show you how to do some of this good stuff elsewhere in this book.

DVD-A

I know that this might break your heart, but even your friend the audio CD is eventually going out to pasture. The likely replacement is a recent format standard named DVD-A, or DVD-Audio. Imagine a standard audio CD that has been to the gym four nights a week for the past 10 years, and you get some idea of what DVD-A is like: either two or four hours of stereo music (depending on the type of media); interactive menus, like with the current crop of DVD-V discs; and even the ability to store video clips.

For me, however, the most exciting new feature of DVD-A is the addition of Surround Sound support. If you're enjoying a Surround Sound system, you know how realistic it is. If not, try out this type of system the next time you're in a stereo and video store. Although the extra data needed for Surround Sound cuts in half the capacity of a DVD-A disc, you're still talking about an hour or two of incredible music.

Additional Toys You Just May Need

Before the sun sets on this introductory discussion of DVD recording, I would be remiss if I didn't tell you that you're likely to need a little additional hardware and software. Why? To make the most of the expanded features of DVD, you need to import, edit, convert, and design — and not necessarily in that order — and there just isn't the room or the need to do most of those things when you're recording a CD-R or CD-RW.

In this section of your palatial mansion, allow me to show you some of the extras you're likely to use.

The MPEG card: Aye, Matey, 'tis indeed a tiny file

If you're serious about creating your own DVD-V discs — or even experimenting with simple video CDs and digital video clips — you should consider an MPEG-2 adapter card for your computer. As I mention earlier in this chapter, MPEG-2 is a compression format; it's somewhat similar to the space you save when you use ZIP compression to shrink a file on your hard drive. And, boy, howdy, do you need it because high-quality digital video that's bigger than a postage stamp on your screen takes up an incredible amount of space. Without compressing (or *encoding*) the video, you're likely to run out of room on even the highest-capacity DVD media.

If you're wondering about that term *digital video* (also called DV, for short), indeed, no film or magnetism is involved. Digital video is composed of the same familiar ones and zeros that are written to a recordable CD or DVD. Unlike with traditional videotape (which can stretch and lose its magnetic properties), you can edit, copy, and play digital video as many times as you like without losing quality.

Most MPEG-2 cards have two functions: They can encode video to shrink it, and they can also *decode* it so that you can watch it on your computer's screen. (If you receive an MPEG-2 card with a DVD-ROM drive, however, it likely just decodes so that you can watch DVD movies.)

Both these chores can be taken care of by software programs as well, but I always recommend a hardware solution for folks who want to do any serious MPEG video work. The advantages of the card over software include

✔ **Speed:** Software encoding and decoding programs are nowhere near as fast as an MPEG card, so a process that can take minutes with a card can take hours with a program. It depends on the raw power and performance of your computer's processor.

✔ **Efficiency:** An MPEG card does all the heavy thinking about MPEG, so even an older PC with an original Pentium brain can keep up.

✔ **Convenience:** Most MPEG cards offer connectors so that you can plug your TV directly into your computer and pipe your DVD movies to The Tube. These connectors are handy little beavers to possess.

The FireWire port: The real information superhighway

No ifs, ands, or buts with this one: If you work with digital video recording, you need one or two high-speed FireWire ports on your computer. Virtually every piece of machinery on the planet that works with DV uses FireWire to connect to everything else, including digital video camcorders and external DVD recorders. Many high-resolution digital cameras and scanners are now using FireWire as their connection of choice as well.

By the way, some manufacturers seem determined to call a FireWire port an i-LINK connection, for some reason. Heck, if you want to be perfectly accurate, the full international title for the FireWire standard is IEEE-1394. You may see several of these names on the same box.

If you're using a late-model Macintosh, you're probably doing the Technological Twist right now, dancing in front of your monitor like a Druid partying around Stonehenge. That's because Apple developed FireWire, and most of the faster Macintosh computers made since Y2K (the year 2000)

include built-in FireWire ports. However, if you're using a PC that didn't come graced with the Wire of Fire, be reassured that you can party just as well by installing a PCI card in your computer. PCI cards average about $100 on the Web, and they provide you with 2 FireWire ports and all the software and drivers. You need an open PCI slot in your PC, naturally.

The digital camcorder: Your digital muse

By law (it's written down somewhere, I know it), you can't record digital video without a *digital camcorder* (sometimes also called a DV camcorder). Note that a DV camcorder is not the same as the VHS-C or Hi-8 camcorder that you already own. Oh, no, things couldn't be that simple, right? Today's typical video camcorder records an *analog* signal, so you can't use that video feed with your computer and your editing software. (The next toy I show you, however, helps you get around this problem.)

Virtually all digital camcorders download their video directly through a FireWire port to your computer, where you can have fun with it to your heart's content. DV camcorders are quite a bit more expensive than their traditional analog brethren, but they're much more versatile: You can take still photographs with most digital camcorders, and most models allow you to perform simple editing jobs onboard ("Can you *please* get the police out of our wedding video?") before you download the video to your computer. For the George Lucas in you, most digital camcorders now allow you to shoot footage in a 16:9 wide-screen aspect ratio.

You now shell out anywhere from $800 to $3,000 or more for a digital camcorder; for example, Figure 3-1 illustrates the Panasonic PV-DV401, which sells for about $900 online. It looks deceptively like a typical VHS-C analog camcorder, but it sports both FireWire and USB ports and a digital camera mode for taking still photographs. You can also add special effects during recording or playback, and it can even record in near darkness.

Figure 3-1:
A digital camcorder like the Panasonic PV-DV401 turns you into a walking film crew.

The A-D converter: A bridge to the past

If you're shaking your head and mumbling, "I can't possibly afford that kind of cash right now for a digital camcorder," I've got a card up my sleeve that may well set things straight. This joker is called an *analog-to-digital converter* — usually called an A-D converter by those who dislike $5 words. The A-D converter freshens up the signal from a "prehistoric" analog TV, VCR, or camcorder, and — voilà — you've turned that analog signal into digital video.

Figure 3-2 shows one of the most popular analog-to-digital converters on the market, the Hollywood DV-Bridge, from Dazzle, Inc. (www.dazzle.com). This alchemist's magic box costs a mere $250 or so on the Web, yet it can

- ✔ Connect your computer, your analog devices, and your DV devices in perfect harmony with a full set of ports (including a FireWire port)

- ✔ Convert digital video to an analog signal so that you can use your VCR to create tapes from a DV source

- ✔ Monitor your DV feed on a TV while it's being converted

- ✔ Mix both DV and analog material in one production

Figure 3-2:
The Hollywood DV-Bridge just plain rocks your analog world.

You also get two different types of Windows video-editing software. I can highly recommend the Hollywood DV-Bridge if you're itching to try your hand at digital video, but you want to spend as little as possible and use the analog equipment you already have.

Video-editing software

Speaking of software, I end this opening gambit in the world of DVD recording by describing the typical software you use. In fact, two of these three programs ship as part of the computer's operating system. (Is DV mainstream these days or what?)

Video-editing software now offers a basic set of tools that take care of all common tasks, such as

- ✔ Importing and arranging video clips
- ✔ Removing unwanted footage
- ✔ Adding basic transitions between clips, like fade-ins and dissolves
- ✔ Adding and synchronizing audio

Figures 3-3, 3-4, and 3-5 illustrate three great examples of these DV Swiss army knives: iDVD, which ships with a number of new Macintosh computers (you may be familiar with its little brother, iMovie 2), Microsoft Movie Maker (Windows Me and XP), and the Adobe Premiere (both platforms). Any one of these programs can deliver a quality digital video production.

Granted, you can spend a heinous amount of money on high-end editing software that toots your car horn and can make doughnuts, but it typically starts at $1,000 (and that's for the cheap seats, my friend). Most programs I cover in this book are free, and even the commercial version of Adobe Premiere costs less than $500 on the Web. (Chapter 13 includes coverage of iDVD and Premiere.) Other programs, like Adobe After Effects, can add everything from a flaming hoop to a scrolling marquee underneath the video.

Because this book is devoted to CD and DVD recording, I can't get more than ankle-deep in the river of DV — however, I can recommend the book *Digital Video For Dummies,* 2nd Edition, written by Martin Doucette and published by Hungry Minds, Inc. He can have you swimming in DV in no time.

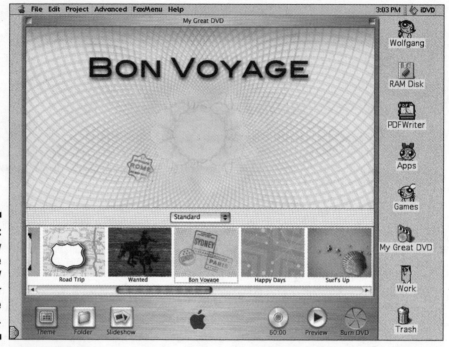

Figure 3-3:
iDVD is my
favorite
basic DV
editor
for the
Macintosh.

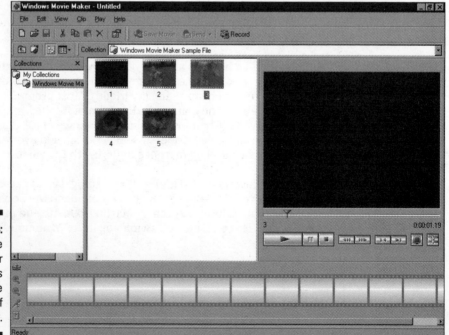

Figure 3-4:
Movie
Maker
follows
in the
footsteps of
iMovie 2.

Figure 3-5:
Adobe
Premiere
ships with
many digital
camcorders.

Chapter 4

Poof! You're a Computer Technician

A certain mystique surrounds today's professional computer technicians: Most folks think that we're one part James Bond, one part Merlin the Magician, and one part Barney Fife. Armed with nothing more than a pair of taped glasses, a Phillips screwdriver, and a spare power cord, techies are supposed to be able to work hardware miracles beyond the ken (reach) of a mere computer owner. (The pocket protector is no longer required equipment; I've never used one.)

If that nerdy stereotype is still your impression of a typical computer technician, this chapter should open your eyes — because *you* can be your own tech. Sure, you can pay someone at your local computer shop to install your new recorder, but why not save that cash and apply it to something else, like your rent? Come to think of it, that $50 you would have paid someone can buy you a stack of 100 blank CD-R discs.

This chapter focuses exclusively on the installation and troubleshooting of CD and DVD recorders — consider it the one-chapter, abridged version of my book *Building a PC For Dummies,* 3rd Edition (published by Hungry Minds, Inc.), which shows that you can assemble an entire PC from the ground up. And yes, I cover possible solutions when the worst happens: when your new drive sits there silently like a bump on a log.

Preparation Is the Key

Ever made a complex dish with a dozen ingredients without first reading the recipe? Or how about climbing on your roof to fix a few shingles and discover that you didn't bring your hammer? Preparation makes all the difference when you're installing computer hardware as well, and in this section I describe the things you need to cover before you get started.

Read the instructions

The steps I cover in this chapter apply to 99.9 percent of the computers and recorders on the planet — but guess who may have bought the drive specifically designed for the other .1 percent of the population? That's right — the Fates may have chosen you as the person who has to cut the blue wire, not the red wire. Certain software may need to be loaded first, or you may need to flip switches to configure your drive correctly, which I don't cover in these generic procedures.

For this reason, you must *read the installation instructions for your recorder* — and that includes external recorders. If the installation process described by the manufacturer is significantly different, follow the general steps I provide in this chapter, jump ship, and follow the manufacturer's steps instead.

Collect what you need

No surgeon (or car mechanic) wants to operate without tools at hand, and you should follow their lead:

- **Gather the stuff you need.** Most installations require just a screwdriver, but bring your drive's installation instructions and any extra parts.

- **Prepare your work surface.** If you're installing an internal drive, prepare a flat, soft, well-lighted surface — several sheets of newspaper on a table work fine.

- **Take your time.** No one's looking over your shoulder with a stopwatch, so relax and follow the steps the right way the first time.

- **Keep those parts.** You're likely to remove small parts, like screws and a bay cover, when installing an internal recorder; keep a bowl handy that can hold everything you remove. You need some of the parts when you reassemble your computer, and anything left over should be saved as spare parts for future upgrades and repairs.

Ask for help

Do you have a friend, loved one — anyone other than your mortal enemy — who has installed a recorder already or who is experienced with computer hardware? If so, buy him a meal and ask his assistance while you're installing your drive. If this is your first time working on the innards of your computer, you can probably benefit from the moral support, too.

By the way, as soon as you've successfully installed an internal drive, don't be surprised if someone you know asks for *your* help with his computer.

Choose a spot to be external

If you're adding an external recorder to your computer, take a few moments beforehand to select the right space for your new drive. The best spot should be

- **A minimum of 6 inches away from your computer:** This space helps minimize interference from your computer's power supply and monitor.
- **Well ventilated:** An external drive can give off a significant amount of heat, so make sure that your recorder has room on all four sides.
- **Free of vibration:** For example, don't park your recorder next to your computer's subwoofer. Vibration can ruin a recording and eventually damage your drive.

Installing an EIDE Drive

As you may have read in Chapter 2, EIDE drives are internal, inexpensive, and fast — no wonder they're the drive of choice for most PC owners. If you've bought an EIDE CD or DVD recorder, now is the time to get down to business and get your new toy installed.

What you need

First, make sure that your PC has these items:

- **An unoccupied drive bay:** Your drive needs a 5¼-inch drive bay that can be opened to the front of your case. Most PC cases have at least two or three of these bays (although a hard drive may be hogging one, even though it doesn't need an opening to the outside world).

✔ **An unused EIDE connector with a cable:** As I mention in Chapter 3, most PCs made in the past two or three years have four available EIDE device connectors (a primary master and slave and a secondary master and slave). You need at least one for your new recorder. You may also need to buy a cable if you're using your secondary EIDE connector because many PC manufacturers don't provide a cable if the connector isn't being used.

✔ **An unused power connector:** No recorder works for long without a power supply. An internal drive uses a connector like the one shown in Figure 4-1. You can also buy a power splitter (or a Y connector) that can convert one power cable into two.

Figure 4-1:
Your internal drive needs a connector to supply the juice.

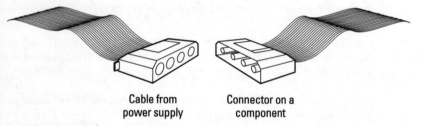

Cable from   Connector on a
power supply   component

The EIDE dance, step-by-step

Let's cover the installation process for an EIDE drive. Follow the steps in this section (and yes, you have to follow them in the order I show here).

Static electricity is not fun, it's not amusing, and it's not your friend: It's the sworn enemy of everyone who's ever installed computer hardware. Static can damage any electronic component in the blink of an eye, and it may not even be easy to spot the damage until you discover that you have a dead drive on your hands. Therefore, you *must* discharge any static electricity on your body before you touch the drive, your PC's motherboard, or any of its internal parts. Touch a metal surface before you open your computer's case — usually, you can just touch the case itself — and touch the internal chassis often during the installation process.

1. **Turn off your computer and unplug it from the AC outlet.**

2. **Remove the screws holding your computer's cover in place and set it aside.**

   Don't forget to put those screws in that high-tech bowl I mention earlier in this chapter.

3. **Every EIDE drive uses a specific configuration that allows your new recorder to cohabitate peacefully with your existing EIDE hard drive(s) or read-only CD-ROM drive.**

   Snazzy Table 4-1 illustrates how you should set up your recorder, although the exact settings for your jumpers vary between brands and models. (If you've never handled a *jumper,* it's the workhorse of the computer hardware world — a tiny, metal-and-plastic crossover that allows you to make connections on the drive's circuit board.) Check your drive's manual for the correct set of pins, and use a pair of tweezers to add or remove jumpers to match that pattern. If you're working with a scavenged drive or you don't have the manual, check the manufacturer's Web site or call its technical-support number.

   - **One hard drive:** Set the hard drive as "multiple drive, master unit" and set your recorder as "multiple drive, slave unit."

   - **One hard drive and one CD-ROM on the same cable:** Set your recorder as "single drive, master unit" and connect it to the secondary EIDE cable. Leave the existing drives alone.

   - **One hard drive and one CD-ROM on different cables:** Set your recorder as "multiple drive, slave unit" and connect it to the EIDE cable that the hard drive is using, and then set the hard drive to "multiple drive, master unit." Leave your existing CD-ROM alone.

   You may have to change the jumper settings on your existing EIDE devices to get things working. For example, if you're adding a CD recorder on your primary IDE connector and you already have an EIDE hard drive on that cable, you have to switch the hard drive from "single drive, master unit" to "multiple drive, master unit." In this situation, your new CD recorder is set to "multiple drive, slave unit."

4. **Check the bay that will hold your recorder.**

   If a plastic insert is covering the bay, you should be able to remove the insert by removing the screws holding it or by carefully prying it off with a screwdriver.

5. **Align the drive into the bay and slide it into the front of the case, with the rear of the drive (the end with the plugs and connectors) going in first.**

   The faceplate and buttons should be visible from the front of the case, as shown in Figure 4-2.

   Naturally, the printing and logo on the front should be facing right side up.

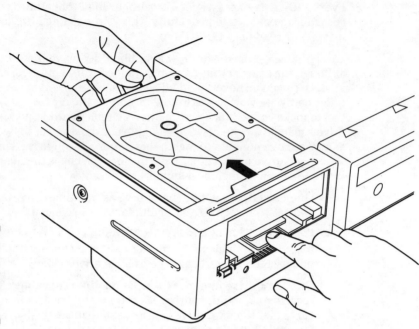

Figure 4-2:
Showing
your
recorder its
new home.

6. **Move the drive forward and backward until the screw holes are aligned with the screw holes on the side of the case and attach the recorder.**

7. **Connect a power cable to the drive and make sure that you press it in firmly.**

   Notice that it goes on only one way, so don't try to force it on backward.

8. **Connect the ribbon cable coming from the EIDE connector on the motherboard to the EIDE connector on the back of the recorder.**

   No need to worry about this connector either because it's notched to fit in only one way. Press it on firmly after it's correctly aligned.

9. **Because pulling and tugging on things inside your computer can result in an unplugged cable, take a moment to check all your connections — even the ones that don't lead to your recorder.**

10. **Replace the cover on your PC with the original screws.**

    Did you read about that parts bowl earlier in this chapter?

11. **Plug in the PC's power cable.**

12. **Turn on your PC and allow it to boot up normally.**

    I love that phrase — like your computer will suddenly grow wings and a tail, leap off your desk, and fly around the room like a dragon. I would say that that would be an "abnormal boot" — wouldn't you?

13. **Uh-oh. I hope that you're not superstitious, and don't mind my ending on Step 13. Anyway, install the software that accompanied your recorder.**

To verify that the installation was successful, try your first recording by jumping to Chapter 8; if things don't fly, read the troubleshooting section at the end of this chapter.

Plugging and Playing with a USB Drive

Made the USB external choice, did you? Notice that this step-by-step section is much shorter than the internal EIDE installation in the preceding section; that's part of the beauty (and the popularity) of USB:

1. **Plug the power cord from your new drive into the AC wall socket.**

   Note that some USB drives are powered through the USB connection itself, so they don't require an external power supply.

2. **Connect the USB cable to the drive (don't connect the cable to the computer's port yet) and turn it on.**

3. **Turn on your computer and allow it to boot up normally.**

4. **Plug the USB cable from your drive into the USB port on your computer, as shown in Figure 4-3.**

   Your next step depends on the software and the operating system you're using; you may see a dialog box prompting you to insert the driver disc that came with your drive, or you may have to install the drive's software separately.

5. **Check your drive's installation instructions to see which path you take.**

That's it. Follow the steps in Chapter 8 to record your first disc and make sure that everything's working well. If your drive's not working, visit the troubleshooting section at the end of this chapter.

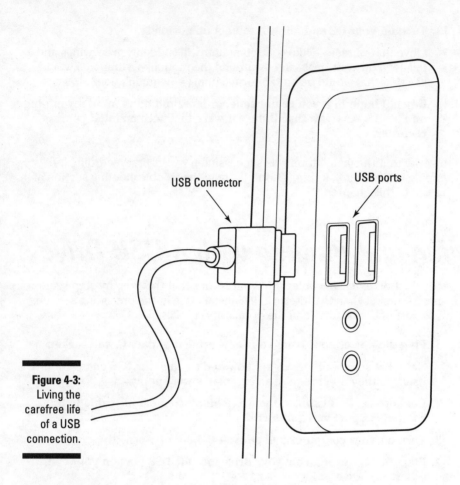

USB Connector

USB ports

Figure 4-3:
Living the
carefree life
of a USB
connection.

Running the SCSI Gauntlet

Decided on an internal or external SCSI recorder? Memorize these two important commandments (add them to the original ten):

Thou shalt assign no two devices the same SCSI ID number.

Thou shalt terminate the ends of your SCSI device chain.

In this section, I explain exactly what I just said — in modern English, without technobabble — and you install your drive.

IDs 'R' Us

Think of a SCSI *device chain* as a "neighborhood on a cable" — to be precise, a chain is at least one SCSI adapter (which may be built-in on your computer's motherboard) and at least one device, which could be your recorder. For your computer to transfer data to or from your drive, it has to know the "address" of your recorder in the SCSI neighborhood. In other words, every SCSI device in your computer needs a unique *SCSI ID number* to identify it, as you can see in Figure 4-4. This sample SCSI device chain has a SCSI card and three devices.

Figure 4-4:
Everyone
got their
own, unique
ID number?
Good!

SCSI card   CDRW drive   SCSI hard drive

SCSI ID: 7   SCSI ID: 4   SCSI ID: 3

Typical SCSI devices can use a range of ID numbers from 0 to 7, with ID number 7 usually the default for your SCSI adapter. (Your SCSI card manual tells you which number the card uses.) Manufacturers of SCSI hardware use different methods of configuring the ID number; most drives use a jumper, which you can set on the correct pins with a pair of tweezers. Again, your drive's manual shows you which jumpers to move when setting the ID number. Some drives also use a thumbwheel you can turn to choose the number.

By the way, there's no reason to assign SCSI ID numbers in sequence; as long as all the device IDs are unique, it doesn't matter what order they're in.

If your SCSI adapter and your SCSI devices are all SCAM ready (man, what an acronym!), you can forget about assigning numbers manually. That's because SCAM stands for *SCSI Configured Automatically:* Enabling this feature on your SCSI adapter allows it to automatically set SCSI ID numbers each time you boot your PC.

Coming to grips with termination

No, I'm not talking about the Flintstones kind of termination, where Fred ends up without a job (again). In the SCSI world, a chain must be correctly *termi-nated* on each end to tell your SCSI adapter where the chain ends. Without termination, your poor SCSI adapter continues to scan the horizon in vain, looking for straggling SCSI devices that aren't there — and your computer either locks up or fails to recognize the last device on the chain. If the termination is set on a device that *isn't* on the end of the chain, it becomes the end anyway, which again leaves at least one SCSI device out in the cold; it either refuses to work or locks your computer. In short, without proper termination, you never get your SCSI devices to work.

Consider the simplest installation of a CD or DVD recorder on a SCSI chain. As you can see in Figure 4-5, this would be just the SCSI adapter and the drive, and the drive could be internal or external. Both these devices naturally indicate the ends of the SCSI chain, so both need to be terminated. When your SCSI adapter looks for terminators, it finds that one device is on one end and the card itself is terminated on the other.

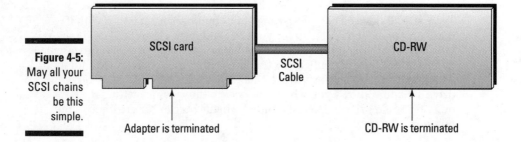

Figure 4-5: May all your SCSI chains be this simple.

SCSI card

SCSI Cable

CD-RW

Adapter is terminated

CD-RW is terminated

However, what if you want to install an internal recorder into an existing SCSI chain that already has a hard drive? If no changes are made and you just added your spiffy new CD-RW drive to the end of the cable, you would invite the disaster shown in Figure 4-6. Because the hard drive is still terminated, your new toy would be useless, and it wouldn't even be recognized within Windows or the Mac operating system.

For this reason, you should *always review all your termination settings when installing SCSI or adding a new device to an existing chain.* Figure 4-7 shows how the same chain *should* be terminated. Now the SCSI adapter can "see" and communicate with the recorder, and all is well.

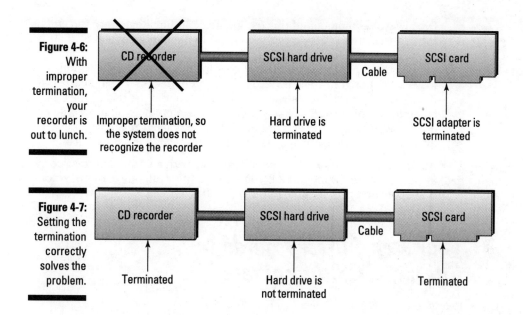

Figure 4-6:
With improper termination, your recorder is out to lunch.

Improper termination, so the system does not recognize the recorder

Hard drive is terminated

SCSI adapter is terminated

Figure 4-7:
Setting the termination correctly solves the problem.

Terminated

Hard drive is not terminated

Terminated

Depending on the manufacturer, setting the SCSI termination usually involves your old friends the Jumper family. You may also encounter a *resistor pack,* which you plug in to add termination and remove to drop termination. Finally, you may set termination by flipping the tiny plastic switches on a *DIP switch* (a tiny switchbox that's wired as part of the circuit board) — use a pencil to set the correct pattern of switches to either On or Off. Again, all these interesting settings appear in your recorder's manual, so keep it handy during the installation process.

What you need

If you're installing an internal SCSI recorder, you need these items:

- **An open drive bay:** Look for a 5¼-inch drive bay that's accessible from the front of your case.

- **A SCSI connector:** Your SCSI adapter should come with a cable, and you should use the first open connector that's closest to the SCSI adapter. If you're adding a drive to an existing chain, select the next open connector on the cable after the last existing device.

I've always recommended this technique of adding devices to the end of the cable (instead of trying to stick them in the middle of a SCSI chain). Why? You have less to worry about come termination time; you simply remove the termination on the last existing device on the cable and make sure that your new device is terminated. Because it's now the last device on the cable, you always know that it marks the end of the chain. Sometimes, this process isn't possible (for example, if you have only one open drive bay and the end of the SCSI cable doesn't reach it), but whenever you can, adding devices at the end of the cable is a good idea.

✔ **An open power connector:** Most PCs come with a veritable forest of available power connectors. If you've used them all, buy a Y connector that splits one power cable into two. 'Nuff said.

Your step-by-step guide to internal SCSI happiness

Ready to dive in? Follow these steps:

1. **Turn off your computer and unplug it from the AC outlet.**

2. **Touch a metal surface to dissipate any static electricity that may be stowed away on your person.**

   Usually, your PC's case suffices just fine.

3. **Remove the screws holding your computer's cover and place it out of harm's way.**

   Put in your parts bowl the screws you took out.

4. **Set the SCSI device ID on your drive to a unique number.**

5. **Determine the correct termination — don't forget that the correct termination includes *all* existing SCSI devices on the chain.**

   Check the position of the SCSI connector you want to use. If the recorder is on the end of your SCSI cable, make sure that the device is terminated (and all intervening devices have had their termination removed).

6. **If necessary, remove the plastic insert covering the drive bay.**

   If the cover is the snap-on type, you can carefully pry it off using a screwdriver.

7. **Slide the drive into the front of the case, with the rear of the drive (the end with the plugs and connectors) going in first.**

   The tray and buttons should be facing the front of the case, as shown in Figure 4-2, and any printing or logos on the front should be facing right side up.

8. **Move the drive forward and backward to align the screw holes on the side of the drive and the case, and attach the recorder with the manufacturer's screws.**

9. **Connect a power cable to the drive and make sure that you press it in firmly.**

10. **Connect the SCSI ribbon cable to the SCSI connector on the back of the recorder.**

    Note that it's notched to fit only one way. Press it on firmly after it's correctly aligned.

11. **Take a moment to check all your power and cable connections — even the ones that don't lead to your recorder.**

12. **Replace the cover on your PC with the original screws.**

13. **Plug in the PC's power cable.**

14. **Turn on your PC and allow it to boot up normally.**

    You should see the SCSI adapter verifying each of the devices on the chain, including your new recorder.

15. **Install the software that accompanied your recorder.**

Sweet! It's time to test things out by taking a quick detour to Chapter 8. If you can't record, remain calm and turn to the troubleshooting section at the end of this chapter.

External SCSI stuff

Like USB and FireWire external drives, an external SCSI recorder carries its house along with it — however, you still have to select a unique SCSI ID and correctly terminate that external recorder before everything starts humming. Use your SCSI adapter's external SCSI port to connect your recorder; a number of different SCSI port configurations are possible, so if your card didn't come with a cable, make sure that you're buying the right type with the right connections.

All external SCSI devices come with two connectors, so you can add more than one external device with additional cables — a classic example is a SCSI system with an external SCSI recorder and a SCSI scanner. The same termination rules you followed for internal drives apply when you're installing multiple external SCSI devices. As shown in Figure 4-8, make sure to terminate the last external device in the chain.

Remember that your SCSI adapter should never be terminated if you've connected both internal and external SCSI devices (in fact, it's now at the *center* of your chain).

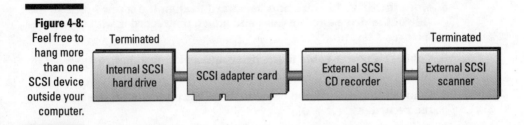

Terminated   Terminated

Internal SCSI hard drive   SCSI adapter card   External SCSI CD recorder   External SCSI scanner

Installing a FireWire Drive

Like USB, the data superhighway that is FireWire makes the installation of your external recorder an easy process. Granted, producing microwave popcorn is easier, but everyone can do that, and it doesn't sound nearly as impressive for the uninitiated. Follow these steps to install your FireWire drive:

1. **Plug the power cord from your recorder into the AC wall socket.**

2. **Connect the FireWire cable to the drive and turn it on.**

3. **Plug the cable from your drive into the FireWire port on your computer.**

4. **Turn on your computer and allow it to boot up normally.**

   Your next step depends on the software and the operating system you're using. You may see a dialog box prompting you to insert the driver disc that came with your drive, or you may have to install the drive's software separately.

5. **Check your drive's installation instructions to see which path you take.**

To double-check your work, rush to Chapter 8 and try burning your first disc. If your drive appears to be suffering from rigor mortis, jump to the troubleshooting section at the end of this chapter.

"Um, It's Just Sitting There"

I *really* hope that you're not reading this — I hope that your recorder went in as smooth as butter, lit up like a Christmas tree when you turned things on, and burned perfectly that first disc of Liberace tunes. Therefore, I'm assuming that you're skipping this section completely. Or, perhaps you've reached this section and you're just curious about what *could* have happened, or you're generally interested in *troubleshooting* (the art of figuring out what's wrong with your computer and how you can fix it).

On the other hand, you may have reached this section with a hunk of hardware that's just sitting there like a dead weight. If so, these sentences are pure gold because they can help you diagnose the problem with your recorder installation and solve it quickly.

EIDE troubleshooting

If you've installed an EIDE drive and it appears to be acting persnickety, here are the problems that folks often encounter and how to solve them.

"The drive doesn't eject the tray, and the power light doesn't turn on."

This problem is usually caused by an unplugged, loose, or broken power connector. Unfortunately, this means that it's time to crack open your PC's case and check your connections.

"I tried to play an audio CD using my recorder, and I can't hear any music."

This problem is common and easy to fix: You forgot to connect the Audio Out cable from the recorder to your PC's sound card. The manufacturer of your drive should provide this cable (and it's often also supplied along with a sound card). Consult the manual for your sound card to determine where you should plug in the Audio Out cable from a CD-ROM drive.

"My drive ejects the tray, but I can't find the drive symbol in Windows, and my software says that it can't recognize the recorder."

The simplest explanation for this problem is an unplugged data cable. Check to make sure that you've plugged firmly into the drive the flat ribbon cable from the EIDE connector. Next, you may have the master/slave jumpers on your recorder configured incorrectly, so check them against the configurations listed in the recorder's manual. Finally — and this is the tricky one — you may have set the jumpers on the recorder correctly, but forgotten to configure the new multiple-drive setting on the drive that's already on that EIDE cable.

SCSI troubleshooting

I think that even Scotty on the original "Star Trek" TV series would have thought twice before sticking one of those silver penlights into a recalcitrant SCSI setup. Just kidding: Although you have more to troubleshoot with a SCSI installation, all it takes to solve a problem is time and patience.

"My computer locks up every time I boot after the installation, and I have to turn it off manually."

I would bet that you're already suspecting that your SCSI termination or ID numbers are configured wrong — and you would be right. Double-check all your termination settings and make sure that they're correct, and then verify that each SCSI device on your chain has a unique SCSI ID number.

"I can't get my SCSI drive to eject the tray, and the power light doesn't turn on."

On an internal drive, check your power cable — if you've added an external SCSI drive, the external power supply is the likely culprit.

"The drive ejects the tray, but my computer acts like the recorder isn't there. (Alternatively, the recorder works, but my existing SCSI scanner is now broken.)"

Poke your drive with a finger to make sure that it's there. (Sorry, I couldn't resist that one.) The real problem is likely your old friends: two or more devices trying to share the same SCSI ID number, or termination that's incorrectly configured for your new drive. Also, make sure that all other SCSI devices on the chain are powered up and connected, and wiggle your data cable to make sure that it's firmly connected.

If your SCSI adapter card came with any SCSI diagnostics programs, running them now and seeing what error messages the programs display is a good idea. Also, check your SCSI adapter manual to see whether you can run a self-test mode.

USB and FireWire troubleshooting

Although both USB and FireWire are Plug and Play (meaning that you can simply connect and disconnect them without rebooting your computer), that doesn't mean that they're troublefree. If your external recorder isn't working, check these possible solutions:

"My computer complains that it doesn't have a 'USB (or FireWire) device driver' when I plug in my recorder."

This message is a clear cry for help from your computer; you either need to install the manufacturer's driver from the disc or the driver you installed has been corrupted. To fix this problem, reinstall the recorder's software. Checking the manufacturer's Web site to see whether an updated USB driver is available is a good idea. If you're using a Macintosh computer and a FireWire recorder, you should check your Extensions list for the device's FireWire extension.

"My recorder has no power; the tray doesn't eject and, no power light turns on."

Your first thought is probably the drive's power supply, and if it does have an external power supply, you're likely right. If you bought your drive locally, take it to the salesperson and ask that person to check it out with another supply. However, if your USB drive is designed to be powered from the computer's USB port, it doesn't have a separate power supply; in this case, the port is probably not providing enough power to meet the USB standard. (This problem happens frequently with USB hubs and keyboard/auxiliary USB ports.) Plug your recorder into another computer's USB port and see whether it jumps into action.

"My drive has power, but my computer doesn't recognize it."

If the recorder's software installation ran without a hitch and the driver is present, this problem is usually caused by a faulty cable, a faulty USB or FireWire hub, or a USB cable that's too long (it shouldn't be more than 10 feet). Try connecting your drive to your computer with a different standard cable and without an intervening hub. Most USB and FireWire devices don't pass a signal when they're turned off, either — this can cause any daisy-chained peripherals that may be connected to suddenly go silent as well. Make sure that all the external devices that connect your recorder to your computer are turned on.

Part II

It's All in the Preparation

The 5th Wave — By Rich Tennant

"You know kids — you can't buy them just any CD creation software."

In this part . . .

Any good cook can tell you that preparation is half the job of preparing a truly great meal — and it's the same with recording a disc. I'll discuss those preparations in this part. You'll find out how to optimize the performance of your PC or Mac, and I'll talk about the recording software you'll use. Plus, I'll decode the engineering-speak that surrounds arcane subjects like CD recording formats, disc organization, and file conversion — they're not dinner conversation, but they are important for a good recording.

Chapter 5

Letting Loose the Software Elves

· ·

· ·

*H*ardware. Are you up to your gills in it? I devote the entire first portion of this book to describing your recorder, buying it, and installing it. Sure, I admit that your drive is the most important part of your computer-based Optical Recording Studio (or ORS), but does it run itself? Can it do anything by itself besides blink a light or two and stick out its tray?

The answer, of course, is a big, fat No. You need software to tame your recording beast. It's like Santa at the North Pole: The old guy gets all the credit, and his elves are constantly toiling behind the scenes all year-round — while he's watching marathon reruns of "The Andy Griffith Show" and eating leftover popcorn balls. Without the elves, who would load the sleigh, make the toys, and feed the reindeer? Not to mention the work that Mrs. Claus must be doing to keep everyone fed and clothed. (Sorry, I tend to get a little carried away — I have three kids.)

In this chapter, doggone it, I change all that. I cover the highlights and special talents of each elf — whoops, I mean *program* — that I use in this book. This information comes in handy if you're considering a shareware or commercial recording package to replace the lame program that came with your recorder. If you decide to buy a different program from the favorites I recommend in this chapter (insert shocked look of chagrin here), make sure that the program you're buying has at least most of these primo features.

The Windows Tool of Choice: The Roxio Easy CD Creator 5 Platinum

For PC owners running Windows, the choice is clear: Easy CD Creator 5 Platinum (which I call Platinum, for short) from Roxio (www.roxio.com). This showpiece has been the solid, reliable Swiss army knife of CD burning for many years. As shown in Figure 5-1, it has the widest range of features of any recording software I've ever used in my travels, it can burn a host of different formats and disc types, and it's simple enough for a novice to use.

Formats and disc types out the wazoo

If you're likely to need just about any specific type of disc on planet Earth, this program can do it. Of course, Platinum can burn simple data and audio CDs using track-at-once or disc-at-once without even lifting an eyebrow, but it can also pump out

- CD-ROM XA (multisession) discs
- Video CDs
- Mixed-mode discs
- CD Extra discs
- Photo slideshow discs

This lineup also includes two types of discs that both deserve special attention: the *bootable* CD-ROM and the *MP3 CD* disc. As you may have already guessed, you can boot most PCs using a bootable CD-ROM, so you can even run your PC without a hard drive — after a fashion, anyway. A bootable disc can also carry other programs and data besides a basic operating system. A Microsoft Windows CD-ROM is a good example of a bootable CD: It uses DOS as a basic operating system, but, after your computer is up and running, you can install Windows from it and *really* screw up your system. (Sorry, Mr. Gates, I didn't mean that. Please don't pull the plug.)

An MP3 disc, on the other hand, is a specialized data CD-ROM. Although it carries music in MP3 (MPEG Audio Layer 3) format, its songs are not recorded in the Red Book digital audio format (refer to Chapter 2), so you can't play the disc in your stereo's audio CD player. MP3 discs are meant to be played exclusively on either your computer, using a program like WinAmp, or on specially designed MP3 CD players.

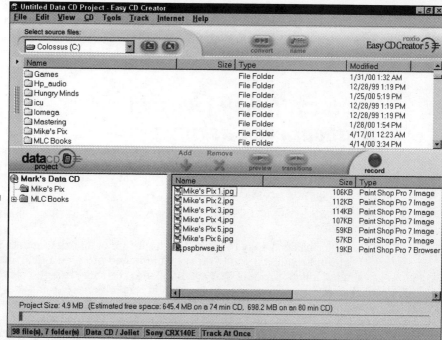

Figure 5-1:
Platinum
is the
recording
software of
choice for
most PC
owners.

Wolfgang woulda loved this

Interested in burning hot music on a compact disc? Whether those songs are in MP3 format or stored on older cassettes and vinyl albums or you're collecting tracks from a number of existing audio CDs, Platinum can do it in style. Although I've tried many different programs that record audio CDs, Platinum continues to be my favorite: It's the easiest to understand and the fastest to use. On the audio side, the program can

- Automatically convert songs in MP3 and WMA (Windows Media Audio) formats and prepare them for recording
- Extract tracks from existing audio CDs and save them as WAV files on your hard drive
- Store CD text for display on many CD players with digital readouts
- Add transition effects, like fade-in, fadeout, and cross-fading
- Preview WAV and MP3 songs before you record them

I especially like how Platinum can venture onto the Internet — it can check online music databases and download all the track names for CDs it finds. This feature can save you both time and sore fingers because you avoid typing all those track names by hand.

Extra stuff they give you (without even asking)

If the Platinum feature list ended in the preceding section, most folks would be satisfied. But, wait — what if I told you that you also get these great stand-alone (separate) programs to boot?

CD Copier

CD Copier makes it easy to produce a duplicate of an existing data or audio CD (without requiring you to start Platinum and produce a disc image, which is a much longer process that accomplishes the same thing). Folks who date back to the glory days of floppies should remember programs that allowed you to copy a disk read from one drive to another. If you have both a read-only CD-ROM drive and a recorder in the same PC, you can use the read-only drive as the source (as I'm doing in Figure 5-2). No "swapping" required. If you have only a recorder, however, you can still use CD Copier — you just have to eject the original disc and load a blank.

I show you how to use CD Copier in Chapter 8.

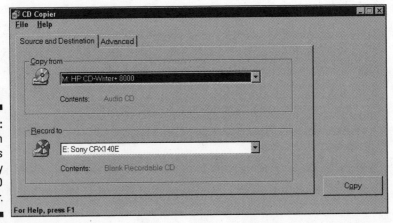

Figure 5-2:
Copying an audio disc is child's play with CD Copier.

Take Two backup

How many times in this book do I harp about backing up your hard drive? Would you mind losing every file you've ever known if your hard drive crashes? If you don't have a current backup, I'll nag you like your mother until you make one. (There's a scary thought, eh?)

With Take Two (as shown in Figure 5-3), you no longer have any excuse. It can back up a drive to multiple CD-RWs as fast as your drive can shovel ones and zeros.

Chapter 8 includes the steps for a typical hard drive backup.

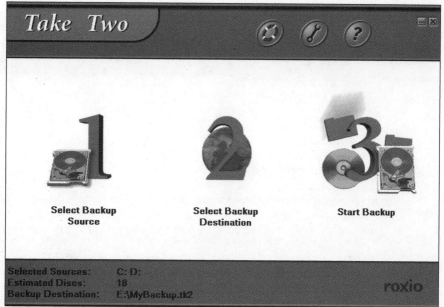

Figure 5-3:
Use Take
Two! Back
up! Do it!

Sound Stream 2

Sound Stream 2 is an exciting program for anyone interested in recording music: You can copy your favorite old cassettes and albums to audio CDs. Those of us with extensive piles of vinyl and tape still occupying the corners of a room know the heartbreak of losing an old favorite that hasn't been released in compact disc format. Scratches and stretched tape can ruin your treasures, but after you use Sound Stream 2 to transfer them to CD, as shown in Figure 5-4, you can keep them for their cover art.

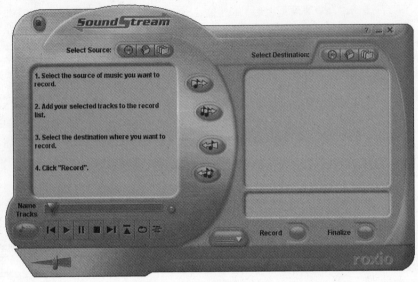

Figure 5-4:
Sound
Stream 2 is
a complete
analog-to-
digital music
solution.

I show you in Chapter 11 how to transfer that "H.R. Puffinstuff" soundtrack album to CD.

CD Label Creator

Let me be honest: I like a labeled disc, but I don't label everything I burn. For example, if I'm going on a business trip and I've just recorded a disc of material for a book I'm writing, I don't go to the trouble of printing a label — I just use my trusty CD-ROM marking pen and write a short title right on the disc.

On the other hand, CD Label Creator (shown in Figure 5-5) is the program you want to use when a disc needs to look its best — if you're giving it to someone else or you're particularly proud of that video CD you made at your cousin's wedding. The program can also produce both front and back jewel box inserts, with classy clip art, photographs, and different fonts. You can also choose one of the themes that's already set up in the program, which can produce a matching set with a label and a complete set of inserts. Neat!

Chapter 14 includes a step-by-step example using CD Label Creator.

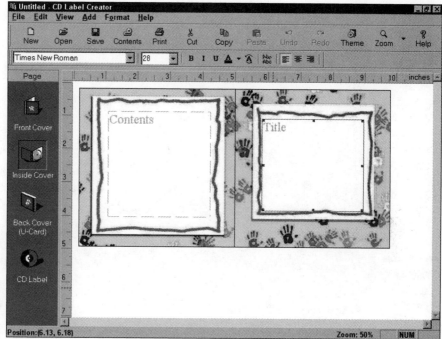

Figure 5-5:
Puttin' on
the Ritz with
CD Label
Creator.

Burning Up Your Macintosh with Roxio Toast

As you can see from Figure 5-6, those Mac folks look different again: This time, it's Toast Titanium, from Roxio, the king of recording programs on the Macintosh. (Don't ask how the program got its name — I'm sure that a funny story is in there, but I don't know it.)

Besides the standard formats — audio, data, mixed-mode, video CD, and CD Extra — that we all expect, Toast can produce a couple of nifty extras:

✔ **Hybrid discs:** These strange beasts can be read under both Windows and the Mac operating system — they're often used for cross-platform applications that have both a Mac and Windows version. Games are often shipped on hybrid discs for the same reason.

✔ **DVDs:** Toast can burn DVD-R discs on supported drives.

If you're burning discs for older Mac operating systems, you can use the Mac standard format. If your disc is used on a newer machine running Mac OS 8.0 or later, however, you should use the enhanced Mac OS Extended mode.

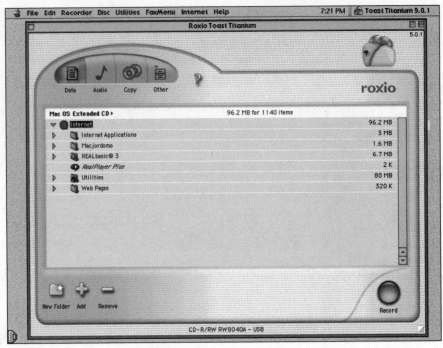

Figure 5-6:
No butter,
no jelly —
just Toast.

As any Mac technotype can tell you, the Mac operating system can mount a disk image as a "virtual" drive on your desktop. Toast can both create and mount these images for you, so you can store multiple images on a single CD or DVD and use them rather than hunt for a physical disc. (I leap headlong into the subject of disc images in Chapter 8.) I also like the Compare feature in Toast, where you can compare two folders or files and view the differences.

Chapter 9 is devoted to burning with Toast. (I'm sorry — that one just slipped in subconsciously.)

Packet Writing Made Easy with DirectCD

Packet writing is almost as foolproof as a burnproof recording: You simply format the disc, write to it just like it's a huge floppy or Zip disk, and then finalize it for reading just like an ordinary CD-ROM. Teamed with a CD-RW drive, packet-writing software can produce the nearly perfect, reusable, low-cost storage solution that everyone has been chasing since the first 1GB drive appeared way back when. Figure 5-7 illustrates the Roxio DirectCD hard at work.

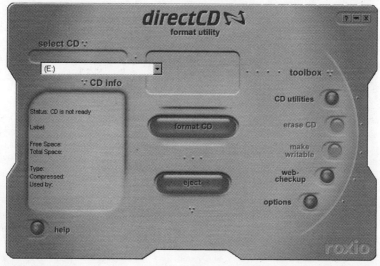

Figure 5-7:
DirectCD is
the key to
oneness
with your
CD
recorder.

You can find a complete rundown on DirectCD in Chapter 10.

Introducing the Editors: iMovie 2, iDVD, and Premiere

Not one of these three programs counts as true disc-recording software: Instead, they're software programs for digital video editing and disc design and the creation of special effects that just happen to have recording features built-in. (As you can tell, these programs cross a number of boundaries when it comes to genre.) Because I use them later in this book, however, I thought that I would introduce at least a little something about each one here.

iMovie, as shown in Figure 5-8, was a groundbreaking arrival for both Apple and the world of digital video. iMovie marked a revolution where practically anyone who could connect a FireWire cable, drag and drop video clips, and select a transition or two could develop their own professional-looking movies. For the first time, you didn't need several hundred dollars to spend just on editing software (it has been shipping free with iMacs since the program was first introduced). iMovie was simple enough to appeal to novices, who definitely didn't want to spend hours understanding the basics of a more powerful, traditional editor. Unfortunately for Windows folks, iMovie 2 runs on only Mac OS 9.1; however, Windows Movie Maker is *very* much like it.

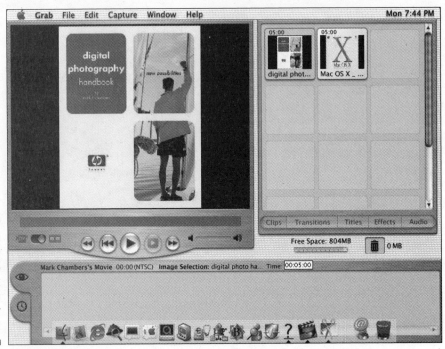

Figure 5-8:
If you buy a
Macintosh
these days,
you pick up
iMovie 2 for
free.

iDVD is the recently released big brother to iMovie 2: At the time I wrote this book, it was available only on Macintosh computers that offer the CD-RW/ DVD-R SuperDrive. With iDVD, you can master your own DVD-ROM titles, complete with basic menu and submenu interaction. For example, viewers can select a video clip to watch or view a slideshow of digital photographs). While designing your disc, you can use a prepared "theme" to automatically set the appearance of your buttons and background, or you can add your own. Finally, iDVD allows you to preview your work and burn the DVD within the program itself. Figure 5-9 shows iDVD in action.

The excellent Adobe digital video editor Premiere (as shown in Figure 5-10) is available for both Windows and Mac OS. Premiere is much more powerful than either iMovie 2 or iDVD, offering professional special effects, better control over audio and timing, output as streaming Web video, storyboarding, and the ability to handle more formats of digital video. However, it's not anywhere near as simple to use as iMovie 2 or iDVD. Because it's a commercial program, you're likely to spend around $500 or so for a copy. Premiere is the right choice for those folks who know that they're in digital video to stay, want to grow into a professional package, and want its tight integration with other Adobe products, like After Effects.

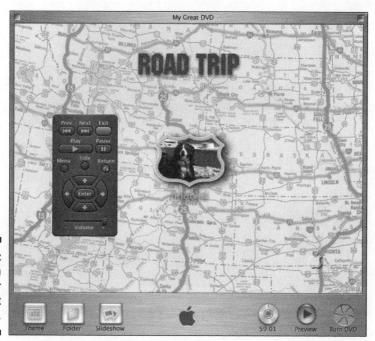

Figure 5-9:
Deciding on
a theme for
my newest
hit DVD title.

Figure 5-10:
You pay for
it, but Adobe
Premiere is
the classic
digital video
editor.

Chapter 6

Fine-Tuning Can Be Fun

"**I**n the beginning, there was Windows 3.1, and the 486 processor, and many did try to record their first CD-ROMs and fell by the wayside. For buffer underruns roamed the land, ruining those discs because the computer could not keep up with the recorder. And many threw up their hands in anger and frustration, and they knew then that they must optimize their systems."

Such tales are few and far between these days because you're likely using a PC or Macintosh that performs much better than the 486-based computers of old. The latest hard drives can deliver data much faster than a recorder can burn it, and today's burnproof recorders no longer fear multitasking and disk-intensive applications. So why do I dedicate a chapter to optimization and fine-tuning? I have two important reasons (besides the fact that I needed a topic for Chapter 6).

First, you may not be lucky enough to own only the cutting edge in hardware. I own and use seven computers, and only one of them is state-of-the-art (meaning that it's less than a year old). If both your computer and your drive have been hanging around for three years, for example, optimization is just as important as ever.

Second, optimization helps your entire system run like the Six Million Dollar Man: better, faster, and farther. I recommend many of these steps even if your computer doesn't sport a CD or DVD recorder right now — you'll thank me the next time you open Microsoft Word or Adobe Photoshop.

Therefore, this chapter is designed to help you tinker and tune. Just hand me a wrench and the proper screwdriver from time to time, and your computer will soon be running at its best.

Creating Elbowroom

No matter how you cut it, 700MB of data takes up a fair chunk of hard drive territory — and that's just what you store on a CD-R or CD-RW disc. As you may have read in earlier chapters, a double-sided DVD-RAM disc can store as much as 9.4GB! You can see how hard drive space can become important very quickly, and there never seems to be enough. You find that your data expands to fill your drive, whatever the size (rather like The Blob). In this section, I cover a number of tips and tricks that can help you clear space for your next burning session.

'Course, you could just buy a bigger hard drive

Although a bigger hard drive is the likely option for the fine folks living in the Gates mansion, I would bet that you would rather conserve space, reduce clutter, and just keep your current drive. Besides the space you need in order to temporarily store the data or audio you want to record, two other important temporary files are taking up space behind the scenes:

- ✔ **Temp files used by your recording software:** If you're recording in Disc-at-Once mode, for example, your software is likely to create a temporary image file of the entire disc — this process typically takes as much space as the data itself!

- ✔ **Virtual memory:** Both Windows and the Mac operating system use territory on your hard drive as *virtual memory,* which is storage space for all those ones and zeros that don't fit into the physical RAM installed in your system. (Ever wonder how a computer with 32MB of RAM can run a 10MB program that opens 256MB files? That's virtual memory at work.) Figure 6-1 shows how limited your system becomes if virtual memory is disabled. I talk more about virtual memory throughout the rest of this chapter.

As you may have guessed from the word *temporary,* these files are deleted after the recording has finished or the additional virtual memory space is no longer needed. (Insert ominous chord here.) However, good people, not all programs are as tidy in cleaning up behind themselves.

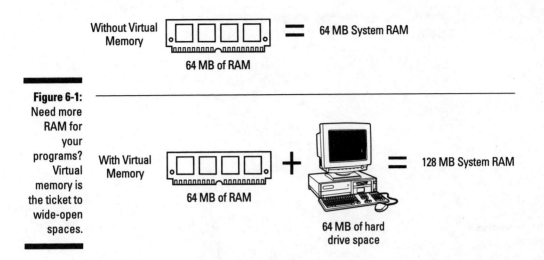

Without Virtual
Memory   =   64 MB System RAM

64 MB of RAM

Figure 6-1:
Need more
RAM for
your
programs?
Virtual
memory is
the ticket to
wide-open
spaces.

With Virtual
Memory   +   =   128 MB System RAM

64 MB of RAM

64 MB of hard
drive space

Locate unnecessary stuff

If you have ever deleted programs and data files manually from your computer, you know that you're waltzing in a potential minefield — never,
never — *never* — delete files willy-nilly! (That's a nontechnical term for opening Windows Explorer and simply deleting an entire folder.) Luckily, programs
that are both built-in to your operating system and available separately at
your neighborhood computer store can help you remove accumulated hard
drive crud safely.

First, though, here's a rundown of which files you can likely kiss goodbye
without sending your computer into a coma:

  ✔ **Demos, samples, and Aunt Harriet's fruitcake recipe:** First things first:
    Get rid of those 10-year old game demos and one-shot software installa-
    tions that you'll never need again! Naturally, you should drag whatever
    unnecessary documents you have created yourself to the Recycle Bin —
    I mean, how many Top Ten joke listings should you save? Anyway, after
    you have decided what to trash, click Start➪Settings➪Control
    Panel➪Add/Remove Programs to display the dialog box shown in
    Figure 6-2. (You should always use this method to delete an entire pro-
    gram!) Click the program you want to delete from the list and click
    Remove to start things moving.

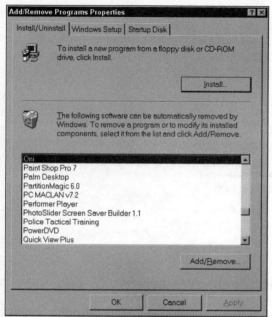

Figure 6-2:
Deleting a
program
(the right
way).

✔ **The contents of your Trash or Recycle Bin:** Hey, you didn't want these files anyway, and they already have one foot in the Great Beyond! To clear the space under Windows, right-click the Recycle Bin icon and select Empty Recycle Bin. Under Mac OS 9.1, click the Special menu and choose Empty Trash; under Mac OS X, click Finder and choose Empty Trash.

✔ **TBR:** That's an acronym of my own — I guess I just snapped from all these silly technobabble terms. It stands for *typical browser refuse*: the images, Web pages, and sound files your browser stores in its cache to speed things up when you reload a page. Luckily, shoveling this stuff out the door is easy because both Internet Explorer and Netscape Navigator allow you to purge their cache directories. If you're a big-time Web walker, you may be surprised at the sheer amount of space you can reclaim!

✔ **Windows temporary files:** Folks running Windows 95 and Windows 98 can click Start⇨Shut Down⇨Restart in MS-DOS Mode to reboot their machines in DOS. (Remember DOS?) Then, type this line:

```
CD C:\WINDOWS\TEMP
```

To change to the Windows temporary folder. Next, type this line:

```
DIR
```

To list the contents of the folder. (Everything in here should end in .TMP — if it doesn't, you're probably in the wrong directory.) Finally, type this line:

```
DEL filename
```

(where `filename` is the filename displayed by the DIR command) to delete a temporary file. You can repeat the DIR and DEL commands as many times as necessary. (Heck, Windows has probably forgotten that these files ever existed!) After you have deleted the files, type

```
EXIT
```

and press Enter to reload Windows.

If you're a Windows power user, you may be wondering why I talk about deleting these files manually instead of using the Disk Cleanup Wizard. I cover the wizard in just a paragraph or two — no fair peeking. Suffice it to say that the wizard may not completely empty the \WINDOWS\TEMP directory, so I still follow this same procedure from time to time to keep things squeaky-clean.

Let the wizard do it!

Fans of J.R.R. Tolkien's classic *The Hobbit* will agree: Dwarves would much rather leave the heavy work to the burglar or the wizard! If your system is running Windows 98 or later, you can turn to the Disk Cleanup Wizard to help you automate the removal of accumulated disk gunk.

To run the Disk Cleanup Wizard, follow these steps:

1. **Click Start⇨Programs⇨Accessories⇨System Tools⇨Disk Cleanup.**

   Geez, can the friendly folks in Redmond hide useful stuff like this any further under the rug?

2. **If you have more than one hard drive on your system, choose Drive C: from the drop-down list box and click OK.**

3. **Windows displays the Disk Cleanup dialog box, as shown in Figure 6-3.**

   As you can see, you save quite a bit of space here! Click OK to begin the cleanup.

4. **Click Yes to assure Windows (which is often slightly paranoid) that you do indeed want to delete files.**

Sit back and watch as the wizard safely sweeps your system clean. Neat!

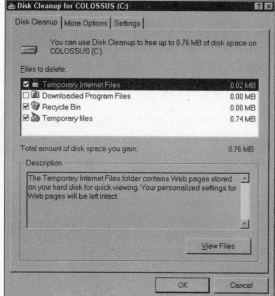

Figure 6-3:
Not even
Gandalf can
clear space
as fast
as the
Windows
Disk
Cleanup
Wizard!

Call in the professionals

I can heartily recommend two commercial programs that can help you clean up either a PC running Windows or a Macintosh running Mac OS 9.1. Figure 6-4 illustrates Norton CleanSweep for the PC, from Symantec (www.symantec.com) — it offers a high level of safety. I especially like the feature that locates and deletes temporary, zero-length, and duplicate files that can nibble at your free space.

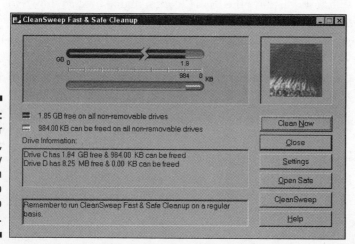

Figure 6-4:
Under
Windows,
you can buy
Norton
CleanSweep
to tidy up
your drive.

On the Macintosh side, I recommend Spring Cleaning, from Aladdin Systems (`www.aladdinsys.com`), which does everything from uninstalling old programs to zapping browser cache files.

Checking Under the Rug

Your computer may be hiding something from you: No, not a winning lottery ticket or a love affair with a coffee machine, but rather nasty errors on your hard drive that may be robbing you of both free space and performance. If you don't look for these errors, I can guarantee that they won't leap up and identify themselves (except, of course, those errors that continue to grow worse and eventually cause you to lose files and data *permanently*). Before you burn — or, for that matter, once every couple of days — running your computer's disk diagnostics program is a good idea to take care of anything hiding under the rug.

These errors fall into two categories:

- *Logical errors* are the most common file problems, and they're usually caused by improper shutdowns, power outages, and misbehaving programs. If you have already encountered lost clusters and cross-linked files, you have already met (and hopefully fixed) logical errors on your hard drive. Most logical errors can be solved with the right software.

- *Physical errors*, on the other hand, are caused by a malfunction in the hard drive itself. The classic cause of physical errors is the infamous and frightening hard drive crash, where either your entire drive croaks or the magnetic platters inside are damaged. Physical errors usually can't be corrected by the layman — if you're willing to spend a rather unbelievable amount of money, some companies can fix the innards of your hard drive, but in most cases it's simply not worth the effort. Therefore, if your drive is acting up and returning physical errors, I strongly recommend that you back up now — this second! — and buy a replacement drive.

Fixing your drive the Windows way

Checking a drive under Windows 98 and Windows Me is child's play, thanks to a program named ScanDisk; using it at least once a day to fix any logical errors that may appear on your drive is a good idea. Follow these steps to put ScanDisk through its paces:

1. **Click Start⇨Programs⇨Accessories⇨System Tools⇨ScanDisk to display the dialog box shown in Figure 6-5.**

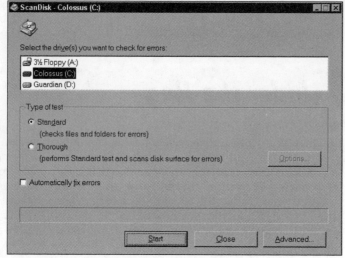

Figure 6-5:
Scanning
for pesky
errors with
ScanDisk.

2. **Use the drop-down list box to select the hard drive you want to scan.**

3. **Click Standard to check for logical errors, or click Thorough to check for both logical and physical errors.**

   Be prepared for a long haul if you choose Thorough, especially on today's huge hard drives.

4. **Click Start to begin the scanning process.**

5. **After the disk has been checked and any logical errors squashed, ScanDisk displays the results.**

6. **Click Close to return to Windows and your work.**

Fixing things with Mac OS 9.1

In the Macintosh world, Apple includes with Mac OS 9.1 a drive checkup program named Disk First Aid. Follow these steps to use it:

1. **From the desktop, click your hard drive and then click Applications (Mac OS 9)⇨Utilities⇨Disk First Aid to launch the program, as shown in Figure 6-6.**

2. **Click the icon for the hard drive you want to scan.**

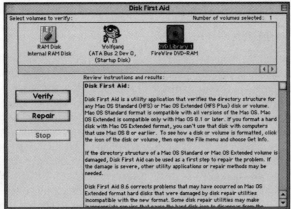

Figure 6-6:
Should I
call this
"iPreventive
iDisk iMaint-
enance"?

3. **Click Repair. Disk First Aid automatically checks the selected drive and repairs any errors.**

   To repair some errors on your startup disk, you may have to boot your Macintosh using your Mac OS 9.1 CD-ROM. To do this, insert the CD-ROM, restart your Mac, and hold down the C key throughout the boot process.

4. **Done? Click File⇨Quit to return to the MacOS desktop.**

Most commercial disk utility programs can also check your drive (such as Disk Doctor, which comes with Symantec Norton Utilities for both Windows and the Macintosh).

Avoiding Fragments

It's time to cover another insidious problem that can rob your computer of the performance you need for recording: *hard drive fragmentation*. Geez, more buzzwords.

I could get into a convoluted description of sectors, files, and your computer's operating system — but this is a *Dummies* book, so I have distilled all that hoorah into a sidebar. If you're interested about what you're doing and why fragmentation occurs, read a little more. Otherwise, just remember this important truth: Defragmenting your hard drive is a good thing to do once a month or so, and it speeds up the overall performance of your computer (including, naturally, your recordings).

Defragmenting For Dummies

No matter how cool I think defragmenting is, I just don't have enough material to write a *Dummies* book about it. I know for sure because I pitched that book proposal to the publisher before I wrote this book. So consider this sidebar your personal copy of *Defragmenting For Dummies* (definitely the shortest book in the series). It has no table of contents, no Part of Tens, no index, and not a single figure or table — but I do tell you what's happening behind the curtain.

Why do files fragment? Well, as you delete and move files from your computer, you open areas on your hard drive for new files. However, these open areas aren't always big enough to hold a new file in one piece, so your computer and hard drive work together to save files in pieces called *segments*. For example, if you're copying a 200MB video clip to your hard drive so that you can record it later, your drive may not have 200MB worth of contiguous, unbroken open space on it — that's when the file is broken up into segments. Perhaps 20MB can fit in one place on your disk, and 100MB can fit in another, and so on. When the time comes to read the file, Windows automatically and invisibly "reassembles" it and sends it to the proper place. All is well, right?

It is until your drive becomes badly fragmented and little chunks of thousands of different files are spread across the surface of your hard drive! If a file is saved as a contiguous whole, your drive can read it efficiently and quickly. On the other hand, it takes a significantly longer time for Windows or the Mac operating system to rebuild a file that's made up of dozens of segments in several different locations. We humans see this lag time in the form of decreased performance and a delay of a second or two. When you're burning a disc, however (especially on an older computer with a fast CD or DVD recorder), that drop in performance can result in a coaster. Scratch another disc, unless you're using a burnproof drive.

You can solve this problem by running your defragmenting program. This slick piece of software reads each file on your disk, combines the segments to form a contiguous file, and then saves the reassembled file back to disk in one piece. Plus, most defragmenting programs can also rearrange the locations of your files so that the programs and data you use most often load the fastest. When the program is finished, your hard drive is a smooth, efficient vista — a storage wonderland. (I think perhaps I need to stop now, before I wax too enthusiastic.)

Windows 98 and Windows Me come with a defragmenting program named (strangely enough) Disk Defragmenter, but Mac OS 9.1 doesn't have a defragmenting program. Mac owners, I feel your pain, and I recommend using a commercial program like Speed Disk (another part of Norton Utilities, from Symantec).

Therefore, here are the steps for defragmenting your drive under Windows:

1. **Click Start➪Programs➪Accessories➪System Tools➪Disk Defragmenter.**

2. **Disk Defragmenter displays the dialog box shown in Figure 6-7. Choose your target from the drop-down list box.**

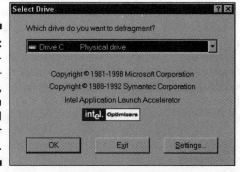

Do you have more than one hard drive? If so, defragmenting all of them is a good idea (especially if you want to record files from multiple locations). If you're pressed for time, however, always pick Drive C because it usually holds both Windows and your virtual memory swap file.

3. **You need to make an adjustment before you begin: click Settings and enable the Rearrange Program Files So My Programs Start Faster check box. Click OK to save the setting.**

4. **Click OK to begin the defragmentation process.**

You can continue to work on other things, but defragmenting takes much less time if you can leave your PC to its own devices. (For this reason, I always defragment during the night, when I'm generally not using my computers.)

Avoiding the Unexpected

"Okay, Mark, how am I supposed to predict the unpredictable?" Good point — I don't mean the *really* unexpected things in life, like a hard drive crash or an honest politician. Instead, I'm talking about that doggone screen saver that pops up while you're burning or that silly guy in the next office who bothers you with constant network messages. Things like these are also unexpected, and they can easily trash a disc.

In this section, I talk about a number of automatic features and functions of Windows and the Mac operating system (OS) that you can disable before you start recording, which can help you avoid these irritating interruptions.

Scheduled events and scripts

Both Windows and the Mac OS allow you to set up scheduled events that run automatically at a certain time or periodically during the day. Although this feature can be a great convenience, I recommend that you disable any scripted or scheduled tasks if you're set to record.

Under Windows 98 and Windows Me, you can temporarily pause scheduled tasks by pausing the Task Scheduler. Click Start➪Programs➪Accessories➪ System Tools➪Scheduled Tasks to display the Task Scheduler, as shown in Figure 6-8. Click Advanced and select Pause Task Scheduler from the menu. After you have finished recording, you can display the Task Scheduler again and restart the schedule: Click Advanced and select Continue Task Scheduler, and click the Close box in the upper-right corner to banish the Scheduler from your screen.

Although Mac OS 9.1 doesn't have a built-in task scheduler, you should disable any scheduling software you may have added before you record; check the program's documentation to determine how to disable or pause automatic events.

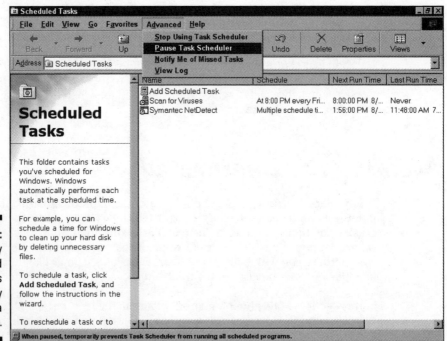

Figure 6-8:
Pause any scheduled tasks that may interrupt a recording.

Network access

Planning on using your recorder on your office or home network? All that network hard drive space makes this idea appealing, but I don't recommend recording a CD or DVD from a network source unless you have no other choice. Depending on the traffic your network carries, your file transfer rate may slow to a crawl and your recording may be interrupted by network messages from your administrator and other users. Someone halfway across the building may decide to copy that unabridged electronic text of *Beowulf* that you have stored on your hard drive.

Worst of all, you may hit a number of hidden snags — restricted or password-protected file access, network drives that suddenly disappear because they were brought down, and so forth. When the network suddenly displays a "dropped connection" dialog box in the middle of your recording session, you have (to put it delicately) hosed a disc.

To wit: Rebooting and recording directly from your local computer's hard drive is a better idea, without logging in to your network unless you're sure of its stability.

If you *absolutely* have to use network storage for your recording, however (for example, if you have a diskless workstation at your desk), I can make three suggestions:

- ✔ **Buy a burnproof recorder.** Burnproof technology prevents a ruined recording caused by a sluggish network and usually avoids optical tragedy even if the recording program is interrupted with a network message. (Naturally, though, it can't fix a disconnected network drive!)

- ✔ **Record using packet writing.** I recommend Roxio DirectCD for packet writing, and I cover it later in this book; even older recorders that don't offer burnproof protection can successfully burn a disc on a busy network when you use DirectCD.

- ✔ **Record early in the morning or late at night.** An empty office generally means an empty network, with far fewer delays and intrusions from other network users.

Power-saving mode and screen savers

Computers are now sophisticated pieces of equipment — they can even fall asleep or switch to standby mode if their lazy humans take a soda or coffee break. Allowing your computer to switch to these power-saving modes is normally a great idea: You save electricity without having to shut your machine down completely. When you're burning a disc, though, your computer may not recognize the activity — after all, you're not really moving your mouse — and a switch to a power-saving mode can be disastrous! I recommend that you either disable your computer's power-saving or standby mode (especially if you're recording on a laptop computer) or set it to at least 30 or 60 minutes before it kicks in.

The same is true of those cool screen savers that keep boredom at bay. They're neat, and I have more than 50 on my own machine, but whenever I use a screen saver, I set it for at least a 60-minute period of inactivity before it starts. This period allows me to complete any recording session before the light show starts and the fun begins.

In Windows, you can configure both your power-saving mode and your screen saver activity delay from the Control Panel. First, click on the Power Options Control Panel icon to display the settings shown in Figure 6-9, and set both Turn Off Hard Disks and System Stand By to Never. To change the inactivity delay for your screen saver, open the Display Control Panel and click on the Screen Saver tab. Click the Wait box and type **30** or **60** for the number of minutes.

If you find yourself continually using the Power Options Control Panel, set up two power schemes you can use to switch back and forth between power-saving and recording modes.

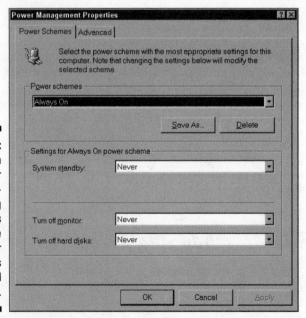

Figure 6-9: You can change your power-saving settings from the Power Options Control Panel.

Macintosh owners, click on the Apple menu and choose Control Panels. Then, click Energy Saver to display the dialog box shown in Figure 6-10. Move all the sliders to Never and click the Close box in the upper-left corner.

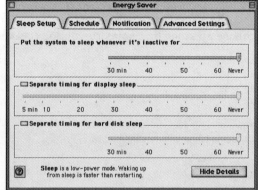

Figure 6-10:
Mac
owners,
saving
energy
while
burning a
disc is not a
good idea!

Terrific Tips and Tweaks

Although I get into specific recording tips throughout the rest of this book, pay heed to these general tricks that apply to all types of recordings.

Avoid disk-intensive, memory-hungry behemoths

Follow this advice while you're recording, anyway. In other words, if you don't have a burnproof drive, launching programs like Microsoft Outlook, Adobe Photoshop, or Macromedia Flash during that burn is not a good idea. They simply take up too much system memory and thrash your hard drive too actively to cooperate well with optical storage.

Give your recording software some elbowroom

Is Mac OS 9.1 your recording environment of choice? Do you have at least 64MB of system RAM? Then I strongly recommend that you reserve additional application memory for your recording software, which can use it for all sorts of good things.

Follow these steps to increase the memory allocated to your recording program:

1. **From the Finder, click the recording program's icon once to highlight it. Click the File menu family and choose the Get Info item.**

2. **Click File and select Get Info from the menu.**

3. **Click Show and choose Memory to display the dialog box shown in Figure 6-11.**

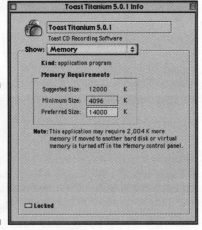

Figure 6-11: Make room! Under Mac OS 9.1, allocating extra memory is a good idea.

4. **Click the Preferred Size box and specify a larger amount of RAM.**

   As a rule, I tend to double the figure, but you should add at least 1024K, or 1 megabyte, of extra memory.

5. **Click the Close box to close the dialog box and save your changes.**

Speed up your hard drive

Here's a great tweak for PC owners running Windows 98 and Windows Me that can help your hard drive's performance! Follow these steps:

1. **Right-click the My Computer icon on your desktop and choose Properties from the pop-up menu.**

2. **Click the Performance tab and click File System to display the File System Properties dialog box (see Figure 6-12).**

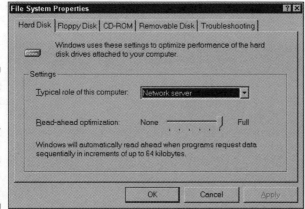

Figure 6-12:
Vroom,
vroom!
Suddenly
your hard
drive acts
more like a
sports car!

3. **Click Typical role of this computer and choose Network server from the drop-down list box. Drag the Read-ahead optimization slider to Full (if it's not there already).**

4. **To save your changes, click OK to exit the File System Properties dialog box and click OK again to return to the desktop.**

   Note that you may have to reboot after this step.

Beware the flagged-out laptop

Laptop owners can be proud of their computers, but a loss of battery power has caused the premature demise of many a recording session. If you're using a laptop to burn a CD or DVD while you're on the road, use your AC adapter if at all possible — and if not, make doggone sure that your battery is fully charged and can last for at least 30 minutes. Also, remember that most laptops automatically switch to standby mode if their battery power levels drop below a certain point, so don't cut things too closely!

Chapter 7

Getting Ready for the Ball

· ·

In This Chapter

▶ Selecting the proper format

▶ Using the correct recording mode

▶ Choosing the right file system

▶ Organizing your material properly

▶ Adding thumbnails to a disc

▶ Converting files between formats

· ·

At this point, you may be ready to throw caution to the wind and start burning ones and zeros — and I can't say that I blame you because I cover a huge amount of ground in this book, and you may not have even recorded a single disc yet! However, I want to devote just one more chapter to preparations; in this case, steps you should take to make your finished discs

✔ Faster during loading and reading

✔ Better organized

✔ Easier to use

✔ Easier to search

See? This stuff is worth another chapter's wait. I promise! I especially recommend that you take care to follow the guidelines in this chapter when you're creating a disc for distribution or creating an archive disc that you will use often over the next decade or two.

Picking a Jazzy Format

I mention formats as features in Chapter 2 — criteria you could use to tell just how high a particular recorder ranks on the evolutionary scale. In this section, I show you how you can make use of those different formats; certain formats are the right choice for certain jobs, and many read-only CD-ROM drives can handle only data and audio CDs.

Data, lovely data

Pure data — your computer lives on the stuff, and that's what data CD-ROMs are for. If you're storing only data or program files — no digital audio — this is the disc format for you. These discs fall into one of two standards: the Yellow Book (for data CD-ROMs manufactured in a factory) and the Orange Book (for data CD-ROMs you have burned with your CD recorder). Some specialized types of discs I mention earlier in this book — for example, video CD and photo slideshow CD-ROMs — are specialized types of data CD-ROMs.

Use a data CD-ROM when you want to

- Store computer files and programs, using the same folder or directory hierarchy as on your hard drive.
- Take advantage of the maximum storage space for data.
- Run programs directly from the disc.
- Load data (like a Word document or a spreadsheet) directly from the disc.
- Save multimedia files, like digital video and digital photographs, as data.

In case you're wondering, your computer's CD-ROM drive is the best playback solution for *any* kind of disc because it can read both audio CDs and data CD-ROMs without blinking. Your audio CD player can't return the favor, though. Don't try to read a computer CD-ROM in an audio CD player: If you hear anything, it's likely to be a screeching wail that will drive away every living thing within a square mile. I'm not kidding; even plants try to escape.

Sweet audio for the ears

Unlike a data disc, a disc recorded in audio CD format — also called Red Book — can store only one type of material (in this case, digital audio). However, it does this really, really well; so well, in fact, that an audio CD player doesn't recognize anything unless it's either Red Book or a subset of Red Book (like a CD Extra disc, which I discuss in Chapter 11).

You can use a number of different sources for audio tracks, including

- MP3 files
- WAV files (a Microsoft Windows standard)
- AIFF files (a Macintosh standard)
- WMA files (another Windows standard)

Man, this band is *horrible!*

Okay, let me get this straight: You have just recorded your Red Book first audio CD from that huge selection of Slim Whitman MP3 files you're so proud of, and the burn seemed to go like butter — you got no error messages, the songs sounded perfect when you previewed them, and your new drive churned the disc out in less than minutes. Excellent! Hold on, though — when you try playing your new disc in your car audio CD player, you get either a screeching wail that sounds like a catfight under an outhouse, or nothing. I mean, absolutely zip. What went wrong?

This is the classic of all classic problems: You mistakenly recorded a data disc format rather than a Red Book audio CD format! Those files are still in MP3 format, and they can be played using WinAmp or another MP3 player program — but only on your computer. To play those songs using your audio CD player, you have to record them again; this time, make sure that you choose Red Book or digital audio or audio CD format (whatever your recording software calls it) when you're setting up the recording.

Oh, one other possibility exists: If your audio CD player doesn't recognize your new CD but your computer's CD-ROM drive (or your recorder) *does* play it, you have rebelled against tradition and used a CD-RW disc rather than a CD-R disc. Of course, this particular rebellion is in vain because your audio CD player simply can't read a CD-RW.

Unlike with a tape cassette, however, you can't record your voice directly on an audio CD. Instead, you have to record your material (usually as an MP3 or WAV file), and then record that disc in audio CD format later.

Are you a musician who uses a MIDI instrument or composes in MIDI format? You can record your compositions on an audio CD as well, but you have to follow this same process and create an MP3 or WAV digital audio file on your hard drive with your MIDI software. After the music is in one of these digital formats, you can burn it to a Red Book audio CD just like any other MP3 or WAV audio.

Remember that a standard audio CD player can't read a CD-RW disc. Use only CD-R discs when you're recording Red Book CDs!

Use an audio CD whenever you want to record a disc for a standard audio CD player.

Straddle the line with mixed mode

There's always an exception, right? (Just like those spelling rules you used to memorize.) In this case, you *do* have a way to record both data and digital Red Book audio on the same disc: mixed-mode format, which is used for multimedia discs and games that need programs, digital video, and high-quality audio on the same compact disc. As you can see in Figure 7-1, mixed-mode discs have two tracks: The first contains data, and the successive tracks are digital audio. Pretty slick!

Because that first track is a data track, however, you still can't play a mixed-mode disc in your audio CD player: This is the idea behind the CD Extra disc, where the audio tracks come first, followed by data tracks. You *can* play a CD Extra disc in your audio CD player — I venture into this territory in Chapter 11.

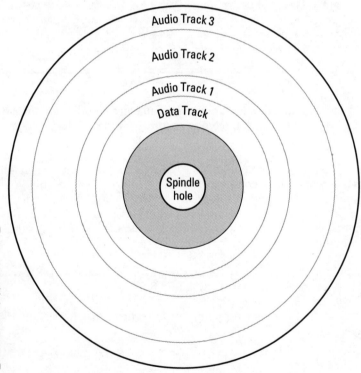

Figure 7-1: Who says data and audio can't mix? (They separate like oil and vinegar.)

Why aren't all discs recorded in mixed-mode format? Of course, there's not much point in it if you're recording only files and programs or recording only digital audio. Other caveats apply:

- **Less operating-system–friendly:** Older versions of DOS, the Mac operating system, and UNIX can't read mixed-mode discs. (Then again, DOS is fading into an indistinct memory for most of us; I use a command line only for Linux these days.)

- **Less compatible:** Older, read-only CD-ROM drives may be able to read only the first or last track on a mixed-mode disc.

- **Decreased capacity:** Working the magic of mixed-mode takes anywhere from 3MB to 19MB of wasted space. Most of that space is required in order to separate the data track from the first audio track. Therefore, don't use mixed-mode format if you need to squeeze every possible pit from your recorded CD.

Use a mixed-mode CD-ROM when you want to

- Store both computer files and digital audio on the same disc.
- Run programs and load files directly from the data track.

Throw caution utterly to the wind with packet writing

I crow enough about packet writing — or, as it's more properly called, Universal Disc Format — in this book that you may already know that it's one of my favorite topics. Packet writing makes it easy to record what you want, when you want it, using either a CD-R or CD-RW disc. Heck, you don't even need to open Easy CD Creator first to write a UDF disc with DirectCD. Just drag-and-drop as you always do, or save directly to the disc from within your applications — if you can do it with a floppy disc or a hard drive, you can do it with packet writing.

Packet writing even allows you to delete files you have written — in a fashion, anyway. The directory entries for the files you're deleting are overwritten, after which the unwanted files effectively vanish. This situation can make it appear that you have erased them completely and regained that space, like you would with your hard drive, but that's not the case: They still take up space on the disc; you simply can't reach them.

Also, you should remember that both CD-R and CD-RW discs must be formatted before you can use them with a UDF program, like DirectCD. Naturally, after you have filled up a CD-R, you can't reformat it and use it over again, but you can reformat a CD-RW disc recorded using packet writing. You lose all the data that's on the disc, of course, but that makes it a great choice for "one-shot" discs. (After all, that's the attraction of CD-RW discs: They can be reused over and over.)

Drawbacks to packet writing? There are only a couple: You can't record a Red Book audio CD using packet writing, and older operating systems (before Windows 98 and Mac OS 8) can't read UDF discs without a separate loader program.

"Disc at Once? Track at Once? Why Not All at Once?"

If you really want to act like a computer technotype at your next party, walk over to a group of your friends and jovially inquire, "So, folks, which recording mode do you use with your audio CDs?" It always gets me a laugh. (I don't get invited to many parties.)

Anyway, this question is indeed a valid one. The recording mode you use helps determine the compatibility of your finished disc and how much data or audio it can contain. Therefore, I cover the four common recording modes now (so that you are ready to answer my question if we attend the same gala bash).

Meet you at the track

In track-at-once recording mode (or, as it's technically known, CD-ROM Mode 1), each data or audio track is kept primly separate from the others: No coed comingling here! As you can see in Figure 7-2, your recorder turns off the laser write head between tracks.

On the positive side, track-at-once mode is supported on every recorder, no matter how old, and can be read on any CD-ROM drive. That's why it's the default recording mode used by most recording programs. Unfortunately, those gaps left by the laser when it toggles off can cause a distinctive "click" noise between each track on an audio CD — whether you hear it depends on the audio CD player, but it can be excruciatingly irritating. Therefore, track-at-once is best used for data CD-ROMs.

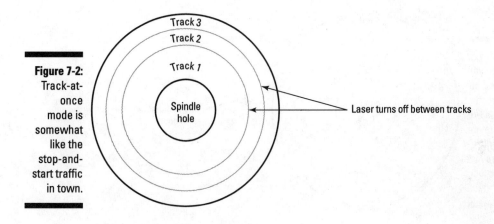

Figure 7-2:
Track-at-
once
mode is
somewhat
like the
stop-and-
start traffic
in town.

Laser turns off between tracks

Do it all at once

Disc-at-once (DAO) recording mode is the best pick for audio CDs. That's
because your recorder's laser is never turned off, and the entire disc is written at once (as illustrated in Figure 7-3). You don't hear a click between
tracks, no matter what type of audio CD player you use.

Disc-at-once mode has three drawbacks, though: First, most older CD
recorders can't write in disc-at-once mode, so if you own an older drive and
you try to select DAO in your recording software, you will probably find that
you can't. Second, your disc takes longer to record in disc-at-once mode.
Finally, DAO recording occupies more temporary hard drive space because
your computer must first create an image file of the entire disc before it can
begin burning.

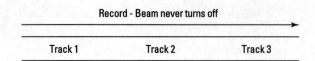

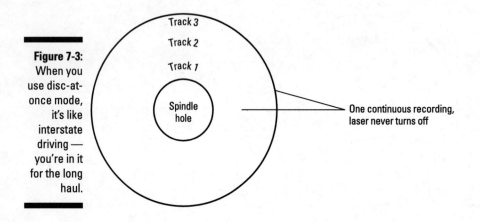

Figure 7-3:
When you use disc-at-once mode, it's like interstate driving — you're in it for the long haul.

Multipurpose multisession

Multisession recording (or, to be technically correct, CD-ROM/XA Mode 2) allows you to add more than one separate session to a disc (think of a chapter in a book), each of which can be read just like a different CD, as shown in Figure 7-4. You can record sessions at different times, too, which makes multisession recording particularly handy for incremental recordings over weeks or months.

Again, compatibility is an issue: Multisession mode is not supported on many older, read-only CD-ROM drives, and you need a separate program that can switch between sessions to read all the material on the disc. (For example, Easy CD Creator has a program named Session Selector.) Also, multisession discs can't be properly read in audio CD players.

Only Session 1, 2, or 3 can be active at one time

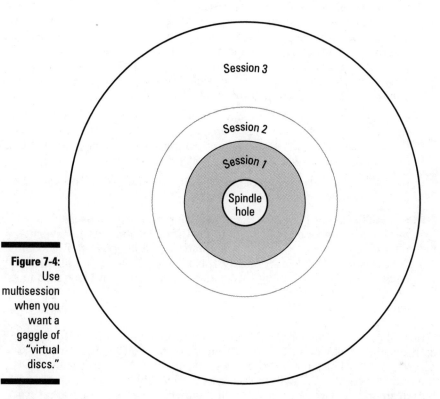

Session 3

Session 2

Session 1

Spindle
hole

Figure 7-4:
Use
multisession
when you
want a
gaggle of
"virtual
discs."

Long Filenames Are Your Friends

While I'm discussing the decisions you must make before recording a data
CD-ROM, I think that now is the right time to mention the four major file systems. A *file system* is a specific set of naming conventions and a data layout
that — whoops, there I go again, letting loose the programmer technical troll
within me. (Sorry about that.)

Let's keep this simple: A file system determines

- What type of computer can read your disc
- The allowable filenames and their length
- The total number of subdirectories (or folders) that can appear on the
  disc and what arrangement they can take

The four major file systems are

- ✔ **Microsoft Joliet:** Supported since Windows 95, Joliet is now by far the most common file system used on PC CD-ROMs. Joliet provides the long file- and folder names that the Windows crowd now finds indispensable, and those names can include niceties like periods, spaces, and most of the characters on your keyboard. A notable exception is the \ (backslash) key, so don't try to use it. If you're burning a disc on a PC for a PC, you have little reason to use anything else.

- ✔ **HFS:** If you own a Macintosh, most of your Mac-only discs use the Hierarchical File System (HFS). Some programs allow a Windows system to recognize and read HFS discs (and, in the same vein, you can find Mac extensions that allow a Mac to read Joliet discs).

- ✔ **Hybrid:** Hybrid discs contain both a Joliet session and an HFS session and can be read on both PCs and Macs.

- ✔ **ISO 9660:** Finally, I come to the oldest file system still in use. ISO 9660 has been around since the dawn of the CD-ROM, and virtually every operating system ever shipped can read it (including heretics like Linux, Solaris, and BeOS). Unfortunately, this high level of compatibility is caused by a vanilla naming convention, so you don't find long filenames on an ISO 9660 disc; also, you can store a far fewer number of files in each directory.

Which one should you use? Luckily, this question is one of those that basically decides itself. For a PC disc, I strongly recommend Joliet; Mac owners can rely on HFS. Folks recording cross-platform PC or Mac discs should use the Hybrid file system. Finally, if you're looking for the widest possible distribution among the largest number of different computers and operating systems, go with the perennial favorite, ISO 9660.

The Right Way to Organize Files

Yes, Virginia, there is indeed a "right way" to add files to a data, mixed-mode, or UDF CD-ROM! Smart organization makes finding that certain data file for your tax return easier — especially if you're being audited tomorrow. No matter what sort of data you're recording, *take the time to think things through*.

Believe me — I have spent many years organizing my data. As an author and consultant, I can't afford to waste time digging through an entire binder of 250 discs, trying to figure out what was burned where. Therefore, heed my words when I say:

- ✔ **Use every character of those long filenames!** The ability to use long file names is the primary reason why you should use the Joliet file system whenever possible. You may know now that the file named AHARCAKE you just burned is Aunt Harriet's fruitcake recipe, but will you remember that after 5 or 10 years?

- ✔ **Put your files in folders!** This problem is a common one with hard drives, too. Storing all your files in the root directory (like C:\) results in the worst kind of anarchy (the computer kind!). Also, file systems such as ISO 9660 can handle only a certain number of files in any directory or folder, including the root directory. The solution is simple: create new folders in the root directory of your CD layout and give the new arrivals logical names, then organize the files within the folders; more on this in a second.

- ✔ **Use a logical file arrangement.** You can help yourself in years to come when you're searching for files by organizing them in a Spock-ian fashion: That is, stick files of the same type or files that relate to the same topic together in separate folders. Or, if you have enough files and you have the time, you can do both, with folder names like Pictures of Fluffy in 2002. Think of the fun you can have! Anyway, when you combine a folder arrangement like this with long filenames, you can suddenly locate that needle in a haystack — and you can still find it three years from now.

- ✔ **Use file-cataloging software.** Some shareware and commercial disk cataloging programs can store the names and locations of every file on a drive. These programs create indexed databases of each CD-ROM you record; with one of these utilities, searching for a single file among 20 of your personal library discs is as simple as using the Windows Search feature. Your operating system may also allow you to search an entire disc. For example, both Mac OS 9.1 and Mac OS X feature Sherlock 2 (see Figure 7-5), which you can use to search not only for filenames but also even strings of text *inside* documents!

Of course, you may not want to spend this kind of time if your disc holds two or three 200MB video clips and nothing else — but it sure helps when you have 300 files to store on one CD-ROM.

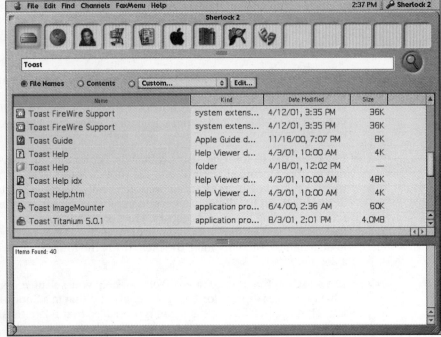

Figure 7-5:
I use
Sherlock 2
to find
everything
but my
socks.

"Thumbnails? You're Kidding, Right?"

Not the human body kind of thumbnails! I mean the postage-stamp–size pictures that represent larger JPEG, TIFF, and bitmap images you have stored inside a folder. When you use a program like Paint Shop Pro (www.jasc.com) that can generate these munchkins, you can build a catalog of thumbnails that make it easy to scan dozens of images in seconds (using the most sophisticated optical hardware ever designed, the human eye). After you have found the right image, just double-click on the thumbnail to load it. Figure 7-6 shows a screen chock-full of thumbnails that I'm searching with Paint Shop Pro.

If you also want to catalog your other multimedia files — like sound files and video clips — you can use Jasc Media Center (again, www.jasc.com). Like digital images, the multimedia thumbnails in this program allow you to preview your stuff by just clicking on icons.

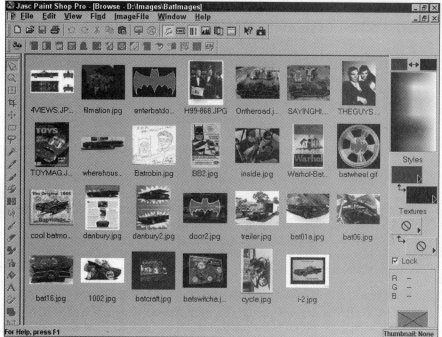

Figure 7-6:
Scanning
more than
100 images
takes only
a few
seconds
with
thumbnails!

No matter what program you use, the trick to remember is that you must generate the program's catalog and add it to the CD layout so that it can be recorded along with the rest of the material. (No sense in keeping the catalog file on your hard drive for 100 years, unless, of course, you use this disc every day.)

Converting Files for Fun and Profit

Before I end this chapter, here's a riddle for you: If you have burned a CD-ROM of photographs from your digital camera in JPEG format (which most cameras produce) and you're using a Macintosh, what have you done wrong? (Because this chapter is about convenience and ease of use, consider that a clue.)

Don't forget that virus check!

As a final preparation before burning, I always run Norton Antivirus and check the contents of those folders that contain the files I have selected — especially for a disc I'm giving to someone else. Can you think of anything more antisocial than sending your friend a virus in a Word document or a program file?

Technically, the answer is "nothing" — until, that is, you try to use those images in most Macintosh applications. You see, most Mac programs that use graphics favor images in TIFF format. Of course, you can use an image editor like Photoshop to open those JPEG images and convert them to TIFF format each time you use them, but talk about a time-wasting hassle! In this case, you would have made a wise decision if you converted all those files to TIFF format before you recorded them so that you can simply pop the disc into your computer and load photos directly from it. (Don't worry if you didn't get that one — it was extra credit.)

With this example in mind, I want to devote this last section to format conversions: which common formats work best in what situations and which programs work best when converting files to other formats. The idea is twofold: You want your material in the form you use it most, and you also want that material to be recognized and usable in years to come.

What exactly is a format? A computer programmer would tell you that a file format is an arrangement of data that corresponds to specific byte positions and data element lengths. (Whew. Thank goodness my days of writing COBOL are over.) We flesh-and-blood humans can simply think of a *format* as a "language" that's recognized by a program for storing and reading files. For example, although an image may look exactly the same when it's displayed in two different formats, one file may be 100K long and another may be 1MB long! The difference in size is caused by the format, which determines the way the image data is saved.

You're likely to encounter four major species of formats when you're recording CDs:

- ✔ **Audio:** Without a doubt, the two most popular — and usable — audio formats for saving your recordings are MP3 and Windows WAV. Between the two, MP3 is probably the best choice because WAV files can reach colossal sizes when recording longer songs at higher-quality sampling rates. Also, Macintosh owners have far more support on their systems for MP3 than for WAV. To convert other sound formats to MP3, I use Musicmatch Jukebox Plus (www.musicmatch.com), as illustrated in Figure 7-7. You can download the basic version for free.

Figure 7-7:
I use
Musicmatch
Jukebox
Plus to
convert
audio
between
formats.

✔ **Video:** Digital video now generally resides in Quicktime MOV format, Microsoft AVI format, or MPEG format — and surprisingly enough, I'm again not recommending the Microsoft standard. Instead, I archive my video clips in MPEG format, which is recognized by just about every editor on the planet; you can be certain that future versions of your editor can import your clips for new projects. For conversion, I use Adobe Premiere on both the PC and Macintosh, which can import all these formats. More expensive commercial programs can handle a wider range of less popular formats, but because I use only the Big Three, Premiere works fine in my case.

✔ **Images:** For archival purposes, select JPEG, TIFF, or Windows Bitmap; the latter two don't use "lossy" compression, so they offer better quality, but both TIFF and bitmap images are much larger than their JPEG counterparts. JPEG is recognized by most image editors (and because JPEG is the format of choice for Web pages, you have the advantage of being able to copy your archived images directly to your Web site). On the PC side, either Paint Shop Pro (from Jasc) or Adobe Photoshop do the conversion trick; on the Macintosh side, use Photoshop or the classic Graphic Converter, from Lemke Software, at `www.graphicconverter.net` (see Figure 7-8).

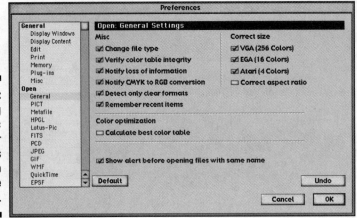

Figure 7-8:
Putting
Graphic
Converter
through its
paces on
the
Macintosh.

✔ **Documents:** I can't think of a better set of tools for importing, converting, and exporting all sorts of document formats than Microsoft Office (www.microsoft.com): On both the PC and Macintosh sides, it can read in most of your ancient, hoary document formats for spreadsheets, word processing files, presentations, and databases. For archival purposes, it's a safe bet that saving your documents in one of the standard Microsoft formats using the Office suite of applications is a good idea.

Part III
Hang On — Here We Go!

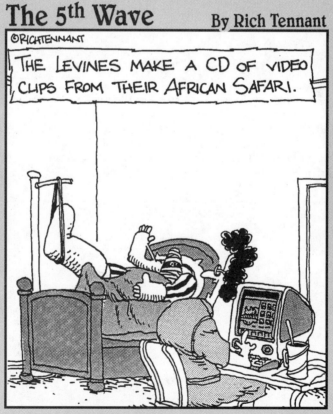

The 5th Wave   By Rich Tennant

THE LEVINES MAKE A CD OF VIDEO CLIPS FROM THEIR AFRICAN SAFARI.

"Do you think the 'Hidden Rhino' clip should come before or after the 'Waving Hello' video clip?"

In this part . . .

Burn, baby, burn! Time to learn the basics of recording — I'll show you how to use the popular Roxio recording programs Easy CD Creator (for the PC) and Toast (for the Mac) to create audio and simple data CDs. You'll see how easy CD recording can be as I demonstrate packet writing with DirectCD.

Chapter 8

Taking Easy CD Creator for a Spin

• •

In This Chapter

▶ Recording data CD-ROMs

▶ Recording audio CDs

▶ Copying an existing CD

▶ Using disc images

▶ Creating multisession CD-ROMs

▶ Erasing a CD-RW disc

▶ Backing up your hard drive with Take Two

• •

*I*t's time to crank up Easy CD Creator on your PC and find out how to make basic data CD-ROMs and audio CDs! You can consider this chapter the bread-and-butter of CD recording: These types of discs are likely to make up 90 percent of the recordings burned by most PCs. First, I describe the basic steps for each procedure, and I close this chapter with three projects that illustrate specific tasks.

Interested in recording DVD-R or DVD-RAM? Unfortunately, Easy CD Creator 5 doesn't support DVD media. However, I fill in the details about DVD-R recording on the Macintosh with Toast in Chapter 9, and Chapter 13 covers DVD-R and DVD-RAM on the PC.

Recording Data: Putting Files on a Disc

The first disc I ever recorded was a data CD-ROM — ah, the memories! Easy CD Creator hadn't been released yet, and the primitive software I used was anything but automatic or easy to use. In fact, I burned a couple of useless coasters before I finally got everything to work.

The great file and folder hunt

"I *know* I put that file somewhere on this drive!" Brothers and sisters, I feel your pain. Searching for one document in the midst of 50 directories and 30,000 files is not my idea of a fun way to spend an afternoon. If you agree, click on the Find Files or Folders button next to the Select source files list box (the button with the folder and the magnifying glass) to call for help from Easy CD Creator.

First, choose the drive you want to search by clicking the Look in drop-down list box. (Boy, those folks in Redmond sure know how to label their fields.) Then, choose your search criteria:

The filename: Even if you know only a part of the filename, you can enter it in the Named field.

(Don't forget to enable the Include Subfolders check box if you want to search the folders below the specified location.)

Text within a file: Search for all files containing a certain string of text by entering the text in the Containing Text field.

The file's time and date stamp: Click the Date tab and enter the date or time range.

The size and type of the file: Click the Advanced tab and choose the type of file and its minimum or maximum size.

When you're ready to go, click Find Now. Good luck, Mighty Hunter!

Just about everything has changed for the better. Easy CD Creator shields you from as much of the drudge work of burning a CD-ROM as possible. Follow these steps to record a basic data CD-ROM with folders and files from your PC's hard drive:

1. **Load a blank disc into your recorder.**

   If you're using a CD-RW disc, it should be formatted (see the section "Erasing a CD-RW Disc," later in this chapter). Easy CD Creator detects that you have loaded a blank disc and automatically displays the rather sexy-looking Project Selector screen (as shown in Figure 8-1).

   To run the Project Selector from the Start menu, click Start➪ Programs➪Easy CD Creator 5➪Project Selector.

2. **Click the funky blue button marked Make a Data CD.**

3. **Click Data CD Project, which automatically runs Easy CD Creator and opens an empty data CD-ROM layout, like the one shown in Figure 8-2.**

   If you would rather run Easy CD Creator directly from the Start menu, click Start➪Programs➪Easy CD Creator 5➪Applications➪Easy CD Creator.

   See the folder tree that fills the top portion of the window? It operates just like Windows Explorer, and you use it to select the folders and files to include in your layout.

Figure 8-1:
Hey, the
Project
Selector
almost looks
like a
Macintosh
program!

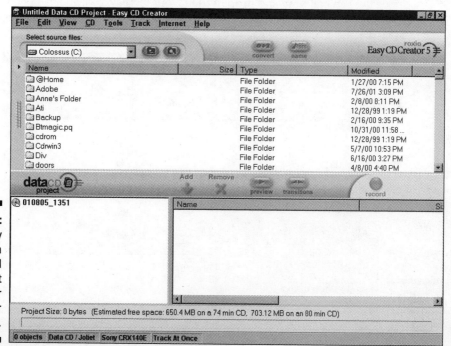

Figure 8-2:
An empty
data
CD-ROM
layout, just
waiting for
your
selections.

4. **To open a folder and display the contents, double-click on it; to move up to the preceding directory, click on the Up one level button (which looks like a folder with an up arrow on it).**

   You can also use the Select source files drop-down list box to navigate to a specific folder. Highlight a folder or file that you want to add by clicking once on the name — you can highlight several by holding down the Ctrl key while you click.

5. **After you have highlighted the folders and files you want to add in the current directory, click the Add button in the center of the screen.**

   Alternatively, you can click and hold the mouse to drag the selected icons from the Explorer tree to the layout display that fills the bottom half of the window. Oh, and if you look at the bottom of the window, you see a truly nifty bar display that tells you how many megabytes you have used in your layout and how much space remains (for both a 74-minute CD and an 80-minute CD) — programs like this one make me proud to be a technonerd.

6. **If necessary, repeat Steps 4 and 5 with other folders until all the files you want added appear in the layout display (as shown in Figure 8-3).**

   You can drag and drop in the layout display, too, so it's easy to arrange files in different folders or in the root directory of the disc if necessary.

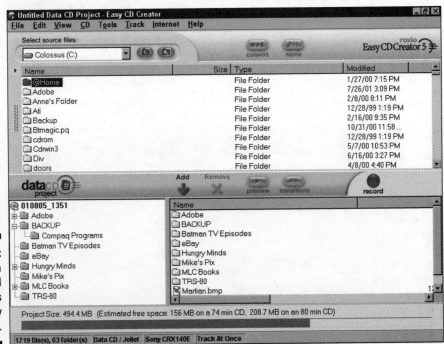

Figure 8-3: The data CD-ROM layout is rapidly filling up.

Arrgh! It never fails: You're almost finished designing your CD-ROM layout, and your Mom calls. Luckily, you can save your current project within Easy CD Creator. Click File and choose Save Project List, enter a filename, and click Save. (To copy the current project under another name, click File and choose Save Project List As instead.) When you're ready to continue with your project, run Easy CD Creator, click File, and choose Open CD Project; highlight the project file and click Open to load it.

You probably won't be satisfied with a name like 010803_0203 for your disc — I don't blame you! Therefore, why not change it? Click once on the CD volume label in the layout window (it's right below that cute Data CD Project logo), and you can change the name just like you would rename a file on the Windows desktop. Remember that you are limited to a certain number of letters, depending on the file system you're using, so keep your name short.

7. **Everything squared and ready? Houston, you're go for recording! Click the Big Red Record button in the center of the screen.**

   The program presents the Record CD Setup dialog box you see in Figure 8-4. For a simple data CD-ROM, the program's default hardware settings should work just fine.

8. **Check to make sure that the correct drive and recording speed are listed.**

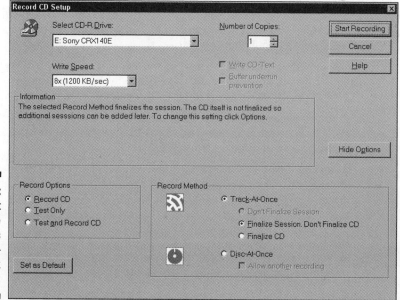

Figure 8-4: Don't let these settings scare you — this is a walk in the park!

9. **Because this recording is probably your first, you can click Test and Record CD if you want to be extra careful. Although it takes twice as long, Easy CD Creator performs a test recording first, and if the test is successful, you can perform the recording.**

   If a problem occurs, you save a blank disc from becoming a coaster. After you have become comfortable with your recorder, however, I recommend that you pick Record CD and press onward.

10. **You can make more than one copy of your disc by specifying the number in the Number of Copies field.**

11. **If you can enable the Buffer underrun check box, do so with all haste — this action turns on your drive's support for burnproof recording.**

   The CD-Text area isn't much fun for a data CD-ROM, so just leave that feature disabled.

12. **If you're recording in track-at-once mode, you can choose one of these options:**

    • **Don't Finalize Session:** Leaves the disc open so that you can record more data later without creating a multisession disc. However, until you finalize either the session or the CD, you can read this disc only in your CD-RW drive. If this field is grayed out, either your drive or the file system you chose doesn't support this option.

    • **Finalize Session, Don't Finalize CD:** Closes the current session so that the disc can be read in any CD-ROM drive; however, the CD itself is not finalized, so you can write additional sessions and create a multisession disc.

    • **Finalize CD:** The entire disc is closed, so you can't write any further sessions. (You can consider it "write-protecting" the disc.) I typically use this option if I'm recording in track-at-once mode.

13. **If you're recording in disc-at-once mode, you may be able to enable the Allow Another Recording check box, which creates a disc with multiple disc-at-once sessions.**

   Naturally, if this check box is grayed out, you can't use this feature. Remember that most older CD-ROM drives do not recognize one of these discs.

14. **Click Start Recording to start the wheels turning!**

   If you used the Windows Start menu method of running the Project Selector and you haven't already loaded a blank disc in the recorder, the program automatically ejects the tray and demands that you feed it one.

   The Record CD Progress dialog box appears, as shown in Figure 8-5, and you can watch the fun. After the disc has been recorded, you can optionally run CD Label Creator or just quit and try out your new toy.

How do you "test" a CD-R?

"Hang on, there, Mark — you said that I could use a CD-R only once. How can my recorder test the disc without messing it up?"

Easy! If you remember my discussion of lasers in Chapter 1, you remember that your CD recorder can toggle between two power levels; when you test a layout, your recorder acts like it's burning the disc, when in fact the laser is

toggled to the lower power setting. At this lower setting, the beam doesn't affect the dye layer (or the crystalline layer, if you're using a CD-RW disc).

The result is a safe test: Easy CD Creator can still detect whether it would encounter an error while recording, but if errors are detected, you don't lose your blank disc!

Congratulations! You're the proud creator of a brand-new data CD-ROM.

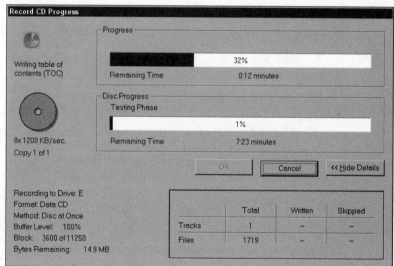

Figure 8-5: This is it, Bucko! You're burnin'!

Recording Your Music

Remember to rip and record only what you've bought, or what's legally available on the Internet. Likewise, don't copy commercial software and blithely hand it over to those who didn't pay a penny for it. I won't turn into a lawyer and start talking unintelligible legalese, but honor the copyrights of the musicians and software developers that worked the long hours. Please.

These days, I find myself recording audio CDs primarily from MP3 files — however, Easy CD Creator can also

- ✔ Copy both individual tracks from existing CDs (in a process sweetly called *ripping*).

- ✔ Copy an entire existing audio CD (find out more on this in the next section, where I show you how to clone things with CD Copier).

With your permission, then, let us create the Ultimate Motorhead Mix CD (or, if you prefer, the Absolute Best of Alvin and the Chipmunks):

1. **Load a blank disc into your recorder, which automatically displays the Project Selector screen.**

   Yes, I'm saying it again: *Do not use a CD-RW disc when recording a standard audio CD for use in a stereo system!* Are you getting tired of that sentence yet? (How about these italicized sentences?) Anyway, you can't say that I didn't warn you.

2. **Click Make a Music CD.**

3. **Click Music CD Project.**

4. **Now it's time to add tracks from the Easy CD Creator screen shown in Figure 8-6. You can choose one of these options:**

   - **Add MP3, WAV, or WMF files:** Use Explorer view in the upper half of the screen to locate folders where your audio files are stored.

   - **Rip tracks from another CD:** Load a disc into either your CD-ROM drive or your CD recorder and then select that drive from the Select Source Files drop-down list box to display the tracks. To load other tracks from other audio CDs, repeat the process.

   If you don't have a track listing for the disc you have loaded, just double-click on a track in Explorer view. Easy CD Creator displays the Preview player, and you can listen to the track before you add it to your layout.

5. **Click once on each track you want to add.**

   To choose more than one track from the same source, hold down the Ctrl key as you click each track name.

6. **After you have selected your tracks from the source folder or disc, click the Add button in the center of the screen to add them to your disc layout or drag them from Explorer view and drop them on the layout list at the bottom of the screen.**

7. **Continue repeating Steps 4 through 6 until your track layout is complete — or until you have packed every second of your blank disc!**

   You can tell how much time you have used on your disc by checking the Estimated Time bar at the bottom of the screen; it tells you how much time the current track list needs and the remaining time you can fill on both a 74-minute and 80-minute CD-R disc.

Figure 8-6:
New music
CDs get
their start
on this Easy
CD Creator
screen.

8. **Arrange the tracks in your layout as you like by clicking a track name to highlight it and dragging it to the new position in the track list.**

9. **Although it's not necessary, I recommend that you enter both a name for your new disc in the New CD Title field and the artist's name in the Artist Name field.**

Need to change or add a name for a track? Just click the entry to highlight it and click again to edit the Track Title field.

10. **Ready to burn those hip ones and zeros? Click the Big Red Record button in the center of the screen.**

If you're loading tracks from an audio CD, Easy CD Creator prompts you to load the pesky thing when it's necessary so that the track can be copied and converted.

The program displays the Record CD Setup screen (shown awhile earlier in Figure 8-4).

11. **If necessary, select your recorder and choose the fastest possible recording speed. You can clone multiple copies of your new music disc by clicking the arrows next to the Number of Copies field.**

12. **You can clone multiple copies of your new music disc by clicking the arrows next to the Number of Copies field.**

13. **Enable the Buffer underrun protection check box if your drive supports burnproof recording.**

    Many audio CD players (and most CD player programs for your computer) display CD-Text while the disc is playing, which includes the disc name, artist name, and each track name.

14. **For a little techno-wow touch to your new audio CD, enable the Write CD-Text check box!**

15. **If your recorder supports disc-at-once mode, select it (to prevent clicks between tracks). Otherwise, choose Track-at-Once mode and choose the Finalize CD option.**

16. **Click Start Recording, you music-producing mogul! If your recorder is empty, Easy CD Creator yells for you to load a blank disc.**

    The program displays the Record CD Progress dialog box (which has already popped up in Figure 8-5), allowing you to monitor the ones and zeros as they're shoveled into the furnace and onto your disc. When the recording is done, you have the choice of running CD Label Creator if you want to print a fancy-looking label or a set of jewel box inserts.

Time to grab your headphones and jam to your latest creation!

Copying a Disc

In this section, I describe how you can copy an existing data CD-ROM or audio CD. Rather than take the time to crank up Easy CD Creator, Roxio provides you with a separate program named CD Copier; it can clone a disc using just the recorder. If you're lucky enough to have either a read-only CD-ROM drive or a second recorder in the same system, you can even copy drive-to-drive and whip out a copy in record time!

Follow these steps to copy a disc:

1. **Click Start⇨Programs⇨Easy CD Creator 5⇨Applications⇨CD Copier to display the screen shown in Figure 8-7.**

2. **Click the Copy from drop-down list box and click the drive where you have loaded the disc you want to copy.**

    It can be any drive on your system that can read a disc, including your CD-RW drive.

3. **Click the Record to drop-down list box and click the recorder that will burn the disc.**

    Remember that it can be the same as the source (the Copy from) drive.

4. **Checking the Advanced settings (see Figure 8-8) before you begin the copy is a good idea, so click the Advanced tab.**

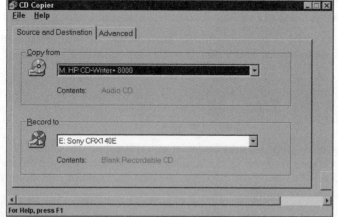

Figure 8-7:
You're on
the road to
Duplication
City with CD
Copier.

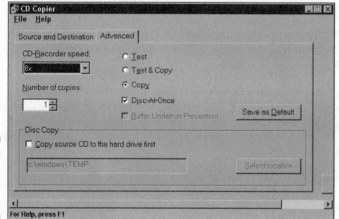

Figure 8-8:
Preparing to
tweak CD
Copier.

5. **You can choose the Test, Test & Copy, or Copy option. Because I'm familiar with my equipment, I skip any testing and jump right to the real thing. However, Test & Copy does the trick as well (it just takes twice as long).**

6. **If you want more than one copy of the original disc, click the arrows next to the Number of copies field and choose, well, the number of copies!**

If you're making more than one copy, enable the Copy source CD to the hard drive first check box. This action saves time because CD Copier can use the temporary image file rather than read the source disc all over again.

7. **Using disc-at-once mode whenever possible is a good idea; enable the Disc-at-Once check box if your drive supports DAO.**

8. **Click Copy to unleash the fearsome power of your laser, and be prepared to load a blank disc if you're using one drive to copy.**

Using a Disc Image

From time to time, you may find that you need multiple copies of a disc, but you don't want to produce them all at one time. Perhaps the data will change within a few weeks or you're preparing discs for sale or distribution, but you don't know how many copies you need.

This situation is where a *disc image* comes in; think of it as a complete CD saved as a single file to your hard drive. In fact, you can even create a disc image for later burning without a CD recorder! I know that sounds screwy, but when you're on the road with your laptop — or you're at the office — and you don't have your external CD-RW drive with you, you can create a disc image file instead. After your computer and external recorder are reunited, recording that disc is a snap.

However, you have to look at the downside: The disc image takes up all the space of its optical sibling, so each disc image you save on your hard drive takes up the space the data occupies on the recorded disc. Therefore, saving 800 or 900MB of free space on your drive is a good idea if you think that you need to create a disc image.

Follow these steps to create a disc image using Easy CD Creator:

1. **Click Start➪Programs➪Easy CD Creator 5➪Applications➪Easy CD Creator. (Alternatively, you can use the Project Selector, as I demonstrate earlier in this chapter.)**

2. **Click File➪New CD Layout and select the type of disc you need.**

3. **Build your CD layout as you normally would.**

4. **Click File and click Create CD Hard Disk Image, which opens the familiar Save As dialog box you see in Figure 8-9.**

5. **Navigate to the folder on your hard drive where the image is saved, type a name for your image file, and then click Save.**

Sit back and watch the fun as the disc image is recorded. The image file carries a CIF extension.

Figure 8-9:
Choosing a
moniker and
a location
for your disc
image.

Later, when you're ready to record the disc, the process is just as easy:

1. **Click Start⇨Programs⇨Easy CD Creator 5⇨Applications⇨Easy CD Creator to run the program.**

2. **Click File and select the Record CD from CD Image menu item.**

3. **The Select File dialog box appears, as shown in Figure 8-10. Navigate to the location of the disc image you want to record. Highlight it and click Open.**

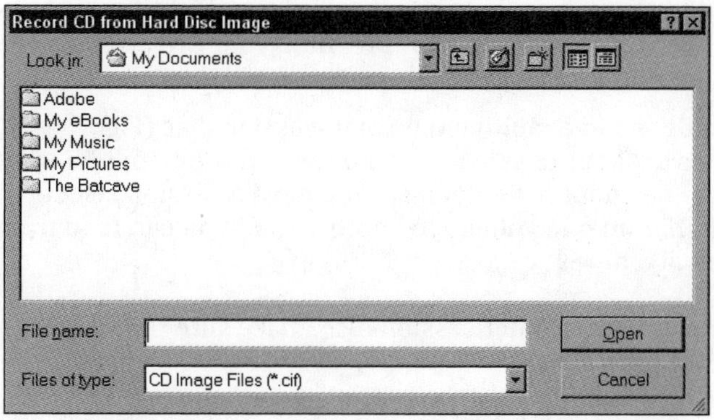

Figure 8-10:
Selecting an
existing disc
image to
record.

4. **Make any settings changes necessary (as I show you earlier in this chapter) and click Start Recording.**

5. **Load a blank disc, and the recorder does its stuff.**

Using Multisession Discs

As I say earlier in this book, multisession discs have fallen out of favor with the arrival of packet writing. Both allow you to record a disc, use it, and then record additional information on it; with a UDF disc, however, you get the same versatility without the extra twists and turns of multisession recording. For example, you don't have to run Easy CD Creator to record another session, and you don't need a separate session-selection program (which allows you to choose which volume you're going to read).

However, I'm a thorough guy, and you may someday have to make a multisession disc for some specific application — therefore, allow me to cover both types of multisession recording in this section.

Keep in mind that not all drives on the planet can read multisession discs! Use them only when a standard single-session CD-ROM doesn't do the trick.

Yes, that's right — I did say "both types" a minute ago:

- ✔ **Incremental:** Use an incremental multisession disc when you know that you want to add data to an existing session later. As you can see in Figure 8-11, successive sessions can add material or "delete" existing material by overwriting it. (Sorry, Charlie, it doesn't mean that you get that space back — your drive simply can't read it any longer.) Because the data in the preceding session is imported into the new one, you don't need a session-selection program. Your drive simply reads the latest session you burned.

- ✔ **Multivolume:** In a multivolume multisession disc (Figure 8-12), all the sessions are kept chaste and separate, and they can't be updated like the data on an incremental disc. You need a session selection program to switch from one volume to another (and you can read from only one session at a time).

To burn an incremental multisession disc, make sure that you record the first session on the disc using

- ✔ **The track-at-once recording method**

- ✔ **The Finalize Session, Don't Finalize CD option** (creates a first session, but doesn't close the disc permanently)

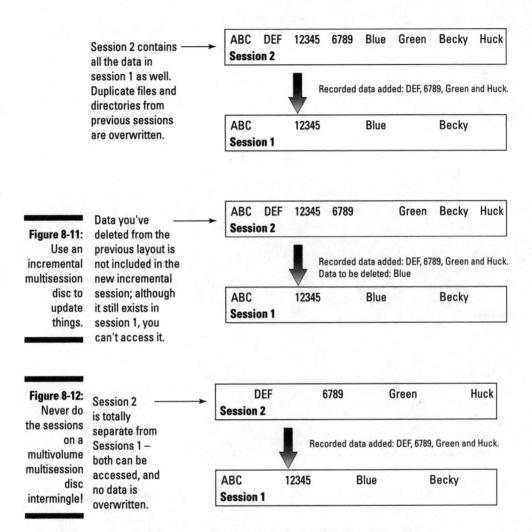

Session 2 contains all the data in session 1 as well. Duplicate files and directories from previous sessions are overwritten.

Figure 8-11: Use an incremental multisession disc to update things.

Data you've deleted from the previous layout is not included in the new incremental session; although it still exists in session 1, you can't access it.

Figure 8-12: Never do the sessions on a multivolume multisession disc intermingle!

Session 2 is totally separate from Sessions 1 — both can be accessed, and no data is overwritten.

When you're ready to record again, follow these steps:

1. **Click Start⇨Programs⇨Easy CD Creator 5⇨Applications⇨Easy CD Creator to run the program.**

2. **Load the original disc in your recorder.**

3. **Click File, select New CD Project, and choose Data CD. (Don't add any files to your layout just yet!)**

4. **Click File and click CD Project Properties (see Figure 8-13). Ensure that the Automatically import previous session check box is enabled and click OK.**

If you want to import a session other than the last one, you can use the Import Session menu item on the CD menu. It lets you choose which session is imported into your layout.

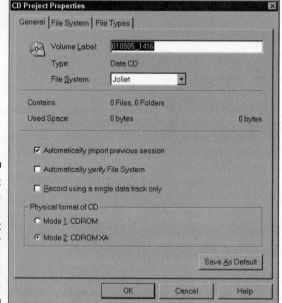

Figure 8-13: Setting the Automatic Import feature for a data CD-ROM layout.

5. **Add files to the layout as you normally would, and the data in the first session is automatically displayed.**

6. **Finish your recording as usual. Remember to choose Finalize Session, Don't Finalize CD if you want to update the session again in the future; if you're all done (and you're sure about that), I recommend that you choose Finalize the CD.**

To burn a multivolume multisession disc, follow the same procedure except for Step 4. This time, make sure that the Automatically import previous session check box is *disabled*.

You can switch sessions using Session Selector (see Figure 8-14). To run it, click Start⇨Programs⇨Easy CD Creator 5⇨Applications⇨Session Selector.

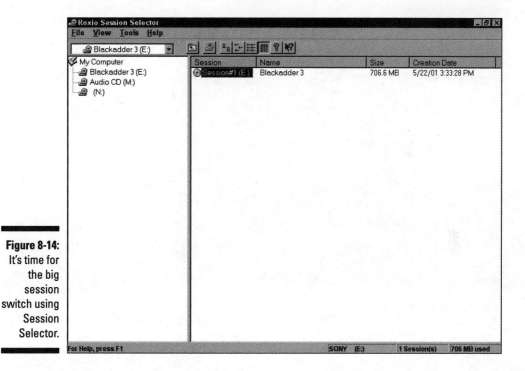

Figure 8-14:
It's time for the big session switch using Session Selector.

Erasing a CD-RW Disc

After you have finished with a CD-RW disc, do you simply chuck it in the nearest wastebasket? No! Instead, you can erase the entire disc at one time (you have no way to erase only part of the disc — it's either all or nothing) and use it all over again.

To erase a CD-RW disc using Easy CD Creator:

1. **Load the offending CD-RW disc into your recorder.**
2. **Click on the Select source files drop-down list box and choose your recorder.**
3. **Click the CD menu and choose Erase Disc, which displays the Erase CD dialog box, as shown in Figure 8-15.**

You can choose a quick erase or a full erase. I agree with the good folks at Roxio and recommend a quick erase in most cases.

When do you use Full Erase? I guess that sometimes you want to be absolutely sure! However, if you're trying to record using a CD-RW disc and Easy CD Creator reports errors with the disc's formatting or TOC (table of contents) information, you probably have to erase the disc to make it usable again. This can happen if a recording session is interrupted by a power failure or if Easy CD Creator should — perish the thought — crash on you.

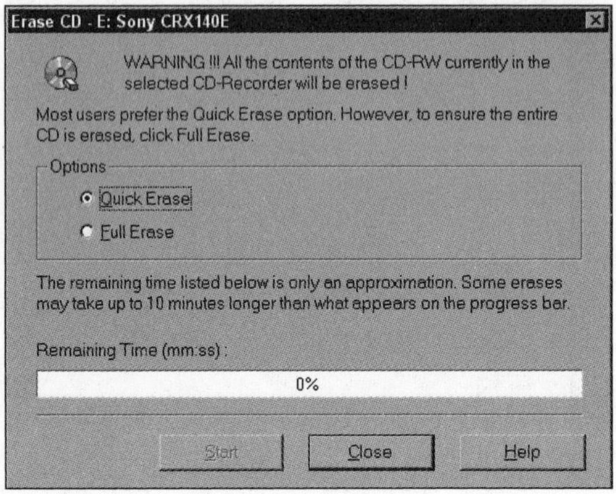

Figure 8-15:
Is that a
quick or full
CD-RW
erasure?

Click Start to begin the process — and take a break for a soda or a cup of java if you have selected the Full Erase option.

Project: Developing MP3 Fever

Friends, I have a hankerin' to hear the King — that's right, Elvis Aaron Presley himself. The trouble is, I have all my Elvis songs in MP3 format on my hard drive and I want to listen to them in my '58 Chevy's audio CD player! If you're in the same boat, you have come to the right project. Let's burn a *Best of Elvis* audio CD. (And yes, neighbors, I own the original commercial CDs for the music I used in this project! I just ripped the tracks into MP3 format for this demonstration.)

1. **Click Start⇨Programs⇨Easy CD Creator 5⇨Project Selector to run the Project Selector.**

2. **Click Make a Music CD.**

3. **Click Music CD Project.**

4. **Click the Select source files drop-down list box and choose the drive where your MP3 files are living. Use Explorer view in the top half of the screen to navigate to the right folder.**

5. **Hold down the Ctrl key and click on the MP3 files you want to add.**

   As you can see in Figure 8-16, I have chosen six songs by Elvis from an entire folder of MP3 files.

6. **Click the Add button in the center of the screen. Figure 8-17 shows the tracks as they appear in the bottom window.**

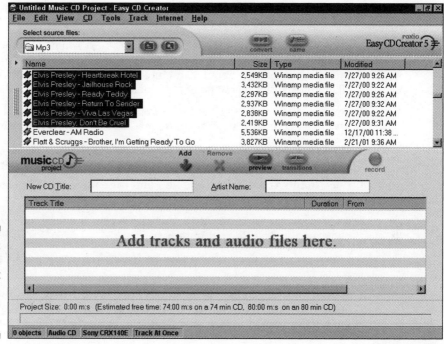

Figure 8-16:
Man, that's some great music — I pick only the best.

Figure 8-17:
The track list is taking shape.

7. **If you want to add songs from another folder, repeat Steps 4 through 6.**

   Personally, I think that these are the King's best songs, so let me stop here. As you can tell by the bar display at the bottom of the screen, these tracks take up about 13 minutes and 15 seconds, and I have about 60 minutes and 44 seconds of additional space.

8. **You can click and drag the track names to rearrange them. I want my disc to start out with "Viva Las Vegas," so I click and drag the entry from Slot 5 to Slot 1.**

9. **Click in the New CD Title field and enter a name for your disc.**

10. **Click in the Artist Name field and enter the name of the performer or band.**

11. **As you can see in Figure 8-18, the disc layout is ready to record, so click the Big Red Record button.**

12. **I need only one copy of this disc, so leave the Number of Copies field set to 1.**

13. **Even if your audio CD player doesn't display CD-Text, you may encounter one in the future; therefore, I always recommend that you enable the Write CD-Text check box for an audio CD.**

Figure 8-18:
Everything
is set to
record.

14. **My recorder supports DAO recording, so I definitely want to pick disc-at-once recording. (If this field is grayed out, your recorder doesn't offer DAO — use track-at-once mode with the Finalize CD option instead.)**

15. **Click Start Recording to start the wheels turning and then load a blank disc.**

16. **When the recording is finished, you can run CD Label Creator (for help, turn to Chapter 14); otherwise, eject your disc and enjoy your Elvis!**

Project: Archiving Digital Photographs

Got a number of family photos you have taken with your digital camera? Why not burn them to a data CD-ROM and free up that hard drive space for other programs? Here's how you can burn a basic archive of digital images:

1. **Click Start⇨Programs⇨Easy CD Creator 5⇨Project Selector to run the Project Selector.**

2. **Click Make a Data CD.**

3. **Click Data CD Project.**

4. **Click the Select source files drop-down list box and navigate to the drive where your images are stored. To move to another folder, use Explorer view in the top half of the screen.**

5. **Click on one or more filenames while you hold down the Ctrl key.**

6. **Click the Add button in the center of the screen, or drag the highlighted files to the bottom window. As you can see in Figure 8-19, my images now appear in the data CD layout.**

7. **To select more images, just repeat Steps 4 through 6 until you have added all the photos you want (or, of course, until the disc is full). Use the bar display at the bottom of the screen to keep track of how much space remains.**

8. **To create a new folder in your CD layout, right-click on the disk title in the Layout window and choose New⇨Folder from the pop-up menu. The new folder appears with the name highlighted; type a name for the new folder and press Enter to save it. To move images in and out of folders, click and drag the filenames wherever you want them.**

   In this example, I have created a folder named Our Dog, and I have dragged three images into it.

9. **Click the disk title to highlight it and click it again to type a new name — I used Photos 2001s for this disc.**

10. **The final disc layout appears in Figure 8-20. Click the Big Red Record button!**

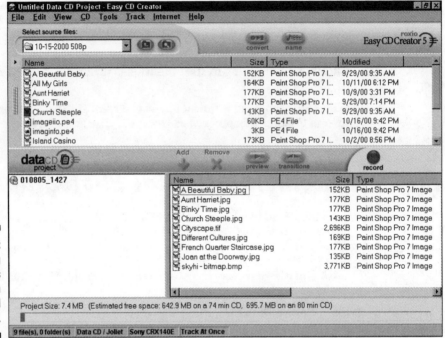

Figure 8-19:
Adding
photographs
to a data
CD-ROM
layout.

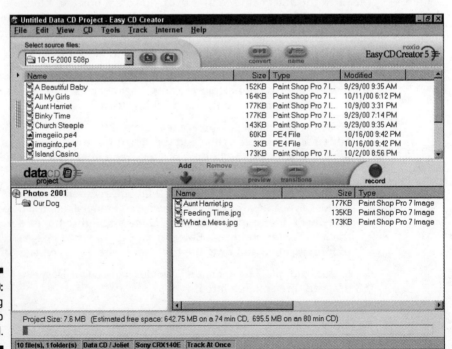

Figure 8-20:
Everything
is set to
record.

11. **If you don't want multiple copies, leave the Number of Copies field set to 1.**

12. **Choose disc-at-once recording if you can; if not, use track-at-once mode with the Finalize CD option.**

13. **Click Start Recording to start the wheels turning and then load a blank disc.**

14. **When the recording is finished, you can run CD Label Creator (for help, turn to Chapter 14); otherwise, eject your disc and hand your photo disc to Grandma!**

Because this is a single session disc and you finalized it, you can't write to it again. If your drive supports packet writing, Chapter 10 shows how to create a UDF disc that you can add files to in the future.

Project: Backing Up Important Files Using Take Two

Before I close this chapter, I want to show you how to back up your hard drive with Roxio Take Two, a separate program that's included with Easy CD Creator Platinum. Take Two is a simplified backup program — you can't pick individual files and folders, just partitions and entire hard drives — but it can still save your skin if you haven't backed up your system! (Plus, you can choose individual files and folders when you restore.) You need at least one blank CD-R or CD-RW disc.

Follow these steps to back up your drive:

1. **Click Start➪Programs➪Easy CD Creator 5➪Applications➪Take Two.**

    The program's main screen appears, as you see in Figure 8-21. ("Hey, Mark, didn't you use that screen shot from an earlier chapter?" Why yes, observant readers. But it's so attractive, I've decided to use it again!)

2. **Click Select Backup Source, which displays the screen shown in Figure 8-22.**

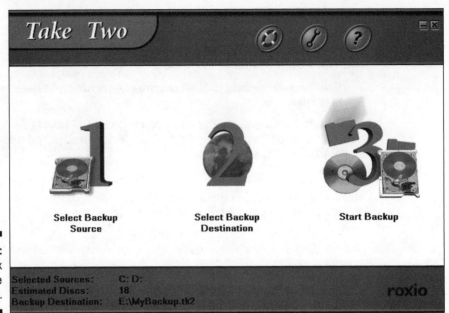

Figure 8-21:
Time to back
up with Take
Two.

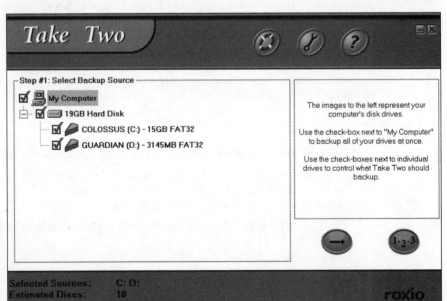

Figure 8-22:
Selecting
the source
for a
backup.

3. **Enable each check box next to the drives you want to back up. Alternatively, you can just enable the My Computer check box, which selects all your drives. To display the partitions on a hard drive, click the plus sign next to it to expand the entry. You can also check to see what drive letters are included at the bottom of the screen. Click the right arrow to proceed to the next screen.**

4. **Enable the check box next to your recorder, as shown in Figure 8-23, and click the right arrow to proceed.**

The program prompts you for confirmation before starting the backup. Closing down all other applications and letting Take Two do its stuff alone is a good idea because too many ongoing changes to files on your drive while the backup is running may cause it to abort.

5. **After you have shut down any other applications, click Yes to continue.**

6. **Load a blank disc when prompted, and the backup automatically starts.**

You are warned if a program has files open that may change; this is almost always the case if you have any programs running in the system tray, but you can still continue with the backup.

7. **You can monitor the progress from the screen shown in Figure 8-24. Be ready to load additional discs when prompted.**

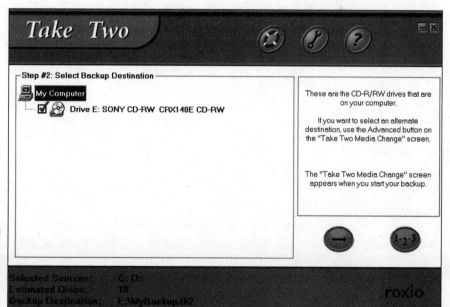

Figure 8-23: Choose your recording weapon.

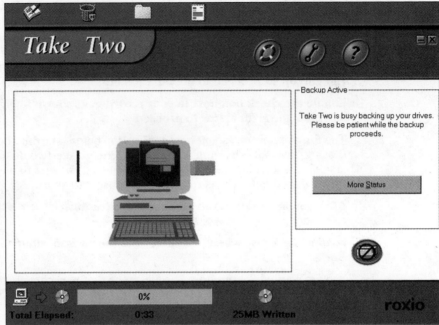

Figure 8-24:
Good for
you —
you're
backing up
your
system!

To restore your system using a Take Two backup, you use Windows Explorer (with Take Two extensions that are installed along with Easy CD Creator Platinum). For complete information about retrieving your stuff, check out the Take Two online Help system by clicking the question mark button on the program's main menu.

Chapter 9

A Step-By-Step Guide to ... Toast?

In This Chapter
▶ Recording HFS data CD-ROMs
▶ Recording audio CDs on the Macintosh
▶ Creating a Hybrid Mac/PC disc
▶ Creating a Temporary Partition
▶ Recording DVD-R with Toast

1 don't even own a toaster, but I use my Toast to burn all the time! (Try explaining that to your friends.) In the Macintosh world, however, that sentence makes perfect sense. Compared to Easy CD Creator, Toast Titanium for the Macintosh (from Roxio) is a lean, mean, and exceptionally attractive recording machine. As you may guess, the program's menu system and appearance are radically different from its Windows sibling, and it has a number of Mac-specific features.

In this chapter, you take a look at both the basics of recording and many of the advanced options available within Toast.

Putting Files on a Disc

Toast can create two different types of HFS disc:

▸ **Mac OS CD:** If your disc will be used on older Macs using System 7 or earlier — those before Mac OS 8.1 — you should use this standard disc.

▸ **Mac OS Extended CD:** Macs running Mac OS 8.1 or later can take advantage of the Extended file system, which allows faster performance and provides a bit more room on the disc for your data.

Therefore, if compatibility is in question, always use the Mac OS CD version of HFS because both older and newer Macintosh operating systems can read it. (Also, as you see later in this chapter, some types of discs require the Mac OS CD file system.)

To record a simple data disc with files from your Macintosh's hard drive:

1. **Double-click the Toast icon to launch the program and display the stylish Toast screen shown in Figure 9-1. (Talk about classy!)**

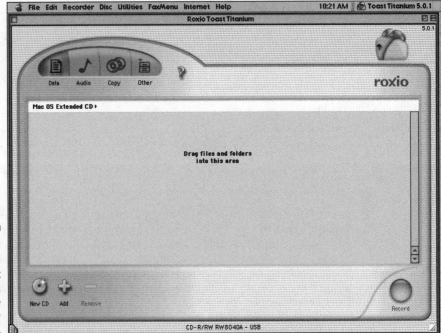

Figure 9-1:
Didn't I tell
you that
Toast is
a spiffy
program?

2. **Click the Data button at the top of the screen.**

3. **To select which type of data disc you want to record, click and hold on the Disc Type display.**

   It's the bold text directly underneath the four buttons at the top. Toast displays the different types of discs you can record in the selected category. For a basic Macintosh-only data disc, you should choose either Mac OS CD or Mac OS Extended CD.

4. **Drag and drop files and folders from the Finder window into the Toast main window.**

   Note that the program keeps track of both the number of files in your layout and the approximate amount of space it uses on the disc.

5. **Repeat Step 4 until you have added all your files and folders or until the disc layout is filled to capacity.**

   You can click and drag filenames to move them into and out of folders, just as you would in the Mac OS Finder when you're using List view. To add a new folder, highlight the parent folder (or the CD itself) and click the New Folder button at the bottom of the screen. To remove a file or folder — just from the layout, mind you, *not* from your drive — highlight the unwanted item and click Remove at the bottom of the screen. Figure 9-2 illustrates a typical disc layout I have created on my system.

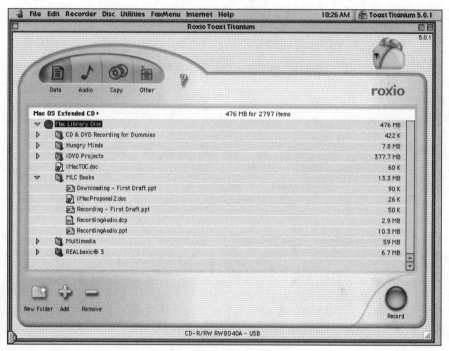

Figure 9-2:
Ready to record with Toast!

6. **Load a blank CD into your recorder.**

7. **Click the Big Pink Record Button.**

8. **The Record dialog box appears, as shown in Figure 9-3.**

   Here, you determine whether you want to finalize the disc:

   • Click Write Session to write a single session and leave the disc open for later recordings. (This action is the same as selecting the Finalize Session, Don't Finalize CD setting in Easy CD Creator.) You can read the disc in your Mac's CD-ROM drive, but you can create a multisession disc by using this disc in the future.

   • Click Write Disc to write the session and finalize the disc so that it can't be written to again. This action corresponds to selecting the Finalize CD setting in Easy CD Creator.

Figure 9-3:
To write a
session or
write a
disc —
that is the
question.

By default, Toast selects the highest recording speed your drive
supports. Also, you can choose to test the recording by enabling
the Simulation Mode check box, but note that this selection does
not automatically record the disc if the test completes successfully.

While recording, Toast displays a progress bar. After the recording is
complete, the program automatically verifies the finished disc against
the original files on your hard drive. Because this process takes several
minutes, you have the option of ejecting the disc immediately and skipping the verification step.

Boot, I say, boot!

Like Easy CD Creator, Toast can burn a self-
booting disc that you can use to start your
Macintosh. Only a Mac OS CD can be made
bootable, so you can't use the Extended file
system.

Also, your new disc has to include a — get
this — *blessed System Folder* to make it bootable. (Don't ask me where the name came from:
In this case, *blessed* means that the icon for the
System Folder has a Mac OS symbol.) Also, that
System Folder has to be appropriate for your
model of Macintosh. For example, you can't
boot an older 68030-based Mac using a Mac

OS 8.5 System Folder because that version of
Mac OS doesn't run on that processor.

To create a self-booting data disc, just drag the
blessed System Folder into the Toast window,
as I have just described. Then, drag any other
files you want to add as you normally would.

If you're recording an entire volume using the
Mac Volume disc type, make sure that you
enable the Bootable check box in the Select
Volume dialog box. (Now is also a good time to
choose a program that runs automatically when
the disc is loaded. Enable the AutoStart option
and choose the appropriate program.)

Recording an Audio CD

Although Apple has released programs like iTunes that can burn audio discs, I still prefer to record audio CDs on the Macintosh with Toast; you have more choices and more control over the finished disc. To record an audio CD from files on your hard drive and existing audio CDs, follow these steps:

1. **Double-click the Toast icon to launch the program.**

2. **Click the Audio button at the top of the screen.**

3. **Add tracks in either of two ways:**

   Add existing sound files you have already saved to your hard drive: For example, drag AIFF or MP3 files to your layout by dragging the files into the Toast window.

   Add tracks from an existing audio CD by loading it into your CD-ROM drive and double-clicking the disc's icon on the desktop to display the track icons: Drag the desired track icons from the audio CD window into the Toast window.

   If you plan to copy the majority of tracks from an existing CD, just drag the entire disc icon to the Toast window, and you can load all the tracks at one time.

4. **You can rearrange the tracks in any order you want by dragging them to their new positions. To rename a track, click on the track name to highlight it and click again to open an edit box. Type the new name. To hear a track, highlight the track name and click the Play control at the bottom of the screen.**

   Before you record your disc, you should extract (a more dignified word for rip) any tracks you're copying from other discs. This extraction eliminates any possible problems your drive may encounter if you try recording directly from the discs themselves.

5. **Highlight each track you have added from another disc and click Extract.**

   Toast displays a Save As dialog box that allows you to pick the folder where the extracted audio is saved. The tracks are saved as AIFF files.

6. **Load a blank CD-R disc into your recorder.**

7. **Click the Big Pink Record Button.**

8. **For a standard audio CD, always choose Write Disc.**

I swear that this is the last time I'll say this — it really is, folks — *do not use a CD-RW disc when recording a standard audio CD!*

After your audio CD has been recorded, you can regain disk space by deleting the extracted audio tracks you saved. Or, if the notion is attractive to you, keep them for another recording, or use them with your MP3 or AIFF audio player.

Ooh! It's a Hybrid!

Next, turn your attention to an important type of disc that's easily recorded with Toast: a PC/Macintosh hybrid disc that can be read on both systems (the Mac portion uses the HFS file system, and the PC portion uses either Joliet or ISO 9660). This disc type is a perfect way to distribute files and programs to a wide audience, especially games, educational material, clip-art libraries, multimedia files, and fonts (all of which are often shared between PCs and Macs).

Note that unless you're running special software, only the native format portion of the disc can be read by each operating system. (Geez, I need a soda. In plain English: The Macintosh can read only the Mac information on the disc, and the PC can read only the PC portion. Sorry about that.)

To create a hybrid disc, follow these steps:

1. **Gather the Mac-only files you want to record and move them to a separate volume (either a separate hard drive partition or a removable disk, like a zip disc or a temporary partition, which I show you how to create in the next section).**

   If you have any files that should be visible on both Macs and PCs, copy them to the volume as well.

   Although a RAM disk is limited in size, it also makes a great temporary volume to use for this purpose. You can add or resize a RAM disk from the Memory Control Panel.

2. **Double-click the Toast icon to launch the program.**

3. **Click the Other button at the top of the screen and hold the button down until a pop-up menu appears. Choose Custom Hybrid from the menu to display the screen shown in Figure 9-4.**

4. **Click Select Mac.**

5. **From the Select Volume dialog box, choose the volume you created in Step 1 and enable the Optimize on-the-fly check box. Click OK to return to the main screen.**

6. **Click Select ISO to display the ISO 9660 dialog box, as shown in Figure 9-5.**

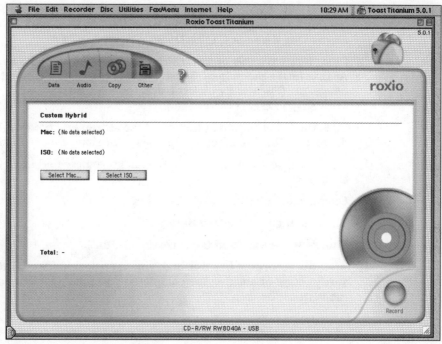

Figure 9-4:
The beginnings of a Mac/PC hybrid disc.

Figure 9-5:
Yes, Mac folks can communicate with PC folks — sometimes.

7. **Drag and drop to the ISO 9660 dialog box the files that should be read on the PC.**

   This folder tree works much like the data CD tree I cover earlier in this chapter. You can click on the CD title or a folder name to rename it — files are automatically renamed to conform to the ISO standard. Click the New Folder button to add a new folder, and feel free to drag files and folders around to rearrange your ISO layout.

8. After you're finished adding ISO files, click the Settings tab. From the Naming drop-down list box, choose Joliet (MS-DOS + Windows), which allows long filenames. Click Done.

9. Okay, let's burn this puppy! Click the File menu and choose the Save As Disc Image menu item. Toast prompts you for a location to save the image file. (I generally pick the desktop because it's easy to find.) Click Save to create the image.

10. Click the Other button at the top of the screen and hold the button down until the pop-up menu appears. This time, choose Disc Image.

11. Click the Select button, choose the image you created in Step 9, and click Open.

12. Load a blank disc into your recorder.

13. Click the Big Pink Record Button.

14. Choose Write Disc, and the recording begins.

15. After the recording has finished, you have the choice of allowing a verify action or ejecting the completed disc immediately and skipping the verification step.

Mounting an image (and not on the wall)

From time to time, you may want to take advantage of the absolutely nifty ability to mount a disc image on the Mac OS desktop, just like it was a gen-u-wine piece of CD-ROM hardware. You can open the mounted disc and even run programs and load files from it. Your Mac applications can't tell the difference, and you don't have to dig through dozens of CDs to find the one that holds the files you need. (You are likely to use a mounted disc image only for data discs because you can listen to audio tracks just by extracting them as AIFF or MP3 files.) As long as you have the available hard drive territory, you can keep a disc image on tap for any contingency.

To create a disc image, build your data CD layout as usual, as I describe earlier in this chapter. (Make sure that you have at least 800MB or 900MB of free hard drive space if your image will reflect a full disc.) Then, rather than burn the layout, click File and select the Save As Disc Image menu item. From the Save Disc Image As dialog box, choose a target folder, type a new name (if necessary), and click Save. Toast acts just as though it's writing to a disc; when it's done, however, you have a brand-spanking-new disc image file.

To mount the file, double-click on it. Toast automatically launches and presents you with two buttons: Select and Mount. Click Mount, and you're ready to go. (After the volume icon appears on the desktop, you can quit Toast.) The mounted volume stays on your desktop until you reboot your Macintosh or drag the volume icon to the Trash. Enjoy!

Project: Creating a Temporary Partition

As I mention earlier in this chapter, while discussing hybrid discs, recording with Toast sometimes requires you to create a temporary partition as a separate volume on your Mac desktop. In fact, you can use the Mac Volume disc type to record the contents of a temporary partition as a complete disc.

In this project, I show you how to create a temporary partition to store the Macintosh files for a hybrid disc. Follow these steps with me, won't you?

1. **Double-click the Toast icon to launch the program.**

2. **Click Utilities and choose the Create Temporary Partition menu item to display the Create Temporary Partition dialog box, as shown in Figure 9-6.**

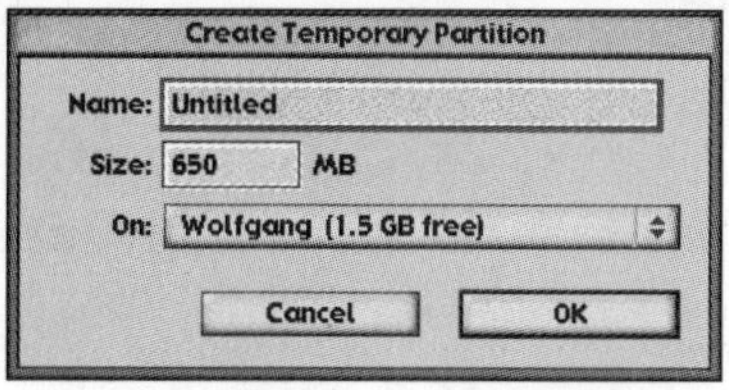

Figure 9-6:
With a temporary partition, I feel so . . . self contained.

Create Temporary Partition

Name: Untitled

Size: 650 MB

On: Wolfgang (1.5 GB free)

Cancel   OK

3. **Click the Name field and enter a volume name for the partition.**

   In this example, I chose Fortisque. (I have my reasons.)

4. **Click the Size field and enter a partition size in megabytes (the default is 650MB).**

   Naturally, this size can't be larger than the amount of free space on the drive you choose in the On drop-down list box. I have only about 150MB of Mac files to record on this hybrid disc, so I show you how to create a 160MB partition on my hard drive. Leaving about 10MB of "breathing space" on your temporary partition is always a good idea. This allows you to add a forgotten file or two more without running out of room.

5. **Click OK. As you can see in Figure 9-7, Fortisque has suddenly appeared on my Mac Desktop.**

   I find the somewhat blunt Toast icon easy to locate!

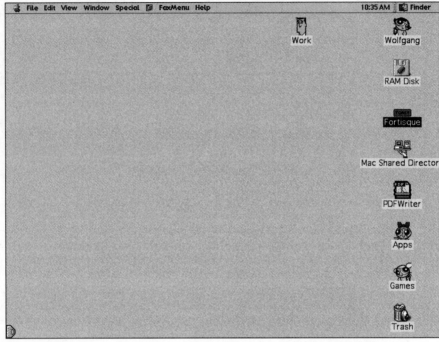

Figure 9-7:
Ah,
Fortisque,
there
you are!

6. **If you're recording in Mac OS Standard format, you're done. Just drag your files to the temporary partition and continue the procedure. If, on the other hand, you need a Mac OS Extended disc, you need to switch formats. Click the temporary partition's icon on the desktop to select it, click Special, and choose the Erase Disk menu item to display the dialog box shown in Figure 9-8.**

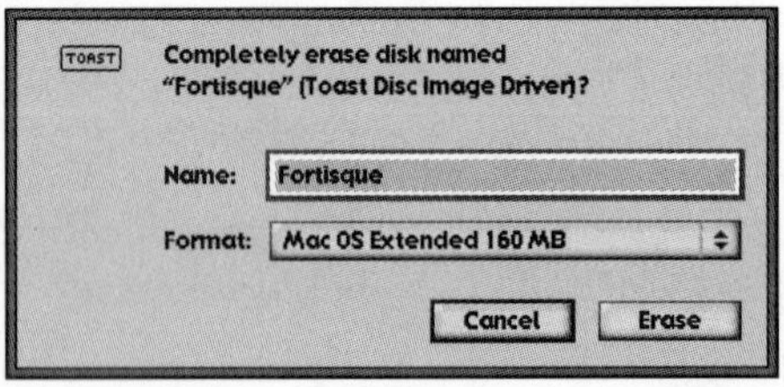

Figure 9-8:
Preparing
to switch
formats
for the
temporary
partition.

> [TOAST] Completely erase disk named
> "Fortisque" (Toast Disc Image Driver)?
>
> Name: Fortisque
>
> Format: Mac OS Extended 160 MB ▲▼
>
> Cancel   Erase

7. **Click the Format drop-down list box, choose Mac OS Extended, and click Erase.**

   After the partition has been reformatted, you're ready to drag your Mac files into it.

After you're done with the partition, you can delete it by dragging it to the Trash.

Project: Recording a Basic DVD-ROM

Toast can burn using DVD-R drives, so it makes a good "quick and dirty" recording program for creating DVD-ROM test discs and *masters* (discs that are to be commercially manufactured). The storage space on a DVD-R makes backing up a decent-size drive easy using only one or two discs. You don't get a full 4.7GB — a 4.7MB disc provides only about 4.25GB when you use the Mac OS Extended format — but it's still nothing to sneeze at.

Let's burn a simple DVD-ROM using video files you have edited and saved on your hard drive. You can use this test disc to check out how your interactive menus operate and how good the video looks when played on a DVD-ROM player. Follow these steps:

1. **Using a DV authoring program that can produce DVD-ROM project files — for example, Apollo Expert Plus, from DV Studio (www. dv-studio.com). Prepare the video and audio streams and create the VIDEO_TS and AUDIO_TS folders.**

2. **Double-click the Toast icon to launch the program.**

3. **Click the Other button at the top of the screen and hold the button down until a pop-up menu appears. Choose DVD from the menu.**

4. **Click the New DVD button at the bottom of the screen to begin a new layout, as shown in Figure 9-9.**

5. **Click and drag the VIDEO_TS and AUDIO_TS folders from your hard drive to the Toast window and any other files or folders you want to add to the disc.**

   If you're just backing up your system, naturally, you can add any files you like to your layout, but these are required for DVD video.

6. **Load a blank DVD-R disc into your DVD recorder.**

7. **Click the Big Pink Record Button.**

8. **Choose Write Disc, and the recording begins.**

Note that Toast can also write a data layout to a DVD-RAM disc, but the entire disc is automatically reformatted first, and the data is recorded as a read-only disc. If you want to record data to the disc again using Toast, you lose the current contents of the disc when it's reformatted. Sorry about that — but then, if you're using a DVD-RAM drive for backups, like I do, automatic reformatting really isn't a problem!

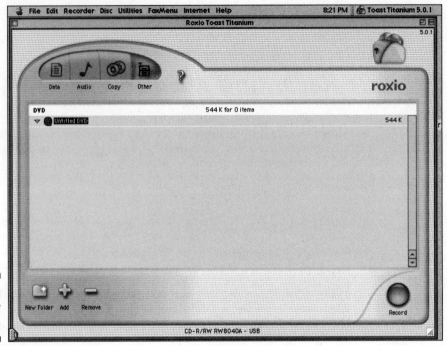

Figure 9-9:
An empty
DVD layout.

Chapter 10

Using DirectCD: Avoid the Hassle!

*O*kay, I trumpet the advantages of the Roxio DirectCD throughout the first half of this book, and it's time to deliver the goods. What makes DirectCD so hot? Here are the facts:

✔ You have no need to open any recording software ahead of time. Just drop a DirectCD disc in your drive, and everything's taken care of for you automatically.

✔ The UDF recording mode — also known as packet writing — used by DirectCD is almost as reliable and foolproof as burnproof recording. You can safely record data on a DirectCD disc while you're working in another application under Windows or the Mac OS (operating system).

✔ You can add files at any time, without creating a multisession disc.

✔ DirectCD works with CD-R, CD-RW, and DVD-RAM discs.

✔ All popular operating systems can read a UDF disc.

Eager to find out more? This is the chapter for you — I put DirectCD through its paces.

"Whaddya Mean, 1 Have to Format?"

Hey, I didn't say that DirectCD is perfect, did I? This program has only two drawbacks:

✔ You have to format a disc before you can use it.

✔ You can't create mixed-mode or audio CDs using DirectCD.

I can't do anything about the latter, but the former is easy to fix — and you have to format a disc only once for use with DirectCD. Follow these steps:

1. **Click Start➪Programs➪Easy CD Creator 5➪Applications➪DirectCD Formatting Utility to display the DirectCD screen shown in Figure 10-1.**

   You can also double-click on the DirectCD icon in the system tray to display this screen.

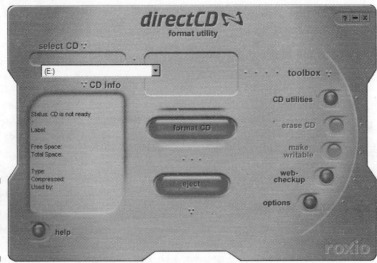

Figure 10-1:
All roads to
DirectCD
start here.

2. **Click the Select CD drop-down list box and choose your recorder. Only recorders show up on this list.**

3. **Load a blank CD-R or CD-RW disc into your recorder.**

   The CD Info window on the left side of the screen should change to show Status: Blank CD, and the Big Blue Format CD Button should turn blue.

4. **Click the Big Blue Format CD Button.**

   DirectCD displays the Format dialog box you see in Figure 10-2.

5. **It's time to give your disc a name. Enter in the Label field a descriptive volume name that's 11 characters or fewer.**

   You see this label displayed in the same places as your hard drive names, including Windows applications, within Windows Explorer, and within My Computer. After you have entered a name, click Finish to start the formatting.

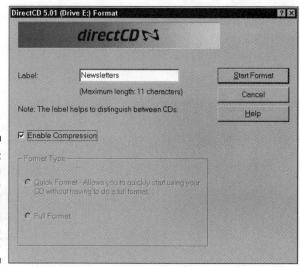

Figure 10-2:
Choosing
a volume
name and
enabling
compression
for a disc.

If you suddenly decide to rename your DirectCD disc — if you change your significant other, for example — click on Options from the DirectCD screen and enter the new name in the Label field.

You can also choose to use compression on your DirectCD disc, which means that files can be reduced in size and you can pack additional stuff on the disc! Roxio says that the compression ranges anywhere from 1.5:1 to 3:1. As with a zip archive, the compression you achieve depends on the data you're adding to the disc. I like to enable this check box because the more space I have to add files, the better; however, this action can limit the number of computers that can read the disc, as you find out when I describe the Eject options later in this chapter. Don't use compression if you want any computer to be able to read the disc!

To read a compressed DirectCD disc on another computer, you have to have either DirectCD 5.0 installed or you have to install UDF support. (Each DirectCD disc has the UDF Reader for Windows automatically copied to it during formatting, so when you load the disc on another computer, you can install the reader from the disc. No need to carry the UDF Reader program around with you like an albatross around your neck.)

6. **Click Start Format to set the wheels in motion, and DirectCD displays the dialog box shown in Figure 10-3 while it's working.**

When the disc has been formatted, DirectCD displays the CD Ready dialog box, which you see in Figure 10-4.

7. Click OK and you can start using your new disc.

After you have become an old hand with DirectCD, you may want to turn off all these newbie (novice) warning dialog boxes. They appear when you format and when you eject a DirectCD disc. To turn off a dialog box, disable the Display this notification again check box at the bottom of the dialog box. You can reenable them by clicking on Options from the DirectCD screen. The fields are labeled Show the CD Ready Notification and Show the Ejected CD Notification.

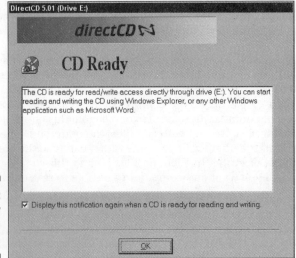

Click on My Computer, and you can see your new drive. Although it appears to be a CD-ROM, it's ready to store data and read it. The DirectCD icon in the Windows system tray now sports a fashionable miniature red padlock, which tells you that you have loaded a DirectCD disc. Remember that you can't eject a DirectCD disc using your drive's Eject button like you can with a regular read-only CD-ROM disc. Don't worry, though: I cover the procedure for safely ejecting a DirectCD disc later in this chapter.

Just Add Files and Stir

"So what programs do I run to use a DirectCD disc?" Programs? You don't need 'em! DirectCD works behind the scenes, so you can forget that it's there. Just read, create, copy, and move files to your DirectCD disc in the same way you use your hard drive or a floppy disk. You can save to the disc within your applications, drag and drop files, or use a file management program like Explorer.

You can also keep tabs on the status of your DirectCD disc by checking its Properties page: Double-click on My Computer to display your drives, right-click on the DirectCD disc, and choose Properties from the pop-up menu. Figure 10-5 shows the Properties for the disc I show you how to create in the preceding section.

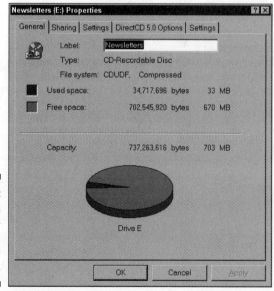

Figure 10-5:
Viewing the properties for a DirectCD disc.

As you can see, the file system is listed as CDUDF compressed. You can see that this disc has approximately 702MB of free space remaining. Remember, though, that it's a "guesstimate" because the rate of compression can vary depending on the type of data you're storing.

That's it! Of all the recording programs I cover, DirectCD is definitely the easiest to master: There's literally nothing to it.

"Wait — 1 Didn't Mean to Trash That!"

When you delete files from a DirectCD CD-RW or DVD-RAM disc, the files are deleted and you recover the space those files used. When you delete files from a CD-R DirectCD disc, the files are no longer accessible, but you don't regain the space.

You can retrieve files you deleted by accident if you're using a CD-R DirectCD disc; however, if you have ejected the disc in the past, you can use Undelete only if you chose the Leave As-is option. (Before you get your hopes up too high, I should note that this action doesn't work all the time.) Follow these steps:

1. **Run the DirectCD Format Utility.**

2. **Click CD Utilities.**

   DirectCD displays the dialog box shown in Figure 10-6.

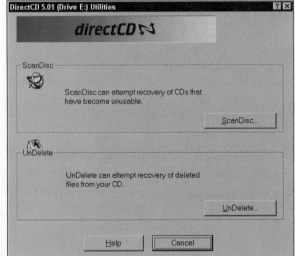

Figure 10-6:
The
DirectCD CD
Utilities —
let's hope
you don't
need 'em.

3. **Click Undelete.**

4. **Select the drive with the DirectCD disc from the list.**

   DirectCD requests confirmation before it begins scanning for deleted files.

5. **Click Yes to continue, and then watch the progress bar while the disc is examined.**

6. **The Undelete dialog box appears, as shown in Figure 10-7. Choose the source folder on the DirectCD disc that held the files. If they can be undeleted, they appear in the list box on the right. Click the file you want; you can attempt to undelete only one file at a time.**

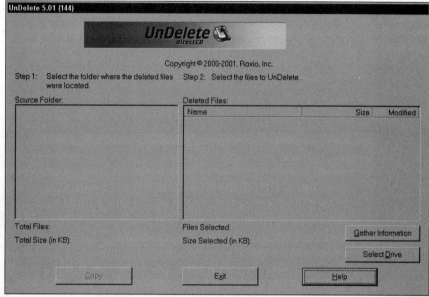

Figure 10-7:
Undelete
doesn't
always
work, but
if it does
it can be a
lifesaver.

7. **Click Copy to attempt to undelete the selected file.**

8. **Choose a destination folder for the file on your hard drive and click Copy.**

9. **Repeat Steps 6 through 8 for each file you want to undelete.**

Eject, Buckaroo, Eject!

A DirectCD disc has one side that's a little tricky, however: You don't just eject a DirectCD disc like any other mundane CD-ROM. (In fact, the Eject button on your recorder may be disabled!) DirectCD has to take care of a few housekeeping tasks, like updating directory entries and preparing the disc for reading.

Follow these steps to eject a disc:

1. **Right-click the DirectCD icon in the system tray to display the pop-up menu, and then click Eject.**

You can also display the DirectCD screen, as I show you earlier in this chapter, or right-click on the drive icon in the My Computer window and select Eject.

DirectCD displays the Eject Disc dialog box you see in Figure 10-8. Choose one close option from the three choices:

- **Leave As-is:** If you want to continue recording later (for example, you need to read something else or record an audio disc with Easy CD Creator and you need the drive), select Leave As-is. You can't read the disc on anything other than a CD recorder, however, so it's effectively out of commission until you reload it.

- **Close to UDF v. 1.5:** The disc is closed so that computers that can read UDF version 1.5 can read the disc — this includes Windows Me and Windows 2000. (You can also pick up UDF extensions for Mac OS 9.1.) With this option, you can either leave the disc open so that you can write more to it later, or you can enable the Protect CD so it cannot be written to again check box to finalize the disc permanently.

Don't have UDF support for your installation of Windows on another computer — perhaps your laptop? Install the UDF Reader for Windows program I mention earlier in this chapter, and you can use the disc.

- **Close to Read on Any Computer:** This option creates an ISO 9660 disc that can be read on just about any computer. Again, you can leave the disc open and write to it again later, or you can enable the Protect CD so it cannot be written to again check box to finalize the disc. You can't use this option if you have elected to compress the data on the disc.

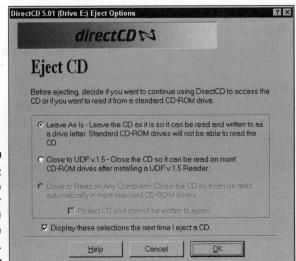

Figure 10-8: Preparing to give your DirectCD disc the boot.

2. **Click OK to eject the disc.**

   Depending on the option you chose, you may have to wait while the disc is finalized, but DirectCD shows you a progress dialog box to let you know how things are going.

Adding Files to an Existing Disc

If you have ejected a disc, you can reload it and write additional data as long as

✔ You didn't choose the Protect CD so it cannot be written to again check box.

✔ Additional space remains on the disc.

When you reload a DirectCD disc, the program may have to open a new session and read the files it already contains. This process can take a few moments, depending on whether you decided to close the disc or leave it as is. However, after the disc is back in the drive, you can use it normally.

Erasing a DirectCD Disc

Like Easy CD Creator, DirectCD allows you to completely erase a CD-RW or DVD-RAM DirectCD disc. To erase a disc:

1. **Run the DirectCD Format Utility.**

2. **Click the Erase CD button.**

   DirectCD requests confirmation that you really want to erase the disc.

3. **Click Yes.**

Sit back while the disc is erased, or go grab yourself another soda.

"Whoops, I Can't Read This Disc"

In case something nasty occurs and you encounter problems with a DirectCD disc (for example, if you are hit with a power failure while copying files to the disc), the program offers a ScanDisc feature that can recover files and fix some errors. Note that this program should not be confused with Windows ScanDisk, which is used only with hard drives and floppy disks.

To scan a DirectCD disc for errors, follow these steps:

1. **Run the DirectCD Format Utility.**

2. **Click CD Utilities; DirectCD displays the dialog box shown earlier, in Figure 10-6.**

3. **Click ScanDisc. DirectCD displays the dialog box shown in Figure 10-9.**

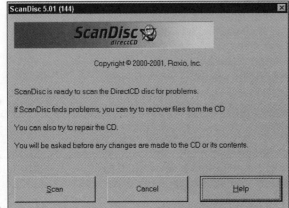

ScanDisc 5.01 (144)

ScanDisc *directCD*

Copyright © 2000-2001, Roxio, Inc.

ScanDisc is ready to scan the DirectCD disc for problems.

If ScanDisc finds problems, you can try to recover files from the CD

You can also try to repair the CD.

You will be asked before any changes are made to the CD or its contents.

Scan   Cancel   Help

Figure 10-9: Running ScanDisc on an ill DirectCD disc.

4. **Click Scan to begin. DirectCD provides a progress bar while it works.**

   If problems are found, you're prompted for confirmation before the program gathers recovery information.

5. **Naturally, this is a definite choice. Click Yes to continue.**

6. **If files can be recovered, ScanDisc allows you to recover them using a system similar to undeleting files. Choose the source folder on the DirectCD disc that holds the files you want to recover.**

   If they can be recovered, they appear in the list box on the right. By default, everything is selected; however, you can hold down the Ctrl key and click on any files or folders you don't need to recover.

7. **Click Copy to attempt to recover all the selected files and folders.**

8. **Choose a destination folder on your hard drive and click Copy.**

9. **Repeat Steps 6 through 8 for each folder that contains files you want to recover.**

Project: Creating a New Employee Disc

Here's the deal: Suppose that you work in the human resources division of your company and it's your job to provide new employees with all the information they need. However, your office doesn't have an intranet (that's another book entirely), so you hit on the idea of a New Employee CD-ROM that contains all sorts of company clip art, press releases, and document templates and the company president's recipe for Heavenly Hash Browns. Your coworkers often take these discs on business trips, too. Your discs are popular because they save plenty of hard drive space on laptops.

That's a great idea, but it has one problem: Your company is continually requesting that new material be added to the discs, and some information is soon out of date and needs to be deleted to make sure that it doesn't get included in a company document accidentally. You need a way to add more data to a disc and be able to selectively delete information whenever you want. Hey, that's the definition of a CD-RW DirectCD disc! Follow these steps to create the perfect employee disc:

1. **Click Start➪Programs➪Easy CD Creator 5➪Applications➪DirectCD Formatting Utility to run DirectCD.**

2. **Click the Select CD drop-down list box and choose your recorder. Only recorders show up on this list.**

3. **Load a blank CD-RW disc into your recorder.**

4. **Click the Big Blue Format CD Button.**

5. **Name the disc (ACMECO, for example), and — because you're assuming that all computers in your company have the UDF Reader installed — enable compression to make room for as much data as possible.**

6. **Click Start Format.**

7. **After the disc is formatted, double-click My Computer on your desktop. Drag to the drive icon all the company files you want to add to the disc to copy them.**

8. **After all the files have been recorded, it's time to eject the disc. Right-click the DirectCD icon in the system tray to and click Eject.**

9. **On the Eject Disc dialog box, choose the Close to UDF v. 1.5 option.**

   Make sure that the Protect CD so it cannot be written to again check box is *disabled* so that you can add and delete files in the future.

10. **Click OK to eject the disc.**

Pass the disc with pride to your next new employee!

Part IV

So You're Ready to Tackle Tougher Stuff?

The 5th Wave   By Rich Tennant

DAD MAKES ULTRA REALISTIC GHOST STORIES CDs FOR THE CAMPING TRIP.

In this part . . .

I'll demonstrate how to create more complex discs, including CD Extra discs, video CDs, and even a digital photo album and slideshow disc. You'll use SoundStream to transfer your music from albums and cassettes to the shiny domain of audio CDs. I'll show you how to create a professional appearance for your discs with labels and box inserts — along with an HTML menu system that will make your data CDs easier to use. Finally, you'll dive into DVD storage. Get ready to create your own DVD-Video disc for your DVD player using the Apple iDVD!

Chapter 11

Heavy-Duty Recording

"*All* right, troops — if you have been following along in this book, you know that I have been easy on you. I have covered the simple stuff, and you can burn simple data and audio CDs until the cows come home. But what if you need to burn a mixed-mode disc? Or record favorite albums and cassettes on audio CDs? Or even record a video CD for use in your DVD-ROM player? Those are heavy-duty recording jobs, Private. Have *you* got what it takes?"

Of course, you do — luckily, those are the specialized discs I cover in this chapter! You may not use them often, but when you do, you can hold your head up high and say "I know how these are made. Step aside, and let the expert show you how it's done."

It's Data, It's Audio, It's Mixed!

Ever felt like you need both digital audio and computer data on the same disc? If so, consider mixed-mode format. You can burn two different types of mixed-mode discs — the one you select depends on the material you're recording and what device will play it.

Putting data before your audio

I mention standard mixed-mode discs in Chapter 7 — they're great for discs that need to combine both digital audio and computer data, but aren't meant to be used in a standard audio CD player. These discs can be played only in a computer's CD-ROM drive.

Typically, the program is installed from the first track (the data portion), which is closest to the spindle hole. After the program is running, it plays the audio tracks that follow: That's why most sophisticated computer games now use mixed-mode format: because the game program can load movies and data files from the first track and still access the digital audio while you're blasting the aliens from Planet Quark.

The extra behind CD Extra

As you can see in Figure 11-1, a CD Extra disc turns regular mixed-mode format on its head: One or more audio tracks come first, followed by a data track. The big attraction here is for musicians; a CD Extra disc can be played in both a standard audio CD player (which really can't tell the difference because the data is at the end) and a computer's read-only CD-ROM drive. This, folks, is the definition of neat!

Groups from the Rolling Stones to the Red Hot Chili Peppers and the Squirrel Nut Zippers have popularized the CD Extra disc with their fans. Although the format costs a minute or two worth of disc space (the blank space that's necessary to separate the tracks), the band's music can share the disc with a multimedia presentation of the latest music video or still pictures of a recent concert — or even lyrics to the songs.

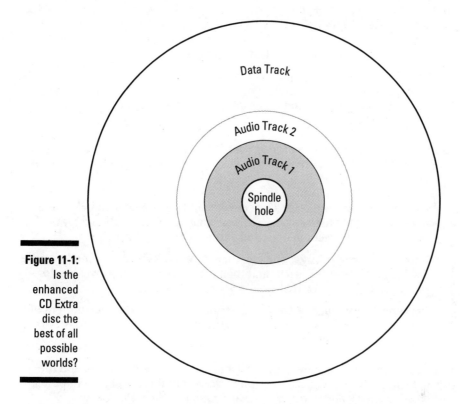

Data Track

Audio Track 2

Audio Track 1

Spindle
hole

Figure 11-1:
Is the
enhanced
CD Extra
disc the
best of all
possible
worlds?

Doing Vinyl with SoundStream

SoundStream is a major program that ships with Easy CD Creator Platinum. Because it involves a little more work than copying an audio CD or recording a new disc from MP3s, I decided not to introduce it until now. In effect, you can consider SoundStream the "bridge" between your existing music collection (vinyl albums, cassettes, and even antique media, like 8-track cartridges and reel-to-reel tapes) and the permanence and sound quality of audio CDs. With the right equipment, you can transfer the music from all these types of old recordings to a brand-new audio CD format.

However, let me make one thing perfectly clear: *I recommend SoundStream for only those recordings in your collection that aren't already available on audio CD.* In other words, using SoundStream to "back up" your Boston albums is simply ridiculous! Here's why:

✔ **Too much effort:** First, why go to the trouble of remastering material that's already available on audio CDs? It's much easier to jump online or walk down to your local record store to pick up a copy of that Police album on audio CD.

- **Subpar sound quality:** No matter how good your equipment and how well you have treated your old media, the sound you achieve is never as good as a professionally mastered audio CD.

- **Less than visually striking:** Unless you have spent a bundle on a compact disc screen printer, your finished disc doesn't look as good as a commercial disc (and it doesn't have those liner notes or that flashy jewel case liner).

"Okay, Mark — exactly when should I use SoundStream?" I would say that if your recording fits these criteria, it's a good bet that they're prime examples of SoundStream material:

- **Unavailable on audio CD:** The college band you loved so much that didn't hit the big time — perhaps it produced an album or a cassette, but those never become ones and zeroes without your help.

- **Rare or live recordings:** The one time that Frank Zappa jammed onstage with Ella Fitzgerald? Burn it, and then *please* send me a copy! I would pay a pretty penny for that one.

- **Personal recordings of you, your family and your friends:** Your grand-parent's family history, or the "soundtrack" to your 16th birthday party, which your Dad recorded.

To use SoundStream, you need the assistance of your home stereo and the original equipment (sorry, this program's good, but it can't play that 8-track cartridge by itself), and you have to make a cable connection or two. Although I cover the procedure in the project at the end of this chapter, you need to connect your stereo's amplifier or tuner to your computer's sound card input jacks. Because computer sound card hardware varies widely between manufacturers (some cards may even need special cables), check the documentation that came with your sound card to determine how to do this.

Adding Effects in SoundStream

While I'm discussing SoundStream, I should also mention that the program allows you to tweak and improve your older recordings while you're remastering them to audio CDs. For example, you can make use of effects like these:

- *Concert Halls,* where a stereo "widening" effect is added to music

- *Sound Cleaning,* where tape hiss and that persistent background hum can be eliminated (unless it's part of your 1960s music and it's actually part of the song)

> ✔ *Pop and Click Removal,* where you can clean older, "low-fidelity" recordings of annoying pops and clicks

I show you how to make use of the Sound Cleaning effect while I'm demonstrating SoundStream later in this chapter.

Giving Your Disc the Boot

I think I have created only one or two bootable discs in my entire burning career — but when you need one, they're absolutely critical. (In both cases, I had to create bootable discs to take care of hardware problems with PCs that wouldn't boot. The drivers, programs, and data I had to store wouldn't have fit on a floppy, either.) A bootable disc contains everything your computer needs to complete the loading of a specific operating system. In most cases, the operating system is DOS, Windows, or Linux — including the required hardware drivers for things like your mouse and your CD-ROM drive.

Here's a great stumper for the next so-called "computer guru" you meet who claims to know all things binary: In the Windows world, a bootable disc conforms to the *El Torito* standard. Of all the strange names I have encountered in my computer travels, that one even beats the acronym TWAIN (which stands for Technology Without An Interesting Name)! My editor's favorite Mexican restaurant was also named El Torito — hopefully, though, they didn't burn anything there.

Let me be honest with you: Creating a bootable CD-ROM is not an easy matter, so it's a project for experienced computer owners. Gathering all this stuff takes careful planning because just a single missing line in your boot files can render the entire disc useless. For this reason, it's good news that Easy CD Creator requires you to create a floppy boot disk it can "import" into your data layout. If your computer can boot from the floppy disk, you know that it can do the same using your bootable CD-ROM. (You can also create a bootable hard drive image and then use that to record, if your hard drive is working.)

I show you how to create a bootable disc later in this chapter. If you have decided to record one, make sure that the computer you use it on supports booting from a CD-ROM. Most PCs built in the past three or four years can use a bootable CD-ROM; check your PC's manual. If the documentation doesn't cover this option, follow the instructions it provides to display the BIOS settings and look for a bootable CD-ROM option.

Creating An Optical Photo Album

Every photo album is "optical," of course — but when I use the word, I mean a photo album that's recorded on a CD-ROM. The photos in a CD-ROM album can be displayed on your computer monitor, saved to your hard drive for use in your documents, or — if you would rather have an old-fashioned hard copy — printed on your inkjet or laser printer.

Easy CD Creator Platinum is thoughtfully accompanied by an excellent "Swiss army knife" for your digital images: PhotoRelay version 2.5, from ArcSoft, Inc. You can use PhotoRelay to create optical photo albums and slideshows (using your digital photographs) and video postcards (using your digital video). If you have a Web site, the program can even create catalog pages for your photographs. A visitor to your site just has to click a thumbnail to display the full-size image. (Remember that if you read the next chapter, won't you?)

I show you in this chapter how to use PhotoRelay to create an optical photo album that can display your images in a slideshow.

Recording that MTV Video

The last advanced specialized disc I discuss is the *video CD* (commonly called a VCD), which stores digital video in MPEG-1 format. You can watch a video CD in a video CD player, a computer CD-ROM drive (with the right software) and most of the latest generation of DVD players. Before the advent of DVD players, video CDs were the primary method of recording and distributing digital video among computer owners.

Easy CD Creator uses a combination of a separate program named VCD Creator and a Windows wizard to help simplify the creation of a video CD. With VCD Creator, you can burn a professional VCD disc, complete with a basic menu system — and I lead you through the process step-by-step in the last project in this chapter.

Project: Recording an Album to CD

I'm the proud owner of a special record album: *Batman and Robin,* recorded in 1966 on the Tifton label and performed by "the sensational guitars of Dan & Dale." You may not believe this, but the guy at my local record shop says that he doubts this classic LP will be released on compact disc any time soon! (In fact, he said something about "a snowball's chance" — I didn't catch the rest.) I have two choices: Either I can continue to play the album and listen to it deteriorate over the next few years, or I can master that music to an audio CD and enjoy it in digital splendor for the next century! (If you think that I'm choosing the former option, you're reading the wrong book.)

Remember that your computer's sound card must be connected to your stereo's amplifier or preamp before you can begin. Follow these steps to master an album to an audio CD:

1. **Choose Start➪Programs➪Easy CD Creator 5➪Applications➪ SoundStream to display the screen you see in Figure 11-2.**

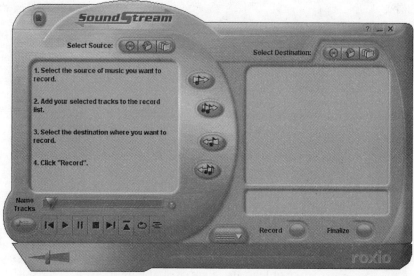

Figure 11-2: I think that Sound-Stream sports an extremely cool interface.

2. **Click the Option Drawer button (it's the down arrow at the bottom of the SoundStream window) to expand the window, and click Spin Doctor to display the screen shown in Figure 11-3.**

3. **If you're lucky enough to have multiple sound cards in your PC, click the Select Source drop-down list box and choose the input or record source.**

   If you have only one sound card, leave this field as is.

4. **Move the sliding selector to Sound Cleaning and click the LP preset button (which, by no coincidence whatsoever, looks just like a tiny record album).**

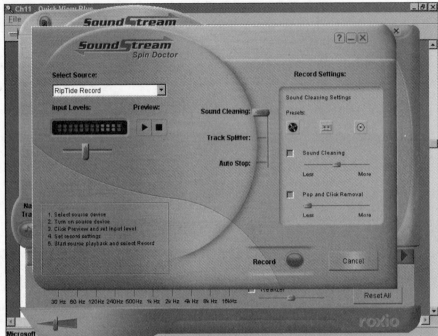

Figure 11-3:
The Spin
Doctor
screen.

This step automatically chooses the best settings for sound cleaning and pop/click removal.

5. **Move the sliding selector a third time to Auto Stop and make sure that it's set to Manual Stop.**

   You have to hang around and listen to the master being played — one last time in analog format, anyway — so that you can stop the recording by hand. However, your PC isn't fooled into thinking that the album is over when only weird silences are being "played." (Fans of The Beatles and The Doors know what I mean on this one.)

6. **Turn on your stereo system and start playing your LP.**

   Optionally, recall the days when the LP was considered "state-of-the-art" and "high-fidelity." Speculate on the future of audio media, and wonder what everyone will be using to record music in another decade.

7. **Click the Preview button — it looks like the Play button on a cassette or CD player — and adjust the Input level slider until the strongest and loudest passage of music lights the entire green portion of the**

level meter. When the level is adjusted, click the Stop button to leave Preview mode.

8. **Click the Big Red Record button to display the Spin Doctor Preliminary Recording Stuff dialog box (that's my name for it, anyway), as shown in Figure 11-4. You have two options: Record directly to CD, or record the music as MP3 or WAV files to your hard drive and then record them later (as I describe earlier in Chapter 8).**

   Roxio recommends the latter, and I agree. That way, you can listen to the tracks and check their quality without wasting a blank CD, and you can also add track names for audio CD players that display CD-Text. If you have an older 2x or 4x recorder, it also helps prevent recording errors. You want to record to your hard drive, so click File.

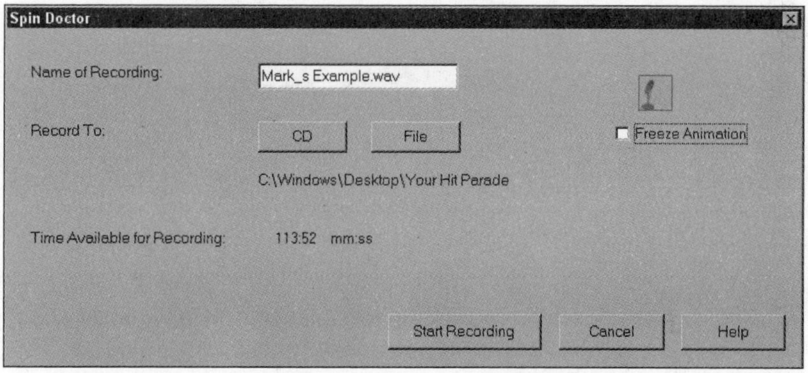

Figure 11-4:
Choosing
the target
using the
Spin Doctor
Preliminary
Recording
Stuff dia-
log box.

9. **The dialog box shown in Figure 11-5 appears. Choose your digital audio format of choice from the Save As Type drop-down list box. Navigate to the folder where you want to store the tracks with Explorer view, and click on the folder to select it and display the contents. (To create a new folder, click the — you guessed it — New Folder button at the bottom of the dialog box.) When you're situated in the right place, click Select Folder.**

10. **Okay, here's the fun part: Start your LP over at the beginning and immediately click Start Recording.**

    Spin Doctor creates separate tracks in the folder you specified.

11. **When the album is over, click Stop and click OK to return to Spin Doctor.**

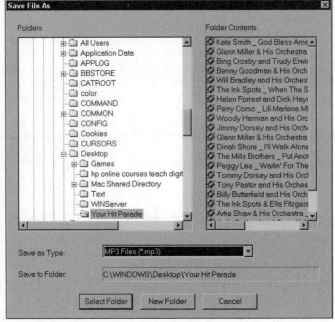

Figure 11-5:
Saving the
*Sensational
Guitars
of Dan &
Dale* as
MP3 files.

That's it! You can now exit SoundStream and listen to your new digital audio files using your favorite MP3 or WAV player. After you're satisfied with the results, follow the instructions in Chapter 8 for recording a typical audio CD from MP3 and WAV files.

Wow, Dan & Dale never sounded so good! Next, I think I'll try that live bootleg album of Iron Butterfly.

Project: Recording a Bootable CD-ROM

Suppose that you work as a computer repair technician for a company and you want to create a test CD-ROM that can boot an absolutely "clean" installation of DOS or Windows. You include diagnostics programs on this CD-ROM, so it becomes a basic "software-toolkit-on-a-disc" for your travels throughout the building. (If this sounds like firsthand experience, believe me — it is!)

This situation is the perfect time to use a bootable CD-ROM. As long as all your company's computers can use a bootable disc, you can guarantee yourself a stable environment (what techies call a "vanilla") for diagnosing troublesome hardware toys.

As I mention earlier in this book, this type of disc requires more preparation than the others I cover in this chapter, and I strongly recommend that *only experienced PC owners and technicians should attempt to burn a bootable CD-ROM.* With that said, you should prepare a floppy disc that boots your system with exactly the same configuration as you want for the bootable CD-ROM. Make sure that it contains the CD-ROM driver, too!

Follow these steps to create your bootable disc:

1. **Choose Start⇨Programs⇨Easy CD Creator 5⇨Applications⇨Easy CD Creator to run the program.**

2. **Click File, choose New CD Project, and select Bootable CD.**

   Easy CD Creator opens the dialog box you see in Figure 11-6.

   Things can get really hairy really quickly at this point — although you can create several exotic types of bootable CDs, I stick with the easiest (and most compatible) type.

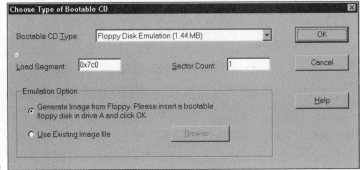

Figure 11-6:
The begin-
nings of
a boot-
able CD.

3. **Click the Bootable CD Type drop-down list box and choose Floppy Disk Emulation (1.44MB).**

   Leave everything else on this dialog box as is.

4. **Load into your 1.44MB floppy drive the floppy disk you have prepared and click OK.**

   After churning for a few seconds while the system files are read, the bootable CD-ROM layout shown in Figure 11-7 appears. Note the two files that have already been added to the layout: *BOOTCAT.BIN and BOOTIMG.BIN must not be erased or moved!* They're the files that make this puppy bootable.

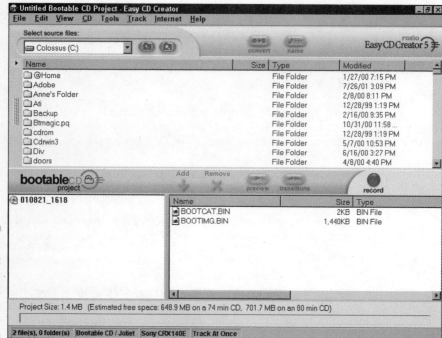

Figure 11-7:
Check out
the all-
important
BOOT files
for this disc!

5. **If you just want the disc to boot your PC (without reading additional files from the disc), you can skip ahead to Step 8. Otherwise, you can locate and highlight more data files, using the same method you used to select files for a data CD-ROM.**

6. **Click Add to add the files and folders to the data portion of the layout.**

   Because a bootable CD-ROM is recorded using the ISO 9660 file system, you may encounter a dialog box like the one you see in Figure 11-8. Unlike other data CD-ROMs you have recorded using Joliet (which allows long filenames), you have to shorten those names to put them on your bootable CD-ROM. Easy CD Creator makes this process easy: Just press Change All. To enter a specific filename for each affected file, type the name you want in the Change Name To field and click Change. Easy CD Creator renames the file, adds it to the layout, and displays the next offending file. Note that this renaming procedure does not affect the file's name on your hard drive — only in the layout.

7. **Repeat Steps 6 and 7 until you have finished adding files to the layout.**

8. **Click the Big Red Record button and start the recording as you would any other data CD-ROM.**

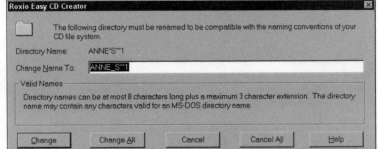

Figure 11-8:
No long
filenames
here, buster.

Project: Recording a Mixed-Mode Disc

Suppose that you need to record a selection of multimedia clips to carry with you on a business trip — some are video clips that you need to store only for the ride, but some of the clips are digital audio that you need to hear to practice your presentation. One solution would be to burn two discs — one, a data CD-ROM for the video clips, and the other, a traditional audio CD. A mixed-mode disc, however, allows you to combine both these types of content on a single disc.

Follow these steps to create a mixed-mode CD:

1. **Choose Start⇨Programs⇨Easy CD Creator 5⇨Applications⇨Easy CD Creator to run the program.**

2. **Click File, choose New CD Project, and choose Mixed-Mode CD to display a special mixed-mode layout, as shown in Figure 11-9.**

   Make sure that the data CD icon is selected at in the lower-left corner, under the label Mixed-Mode CD Project.

3. **Locate and highlight the data files, using the same method you have used to select files for a data CD-ROM.**

4. **Click Add to add the files and folders to the data portion of the layout.**

5. **Repeat Steps 3 and 4 until your data layout is complete, as shown in Figure 11-10.**

   Don't forget to click the CD label and name the data portion of the CD-ROM something descriptive. The default name, which is built using the current date and time, is rarely what you want.

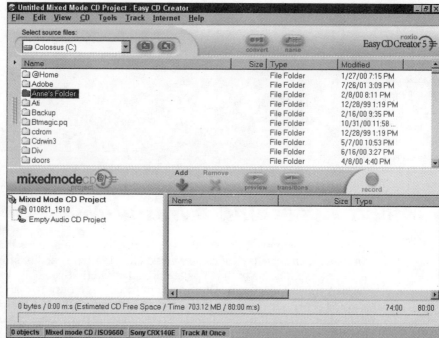

Figure 11-9:
A blank
mixed-mode
CD layout
in Easy CD
Creator.

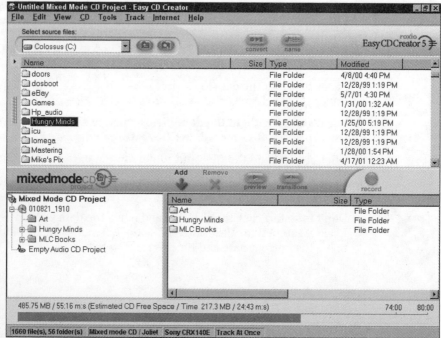

Figure 11-10:
The data
part of this
mixed-
mode
layout
is now
complete.

6. **Click the music CD icon next to the label Empty Audio CD Project to add the digital audio tracks.**

   As you can see in Figure 11-11, the lower-right portion of the screen changes to the familiar audio CD track layout.

7. **Locate and highlight the MP3, WAV, or WMF digital audio files you want to record, just as you do in designing a standard audio CD.**

   Remember to watch the free-space display at the bottom of the screen to make sure that you don't run out of space while adding audio files.

8. **Click Add to copy the files to your track layout.**

9. **Repeat Steps 7 and 8 until your audio track layout is complete, as illustrated in Figure 11-12.**

10. **Click the Big Red Record button and finish the recording, just like with a typical data CD-ROM.**

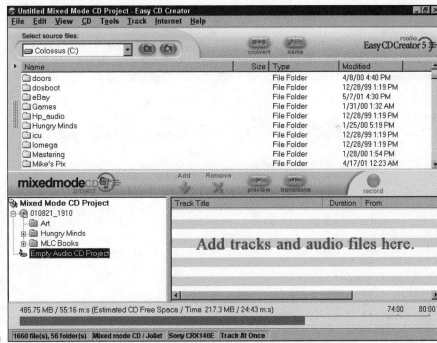

Figure 11-11:
Whoa! Now you have switched to digital audio — on the same disc.

Figure 11-12:
I think this
disc is
ready to be
burned,
don't you?

Project: Recording a CD Extra Disc

As you may have guessed, I could also have created the disc I showed you how to burn in the preceding project using a CD Extra disc. Like a mixed-mode disc, a CD Extra (or Enhanced) disc can hold the same unique combination of digital audio and computer data. The big difference is that you can play the audio tracks from a CD Extra disc in your standard audio CD player, and you need a computer's CD-ROM drive to access the digital audio on a mixed-mode disc. That's great for adding that video of your garage band to that *Best of Deep Purple* disc you burned!

Follow these steps to record a CD Extra disc:

1. **Choose Start⇨Programs⇨Easy CD Creator 5⇨Applications⇨Easy CD Creator to start your favorite program.**

2. **Click File, choose New CD Project, and choose Enhanced CD. Again, Easy CD Creator has a special layout screen for a CD Extra project, as illustrated in Figure 11-13. If the Empty Audio CD Project audio CD icon isn't already selected in the lower-left corner, click it now.**

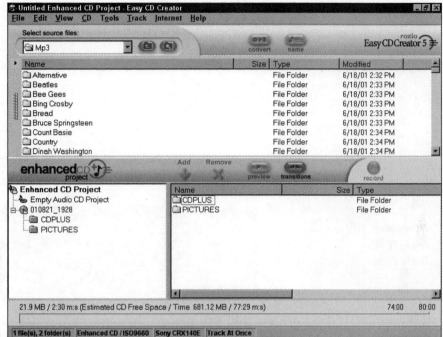

Figure 11-13:
A CD Extra
project
layout.

3. **Locate and select the MP3, WAV, or WMF digital audio files to record, just as you do in designing a standard audio CD.**

4. **Click Add to copy the tracks to the audio CD portion of the layout.**

5. **Repeat Steps 3 and 4 until you have added all the audio tracks you want.**

6. **Click the volume label for the data CD icon in the lower-left corner and change the label to something descriptive.**

   Leave the CDPLUS and PICTURES folders as they are. Don't delete these folders or add files within them because they are used in conjunction with the audio tracks on the disc! (You can find out more about this topic in the nearby sidebar, "Documenting your CD Extra discs.")

7. **Locate the files and folders to add in the usual manner using the Explorer display in the upper half of the screen, and highlight them.**

8. **Click Add to copy the selected files and folders to the data portion of the layout.**

9. **Repeat Steps 7 and 8 until all the files you want are added. Figure 11-14 shows a finished data layout for your CD Extra disc; note the location of the data files in the layout.**

10. **Click the Big Red Record button and finish the recording as you would with a typical data CD-ROM.**

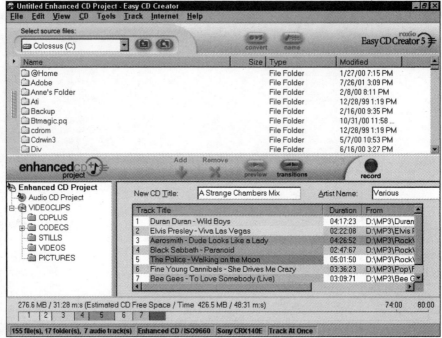

Figure 11-14:
The finalized
audio and
data layouts
for your CD
Extra disc.

Project: Recording a Photo Disc

Aunt Harriet canning preserves. Pictures of the kids at Christmas. Those
home inventory photographs. 'Nuff said! Whatever the subject of your digital
images, you can create a photo disc using PhotoRelay that can be viewed on
any PC running Windows 95 or later.

Follow these steps to burn a photo disc:

1. **Choose Start⇨Programs⇨Easy CD Creator⇨Applications⇨PhotoRelay
   to run the program, which displays the screen shown in Figure 11-15.**

2. **By default, the program starts with a new, empty album, so click
   Album and choose Add Image from the menu.**

   Alternatively, click the first button on the toolbar, which represents
   a photo album with a green arrow pointing to the images. Whichever
   method you use, PhotoRelay displays a standard File Open dialog box.

Documenting your CD Extra discs

I mention CD-Text earlier in this chapter, which is a nice feature that allows many audio CD players to display the CD title and the artist and track names while you listen. That's all that most people need. However, a CD Extra disc can store even more reference information describing the audio tracks, including the artist name, CD title, and publisher. If your audio CD player can't show this additional stuff, your computer probably can when you play the disc in your CD-ROM drive.

If you want to store this extra information, you must enter it after you have added your tracks (see Step 5 in the section titled, "Project:

Recording a CD Extra Disc"). Click File, choose CD Project Properties, and click the Enhanced CD tab to display the dialog box shown in the following figure. Click the Created and Published drop-down boxes to choose these dates from a miniature calendar; the other fields can be entered by just clicking in the field and typing away. Click OK to save the information you entered and return to the CD Extra layout.

Personally, I don't use these fields, and you don't have to enter any of this stuff — but the fields do come in handy when you're recording a disc that will be used as a master for a manufacturing run.

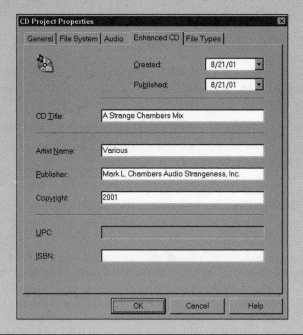

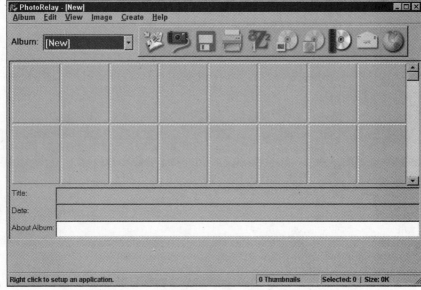

Figure 11-15:
PhotoRelay
waits for
the action
to start.

3. **Navigate to the folder that holds the images you want to add to the album. Click an image to highlight the filename; to add multiple images, hold down the Ctrl key while you click. Click Open to add the selected images to the album.**

Figure 11-16 shows the thumbnail display for an album.

4. **Repeat Step 3 until you have added all the images you want to include on your photo disc.**

To view an image in full-size mode, double-click the thumbnail image.

5. **If you like, you can add a little descriptive information for each image. Click a thumbnail and type the photo's title, the date it was taken, and a 1-line description at the bottom of the window.**

6. **Save the album: Click Album and choose Save Album from the menu. Enter a descriptive name in the field (note that the PHB extension is added automatically) and click OK.**

You're ready to create the slideshow.

7. **Click the Create a Slide Show button on the toolbar.**

It's a disc with an old-fashioned photographic slide. PhotoRelay displays the dialog box you see in Figure 11-17.

Figure 11-16:
The photo album is rapidly filling up with thumbnails.

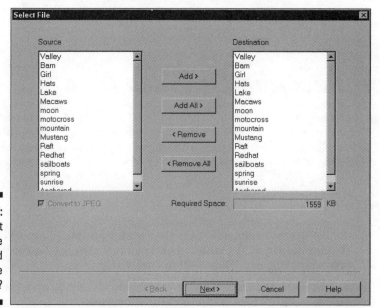

Figure 11-17:
What should be included in the slideshow?

8. Hold down the Ctrl key and click each photo you want to add to the slideshow in the left list box. Click the Add button. If you're like me, you want to add all images in the album, so you can just click Add All. Click Next to continue.

   Next, PhotoRelay allows you to add a single digital audio file in WAV or MP3 format that plays in the background during the show.

9. If you want to do this next step, click Play Single Audio File and click the Browse button to select the file. If you would rather skip the audio accompaniment, leave things set to No Audio. Click Next to continue.

10. Time to burn! Load a *blank* CD-R disc into your recorder — don't use a disc with an existing session. To create the slideshow in a separate folder, click the Slide Name field and enter the name you want. To create the slideshow in the root (top level) of the disc, leave the Slide Name field blank. (I recommend leaving the field blank because some folks may find it inconvenient or difficult to change to the folder.) Click Finish to start the recording, and watch PhotoRelay load Easy CD Creator to take care of the burn. Talk about teamwork!

To watch your slideshow, just insert the disc into your CD-ROM drive, and Windows should automatically start things going! You can also start the show manually: Use Windows Explorer to locate the file SLIDE.EXE on the CD-ROM and double-click it.

Project: Recording a Video Disc

To end this chapter on advanced recording, I show you how to create a video CD of a child's birthday party. Suppose that you have a series of short video clips you have edited using Adobe Premiere and you have saved them in MPEG format on your hard drive. The VCD disc should show the clips in order.

Follow these steps:

1. Choose Start➪Programs➪Easy CD Creator➪Applications➪Video CD Creator to load VCD Creator. As shown in Figure 11-18, the wizard runs automatically. Click Next to continue.

2. Because you don't need a menu system to simply display the clips, choose Simple Video Sequence and click Next.

Figure 11-18:
The opening
gambit used
by Video CD
Creator.

3. **Click Add to display the Add Play Items dialog box. Select the folders where you have stored your MPEG files and double-click the clip you want to appear first on your video CD.**

   The clip appears in the Add New Play Item dialog box (see Figure 11-19), where you can preview it by dragging the slider bar that appears under the Video Clip Preview window.

4. **Click OK and VCD Creator adds the clip to your Video CD layout as a thumbnail-size icon.**

Figure 11-19:
Adding a
new item to
the VCD
layout.

5. **Add the rest of your clips by repeating Steps 3 and 4. When all the clips have been added to the layout, click Next to continue.**

6. **Click Next again on the Creating Play Sequence screen to display the dialog box shown in Figure 11-20.**

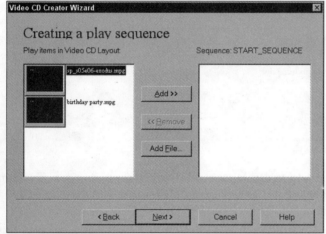

Figure 11-20:
Selecting the order in which video clips will play.

7. **Click the icon in the left list box to highlight the clip that should appear first, and then click Add to copy it into your sequence. Add the remaining icons in order using the same method. To remove a clip from the sequence, click the icon in the right list box to highlight it and click Remove.**

   If you have forgotten a clip, you can add it to the left list box by clicking the Add File button.

8. **When the sequence in the right list box is completed, click Next to continue.**

9. **Click Playback to view the entire sequence.**

   The program displays the high-tech control panel you see in Figure 11-21, complete with familiar controls like the buttons on a DVD player.

10. **When you have finished your preview, click the Close button on the control panel and click Next to continue.**

   From the dialog box you see in Figure 11-22, you can choose to record your VCD immediately, create a disc image for later recording, or make changes from the VCD Creator layout.

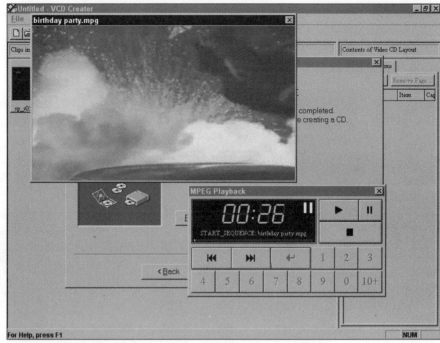

Figure 11-21:
Previewing
the goods
before you
record.

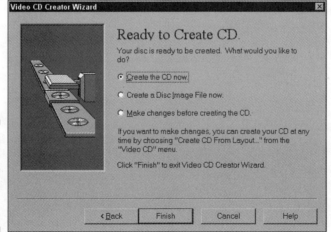

Figure 11-22:
Choosing
recording
options
for the
video CD.

11. **To record now, click Create the CD Now, load a CD-R disc (always use
    a CD-R disc, not a CD-RW disc, for a video CD), and click Finish to
    display the familiar CD Creation Setup dialog box.**

12. **Finish the recording as you would do for a standard data CD-ROM
    layout.**

Chapter 12

BAM! Add Menus to Your Discs!

Your cell phone uses a menu. Your computer programs use menus. Some cars now use menus to display information to the driver. I'm sure that someone somewhere is trying to add a menu to bathroom fixtures — all in the name of those two powerful deities, Convenience and Ease of Use.

In this chapter, I show you how you can add a professional-looking point-and-click menu system to your recorded data CD-ROMs — without spending a fortune on strange programs, dedicating half of next year to learning any strange scripting language, or hiring some strange programmer for half of next year's income to do it for you. (If you like, you can send your thanks to mark@mlcbooks.com — there's nothing better than e-mail from happy readers!)

Everything Uses Menus These Days

Can you imagine buying an application or a game program, installing it, and discovering that it had no menu system? Why, you would think that our civilization had returned to the archaic Dark Ages of DOS, with commands you had to type by hand. That's why I add, for one reason or another, a menu to about half the discs I burn. I think that any disc that falls into one of these categories needs a menu onboard to make it, well, more convenient and easier to use.

(By the way, I still remember about 90 percent of those archaic DOS commands. Who knows when I may need them again, but I'm too nostalgic to forget my first operating system!)

Discs chock-full of images, video, and sounds

If you want to display digital photographs, play sound clips, or show video clips, you have come to the right place — HTML provides support for all these files, and they sound and look as nice as they do when you're receiving them over the Internet (just much, *much* faster). Whoops, I almost forgot: You can add cool extras, like Flash animation, Adobe PDF files, and Java applets to your HTML menu, too.

Discs burned to distribute to others

Convenience and ease of use are both doubly important when you're recording a disc for distribution. As a shareware author, I can attest that what seems to you like a piece of cake to use can be a hunk of lead the size of an anvil to a computing novice. For example, rather than try to figure out what program to run and where it is on your disc, your customer may decide to chuck your demo CD-ROM into the trashcan.

Besides making your disc easier to use, an HTML menu system allows you to pull out all the stops for a professional first impression: Your menu can make liberal use of graphics, music, and even video (without requiring a connection to the Internet) while providing the point-and-click functionality everyone wants. A multimedia menu tends to draw people; as anyone in advertising can tell you, using eye candy helps to deliver the message.

Discs with Internet links

If an Internet connection is available, your discs can offer direct links to your online Internet presence. You can take visitors directly to your Web site, prepare an e-mail message that's automatically addressed to you, and load resources from your Web server (like the latest program update or your latest newsletter in PDF format).

Discs with text files galore

If you take the time to convert your text into HTML (which I demonstrate to you later in this chapter), you can display them directly within the friendly confines of a Web browser, complete with links to other documents, search commands, and basic text formatting.

Discs that include a Web site

Yes, Virginia, you can indeed store an entire Web site on a disc, complete with every graphic, sound, and animation found on the Internet site. (The only thing that would have to be left by the wayside would be streaming video because it requires a connection to the Internet for you to download.) Because both Netscape Navigator and Microsoft Internet Explorer can load a Web page from a CD-ROM or a hard drive rather than from a Web server, anyone with a browser can "visit" your site — just by loading your disc.

Discs with dozens and dozens of folders

If your disc has only one or two folders, no big whoop (although you're still betting that the person who has your disc knows how to use Windows Explorer or will read your printed instructions). But what if your disc has nested directories three or four levels deep and that person has to dig for a specific piece of clip art or a certain Adobe Acrobat PDF file?

With an HTML menu, you can provide hyperlinks that automatically open these files or "download" them directly to the computer's hard drive for later use — no digging, no searching and, very likely, a satisfied customer.

Designing Menus (But Not for Food)

What's the secret to designing a good menu? What elements should it have? Of course, the appearance of your menu is completely up to you — and the flexibility of HTML makes it easy to add a menu that's as flashy or mundane as you like. However, I can provide you with a few guidelines that apply equally well to any CD-ROM menu:

> ✔ **Plan your menu in advance.** Before you run your HTML editor, sit down with a piece of paper and a pencil (remember those?) and write down precisely what commands your menus should include and how many menus you need. For example, if you need only an e-mail link, a couple of text links, and a download link, you can place all those on one

menu. If you're selling different products and you want each to have its own page, make notes of what commands each page needs.

✔ **People like consistency.** Think of the best sites you find most attractive on the Web: I would bet that each site has its own graphic design elements (like buttons, separation bars, fonts, and incidental graphics) that set it apart. Those elements work only when they're used consistently, so avoid a hodgepodge of different looks. Also, decide ahead of time what common controls should be on every page — for example, if your menu will have more than one page, don't forget to plan the navigational controls you need. As with a standard Web page, you need links to advance a single page or send your user back to the home page — and it's a good idea to add a link to back up a single page, too.

✔ **"What's my motivation?"** Okay, sorry about the actor-speak: Ask yourself what kind of an impression you want to make on those using your disc. Do you need the multimedia pizzazz, or would your purpose be better served with a simple menu and a few animated images? If you're recording a disc just for reference purposes, for example, your customers probably don't need anything fancy — clarity and speedy retrieval are more important. A demo disc that offers a product, on the other hand, may pull out all the stops and offer plenty of eye candy.

✔ **How will the information be used?** Will the information on your disc be viewed directly within the browser (like a PDF or HTML text file), or do users have to download programs and data to their hard drives first? It's always a good idea to add text to your menus that helps guide novices if something has to be done.

Whether your menus are plain and simple, somewhat attractive, or downright Hollywood, they must be arranged in a logical manner. If your disc offers primarily a catalog of images, why put the links to the sample images on a secondary menu? Your menu system should save as many mouse clicks as possible, so it's always a good idea to "put the best stuff in the window."

Using HTML for Your Menus

HTML (short for *Hypertext Markup Language*, as though anyone really worries about it any more) is just plain neat. When it was first developed, it was heralded as the beginning of a new age of communication as the foundation of the World Wide Web; and indeed, it has proven to be exactly that. HTML could rest on its laurels for the rest of history, known as nothing but the cornerstone of the Web.

But a great concept like HTML is hard to contain to a single facet of the computing world: Software developers and engineers have this funny habit of using something that works well in ways that the original designers would have never considered. For example, HTML has now become the basis of today's disc-based help and documentation; many applications, utilities, and games now ship with no printed manual. The entire manual is saved in HTML format to the disc itself. (In fact, that was what prompted me to develop my first HTML menu for a disc, sometime back in the hoary days of 1996: I was fascinated by my first experience with an on-disc HTML manual.)

So why does HTML make such a good foundation for a CD-ROM menu system? Reflect, good reader, on these facts:

- ✔ **Free, free, *free!*** That got your attention, didn't it? Not only are Web browsers generally free, but you can also choose from a wide range of free HTML editors (with a generous handful of inexpensive shareware editors around to boot). Probably the best known of these is Microsoft Front Page. Even programs like Microsoft PowerPoint and Word can create simple Web pages.

- ✔ **It's available on everything.** HTML is such a pervasive force these days that every operating system either displays it or includes a browser; that includes the Big Three (Windows, the Mac operating system, and Linux) as well as strange and wonderful beasts like BeOS and Solaris. Because operating systems now install a Web browser automatically, you're also virtually assured that your customers can use your menu. If, in some cosmic irregularity, they haven't installed a browser, you can even include the distribution versions of Netscape Navigator or Microsoft Internet Explorer on the CD itself.

- ✔ **Customers already know how to use it.** These days, the vast majority of folks already know how to use their Web browsers, and those browsers can automatically display common multimedia file formats; no need to manually run external programs. (I know a friend who's uncomfortable with any programs other than Outlook Express and Internet Explorer, and even he could use your disc.)

- ✔ **A complete menu toolbox.** HTML has evolved into a powerful language, complete with tools to display formatted text; search that text for specific words and phrases; play movies, music and sounds; display images; link files; copy files from disc to hard drive; send e-mail; and visit other Web sites. Whew!

- ✔ **A normal person can understand HTML.** Compared to a "serious" programming language like C or assembly, understanding HTML is a walk in the park. To be honest, you really don't need to study it anyway because a good HTML editor can create a menu without your writing a single line of code. (For example, I use Netscape Composer in the menu project at the end of this chapter.)

- ✔ **You can use third-party plug-ins to add even more features.** Need Flash animation for your HTML menu? How about specially written Java applets? (If you don't know what either of these is, feel free to ignore them.) If you can program in Java or you have an application to build Java applets for you, your menus can run these toys with a click of a mouse (or automatically with the menu).

For those with knowledge of HTML

I often make quick changes to Web pages with Windows Notepad — it's easy to modify a word here or there or change the color of a font. However, I use a "careware" HTML editor when I'm designing or making major changes to an existing page, and I can heartily recommend it as a powerful addition to your HTML toolbox. The program, Arachnophilia, was written by Paul Lutus. You can download your copy at `http://www.arachnoid.com/arachnophilia/` (it comes in flavors for all versions of Windows).

Arachnophilia offers support for format templates, tables, keyboard macros, global search-and-replace, page frames, and much more. It

even includes a built-in ftp client for transferring Web pages and files. The program can display with its internal browser a preview of a page you're developing, too. The following figure shows Arachnophilia at work on my personal Web site. Note that this is not a WYSIWYG (short for What You See Is What You Get) HTML editor per se (like Front Page), so you do need knowledge of the HTML language.

(By the way, careware is a simple concept: Simply repay the author with deeds of kindness in your general area, and be thankful for what you have. It's a great program at a great price.)

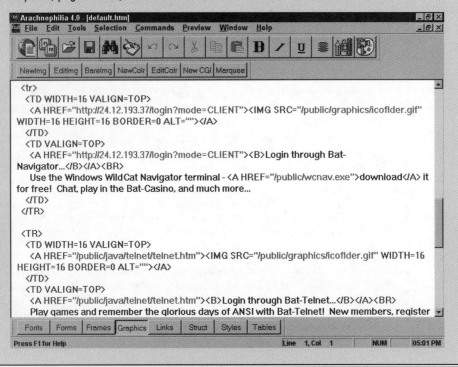

"So how do I *add* to my CD layout the menu system I create?" That's the simplest part. The HTML files you create (along with the files they use, like graphics and sounds) are copied to a separate folder you create in your CD layout. The person using your disc can open the folder manually and double-click the top-level HTML menu file, or you can create a shortcut (in Windows) or an alias (in the Mac operating system) in the root directory that loads the top-level menu.

While I'm discussing HTML within specific margins in this chapter, you can find out all the details of the language and what it's capable of in the book *HTML 4 For Dummies,* by Ed Tittel, Natanya Pitts, and Chelsea Valentine (published by Hungry Minds, Inc.).

Mentioning Animation

If you're interested in animating your menus, I would recommend these two methods:

- ✔ **Animated GIF images:** You can use Animation Shop 3 (from Jasc) to create animated GIFs. It's simple stuff, but all browsers can display them without additional plug-ins, and they can add basic animation to a title or a background. Figure 12-1 shows Animation Shop 3 at work; it's a steal at $40, and you can buy it directly from Jasc at their Web site (www.jasc.com).

- ✔ **Macromedia Flash:** Flash, from Macromedia (www.macromedia.com), is the standard for creating interactive animation for HTML pages. Unlike with an animated GIF image, you can control what happens and what runs when your customer clicks on a Flash control or animation. Flash animations can use sound, images, and graphics you have drawn yourself and imported from your favorite drawing program. If you have visited a Web site recently that uses fancy "drop-down" menus, they were likely created in Flash. The latest version even adds support for MP3 music.

Figure 12-2 illustrates the Flash design environment. Although Flash takes some time to master and costs about $400, I often recommend it to folks who are looking for professional-quality Web animation. If you take the time to study the program, Flash can produce browser-based games, deliver interactive education, and — oh, I forgot — create CD-ROM menus worthy of Microsoft or Adobe.

I don't go into detail on Flash, but Gurdy Leete and Ellen Finkelstein do, in their book *Flash 5 For Dummies,* published by Hungry Minds, Inc.

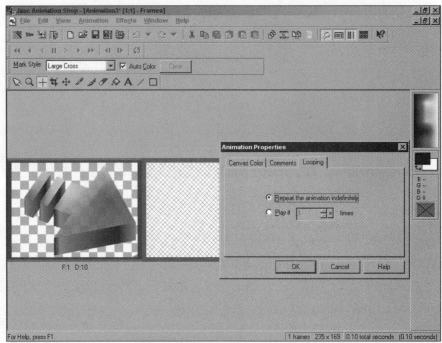

Figure 12-1:
Creating an
animated
GIF in
Animation
Shop 3.

Figure 12-2:
Putting
Macromedia
Flash
to work
creating
serious
animation.

Project: Creating a Disc Menu with HTML

Time to get your hands dirty with HTML. Let's create a typical basic CD-ROM menu for a shareware disc. The program is Handsome Prince 2.0 ("Turns a regular guy into a mate fit for a princess"), and you need to add these functions:

- A link to download the program from the disc to the computer's hard drive
- A link to the READ ME file so that it can be read directly from the disc
- A link to send e-mail
- A link to the program's support Web site

Because the customer has already bought the program, you don't need anything flashy — a simple menu that offers fast access to the program and the other links is perfect. I use Netscape Composer, the free HTML editor that ships with Netscape Navigator (www.netscape.com), to show you how to create the menu. Follow these steps:

1. **Choose Start⇨Programs⇨Netscape 6⇨Netscape 6 to run Navigator. From the Navigator menu, click File, choose New, and then click Blank Page to Edit.**

   The Netscape Composer screen shown in Figure 12-3 appears.

2. **First, select a title for the page: I typed** Handsome Prince Version 2.0. **Click and drag to select the text and then click Format and choose Font. I use Helvetica. Click Format again, choose Align, and click Center on the pop-up menu.**

   You now have a dramatic-looking title for the CD-ROM menu, as you can see in Figure 12-4.

   Now you create a line to separate the title from the rest of the menu.

3. **Press Enter twice and then click the H. Line button on the toolbar to add the bar (see Figure 12-5).**

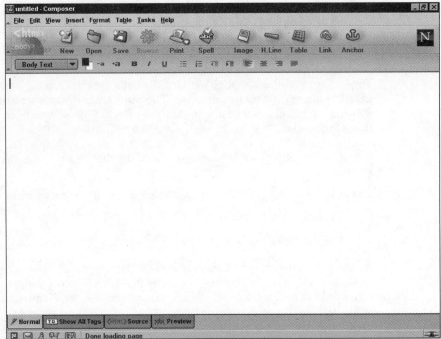

Figure 12-3:
Netscape
Composer —
before your
inspiration
hits, that is.

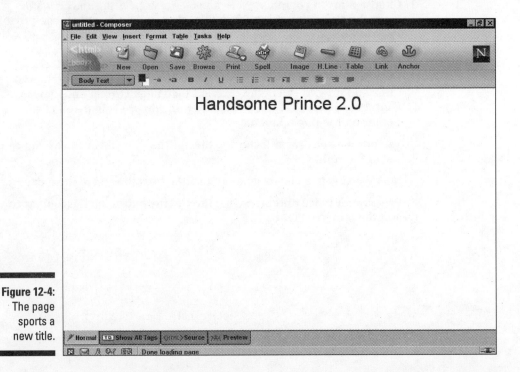

Figure 12-4:
The page
sports a
new title.

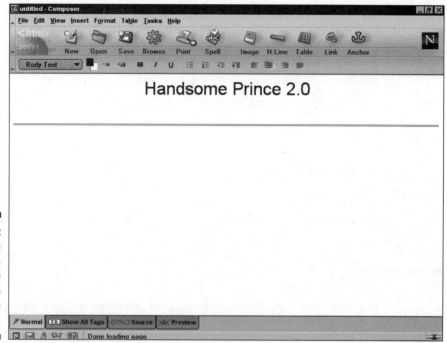

Figure 12-5:
Adding a
line to sep-
arate the
menu items
from the
title.

4. **Add the first link — a download link for a file (for example, HPRINCE2. EXE). Click Link to display the Link Properties dialog box (see Figure 12-6) and type the link description (I'll use the words** Copy Handsome Prince 2.0 to your hard drive) **in the Link Text box. Click the Choose File button to locate the file (make sure that you choose the All Files view in the Files of Type drop-down list box). Highlight the filename and click Open. Click OK to create your first link, as shown in Figure 12-7.**

Before you celebrate too much, though, you have to change the location of the file you chose because that file will be on a CD-ROM rather than on your hard drive. Right-click the link you just created and choose Link Properties from the pop-up menu. In the Link Location field, erase the rather cryptic file location that Composer created and just type the name of the file to download (in this case, **hprince2.exe**). Click OK to save your changes. With this change, your browser looks for the file in the same location as the HTML file itself, which is in the root directory of the CD-ROM.

You may be wondering how the program is copied to the hard drive. Because HPRINCE2.EXE is a binary application, your browser knows that it can't be displayed, so you receive instead the familiar prompts asking whether you want to copy it to your hard drive. Neat, eh?

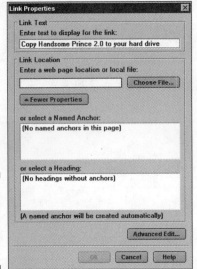

Figure 12-6:
Configuring
the
download
link.

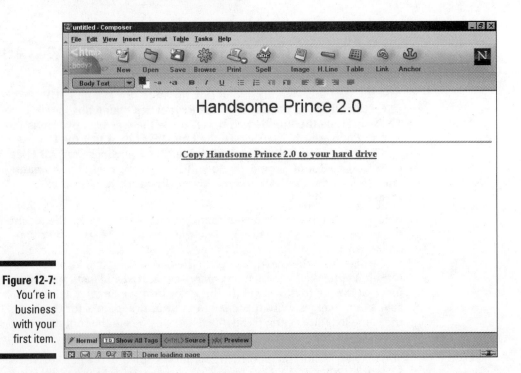

Figure 12-7:
You're in
business
with your
first item.

5. **To display the formatted HTML READ ME file (which I show you how to create in the next project), repeat Step 4.**

For this example link, type the title **Read the Handsome Prince 2.0 READ ME File** in the Link Text box and choose the README.HTM file.

If you need to remove a link, click it to select it and then click Format and choose the Remove Link menu item.

6. **Now you need the e-mail link. You enter this code directly — click Insert HTML to display the dialog box you see in Figure 12-8. Type this text into the box:**

```
<A HREF ="mailto:mark@mlcbooks.com">Send An Email to the
        Author of Handsome Prince</A>
```

7. **Change the e-mail address (the part immediately following the `mailto:`) to your address and click Insert.**

Voila! Your menu with its new e-mail link is shown in Figure 12-9.

Again, things are about as automatic as they can get. If the computer using your disc is connected to the Internet, clicking this one link in a Web browser connects to the Internet and displays the person's default e-mail program, complete with a new message already addressed to you.

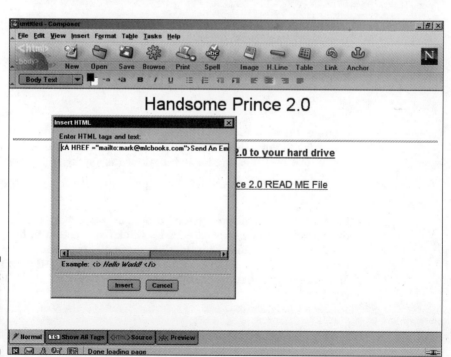

Figure 12-8: Entering HTML code directly into Composer.

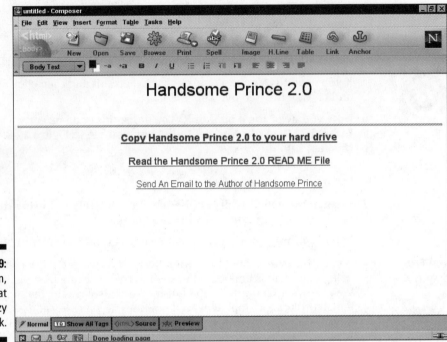

Figure 12-9:
Wow, man,
dig that
crazy
e-mail link.

8. **Press Enter twice and repeat Step 6 to create your Web site link. This time, type this text:**

```
<A HREF ="http://home.mlcbooks.com">Visit the Handsome
        Prince Support Site</A>
```

9. **Change the Web address (the part immediately following the** http://**) to your Web site address. Click Insert. Your new CD-ROM menu now includes the basic functions (as shown in Figure 12-10).**

    Before you declare things finished, how about sprucing up the background a little bit?

10. **Click Format and choose Page Colors and Background to display the dialog box you see in Figure 12-11. Click Use Custom Colors and click the Background color sample. Composer displays a grid of possible colors you can use. Click a color that coordinates well with the black and blue of the text (like a light orange or gray) and click OK to change your background color.**

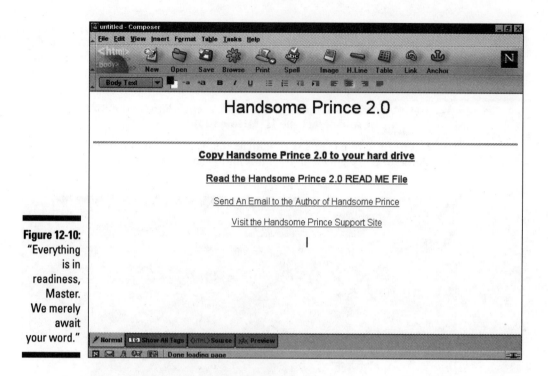

Figure 12-10: "Everything is in readiness, Master. We merely await your word."

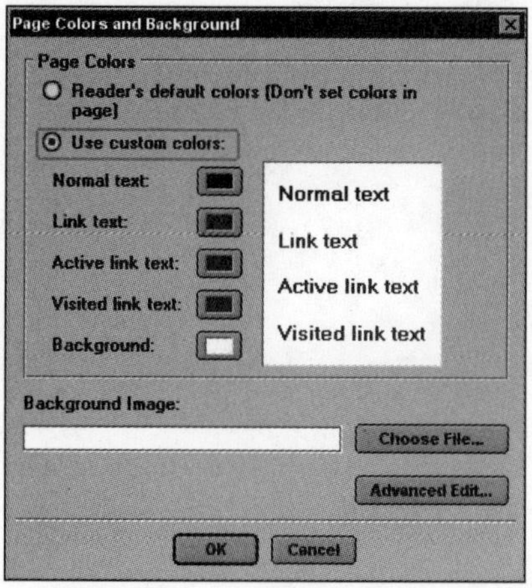

Figure 12-11: Selecting text and background colors for the menu.

11. **To save your page, click File and choose Save As. Composer prompts you for a title to be displayed on the title line of the Web browser; I typed** Handsome Prince 2.0 CD-ROM. **Click OK. From the Save Page As dialog box, select the folder where the menu should be saved. Type a descriptive name (I suggest something like** MENU.HTM) **and click Save.**

Because your files reside on a CD-ROM, you must make sure that the locations of any linked files match the locations they have within the CD layout. In the example, HPRINCE2.EXE must reside in the root directory, just like the MENU.HTM and README.HTM files. If these files are in different folders, your download link doesn't work.

12. **To test your menu, open your browser, click File, and choose Open. Then locate and select the HTML menu file.**

   Figure 12-12 illustrates the menu as displayed within Internet Explorer. Don't forget to check all the links and make sure that they work.

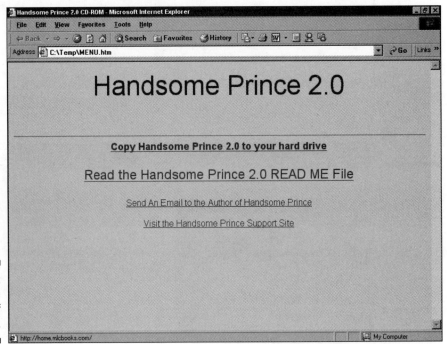

Figure 12-12:
Viewing the fruits of your labor.

Project: Converting a Text Document to HTML

Personally, I like viewing text as a file within a browser. It somehow seems more of an elegant solution than just opening Windows Notepad. When you need to show a text file within your CD-ROM menu, though, converting that text to HTML becomes a requirement (there's no View a Text File command).

For a simple text file, like the READ ME file for Handsome Prince 2.0, Microsoft Word makes the conversion easy.

Because Word does a simple conversion job, you have to use an HTML editor to add graphics, add a table, or change a dotted line to a solid separator bar (like the one you used in the preceding project). Even if you have to add graphics and special formatting in another program, however, Word makes a great conversion tool for the text.

Follow these steps to convert a text file to HTML with Word:

1. **Choose Start⇨Programs and choose Microsoft Word from the menu. From the Word menu, click File and choose the Open menu item; navigate to the location of the original text file and double-click to load it.**

   Your text file should look something like Figure 12-13.

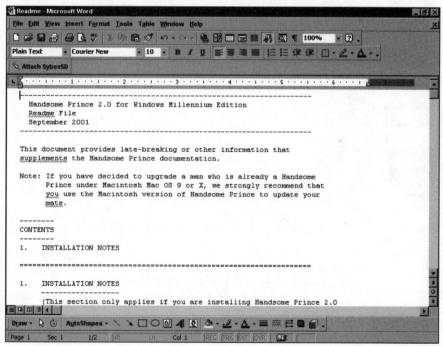

Figure 12-13: Opening a text document in Word — nothing up either sleeve.

2. **Because HTML text can be formatted with bold and italic text, take a moment to change to either bold or italic any text that needs a little emphasis. Select the text you want and click either the Bold or the Italic button in the Word toolbar.**

Avoid the underline text attribute because it can be easily mistaken for a link in the finished HTML file. Also, you don't need to choose an alternative font because a simple HTML file uses the default font set by the browser's configuration.

3. **After the text is italicized and bolded as you like, click File and choose Save As. Navigate to the location where you want to save the file and choose Web page from the Save as drop-down list box.**

4. **As shown in Figure 12-14, the Save As dialog box for a Web page has an additional field you should enter. Click the Change Title button and type a descriptive title (it's displayed in the browser window). Click OK to return to the Save As dialog box.**

   Note that the title is not the same as the filename, which you should enter now. I use the filename README.HTM, from the preceding project.

5. **Click Save to begin the conversion.**

Figure 12-14:
With an HTML Web page, you get a title thrown in for free.

6. **After the file has been saved, click File and choose Exit to exit from Microsoft Word and return to Windows.**

Figure 12-15 shows the finished HTML file README.HTM loaded in Internet Explorer. Not a bad job!

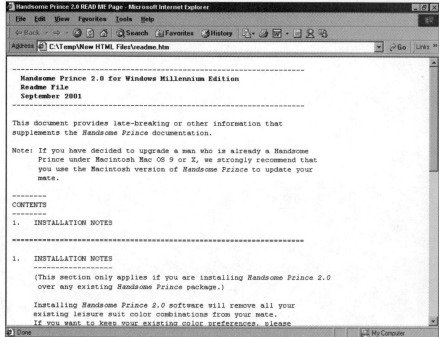

Figure 12-15:
The finished README file dressed as a Web page.

Chapter 13

Storing Megastuff with DVD

*W*hether it holds 60 minutes of digital video or it's simply crammed full of backup files, a DVD recordable disc is a wonderful thing — only current prices are holding most technotypes back from investing in a DVD-R or DVD-RAM drive. But those prices have already fallen from $1,000 to less than $500 for a DVD-RAM drive, and the cost of blank media has dipped more than 50 percent over the past two years. It's simply a matter of time until DVD recorders pack the shelves at your local discount store; they will replace the CD-RW drives that are now standard equipment on today's PCs and Macs.

My job is clear: I must prepare you for the rigors of DVD recording so that you're ready for the coming wave of new hardware! It's a daunting job, but, well, it's not *really* all that daunting. If you're interested in backing up your system or simply saving 4GB of data at once, burning a DVD is a process similar to burning a CD-R or a CD-RW. I show you how in this chapter.

If you're interested in mastering a DVD with digital video for use in your home DVD player or your computer's DVD-ROM drive, you are indeed walking into an unfamiliar land — and this chapter shows you the way there!

Let me be honest with you (as always): This isn't a book about either digital video editing or DVD authoring. The topic for this particular tome is recording CDs and DVDs, and I need all the space that Hungry Minds will give me just to tackle those topics! However, if the basic introduction to editing and authoring in this chapter is enough to pique your interest, I can recommend *iMovie 2 For Dummies,* written by Todd Stauffer, and *Digital Video For Dummies,* 2nd Edition, written by Martin Doucette (both published by Hungry Minds, Inc.).

What's Involved in Recording a DVD-R?

In a word, what's involved in recording a DVD-R are the same four things required in order to burn a CD-R:

- A recorder
- A blank disc
- Your source material
- The appropriate recording software (either UDF/packet writing, a DVD authoring program with built-in burning capabilities, or a full-blown mastering program similar to Easy CD Creator)

With this close resemblance to the now-familiar process of CD recording, what gives DVD recording that James Bond feeling — at least at the time this book was written? Here are a number of reasons:

- **Prices are still high.** The painful side of DVD-R and DVD-RAM recording simply *starts* with the cost of the drive. Then you're hit with the cost of the blank media! A single DVD-R disc sets you back around $15, and a typical DVD-RAM disc is a hefty $35. The higher the cost, the less appealing DVD recording remains to average computer owners.

- **DVD standards are still evolving.** "Should I invest in DVD-RAM or wait for DVD-RW? Will my DVD player read the discs I record?" Unfortunately, far too many question marks still surround the different DVD formats, and many computer owners are holding back another six months to a year, hoping for one to become a clear winner.

- **Perceived value.** At this point, many folks just don't feel that they *need* the space offered by recordable DVD. DVD is attractive for digital video and system backups, but 700MB per CD-R disc is still a fair chunk of territory (at a mere pittance of a price, too).

- **DV is still not a mainstream technology.** As DV camcorders drop in price and Uncle Milton decides to try out digital video editing, DVD recording is sure to heat up (pun intended). Right now, the analog camcorder and the VHS VCR are still King of the Mountain.

The Heavy Stuff: Introducing DVD Authoring

If you have been reading up on DVD technology, you know that DVD *authoring* (that's the process of creating an interactive DVD-ROM title, usually involving digital video, still images, and custom-written programs) and DVD burning go hand in hand.

Authoring a disc involves a little bit of "flowchart" design (the creation of a logical menu system), a little bit of artistic talent (the development of a distinctive "look and feel" for the buttons, images, and background), and at least a basic knowledge of digital video. Of course, the DVD video discs you buy at your local video store are authored by professionals using hardware and software packages that cost many thousands of dollars; you may be surprised, however, at the results *you* can achieve with the right software, as you see in the iDVD project at the end of this chapter. (My first DVD amazed my family. After they played with the menu system for several minutes, I was such a hit that I could have sold them oceanfront property in Kansas.)

Although the recording is only a small part of the authoring process, I want to give you a small taste of two authoring programs. iDVD is a free package that's exceptionally easy to use, and DVD Studio Pro is a full-blown professional authoring package that sets you back $1,000. (If that's not a wide range, I don't know what is.) Both these programs were developed by Apple (www. apple.com).

Welcome to the World of iDVD

iDVD, a Mac OS 9 application, ships with the current crop of high-end G4 Macs that offer the DVD-R SuperDrive. Because iDVD is aimed squarely at novices, it has none of the more powerful features offered by the Big Guys. For example, iDVD can use only QuickTime movies, and you can't create discs using a 16:9 wide-screen aspect ratio. But, friends and neighbors, the kids at the local elementary school are now using iDVD. It's easy — and if it's easy, *normal* people will try it!

DVDs created with iDVD are limited to displaying digital video and still images (using a slideshow format). These displays are organized into media folders (which, in turn, can hold subfolders). I especially like the fact that discs created with iDVD take advantage of the DVD player remote control (even though you don't have to know anything about how the remote on your DVD functions). It's all taken care of automatically by iDVD, leaving you free to concentrate on where to put what and how it should look.

An iDVD disc can contain about an hour's worth of digital video or a combination of DV and slides. After you have completed your design, you can use the program's Preview mode to try out your disc before you burn it (complete with a virtual remote).

For a guided tour through the creation of a DVD video disc using iDVD, check out the second project at the end of this chapter.

Letting Loose with DVD Studio Pro

On the other end of the spectrum, you have a heavyweight of DVD authoring: DVD Studio Pro includes commercial features, like Macrovision copy protection, support for today's popular widescreen aspect ratio, a total of nine possible camera angles, MPEG format support, region coding, and much more. You have complete control over your menu creation, with layered images taken from Adobe Photoshop. Unlike with iDVD, you choose what actions are taken when the different buttons are pressed on the DVD player's remote control. Whereas iDVD can use only one audio track — the audio from the video itself — a high-end package like DVD Studio Pro allows as many as eight tracks, so you can mix music with your DV.

As with iDVD, you get a Preview mode with DVD Studio Pro, so you can double-check all your work before burning. Speaking of recording, that too is supported internally. As extra options, you can also write your completed project to a disc image or DLT tape.

If you're already well versed in digital video editing, you should feel right at home using DVD Studio Pro (and you should be better prepared for the high prices for DV hardware and software). If you have just bought your Macintosh and you have never shot a frame of DV, I recommend that you pass on both the complexity and the price. This package will likely take you places where you don't want to venture, so stick with iDVD (or, on the Windows side, Windows Movie Maker).

Project: Recording a DVD-RAM disc with VOB InstantWrite

Here's another of my patented Nuggets o' Knowledge: "What works with CD-RW usually works just as well with DVD-RAM." (Look out — you could soon see this catchy phrase on bumper stickers and T-shirts.)

In this case, what works is UDF — otherwise known as your old friend packet writing, which is compatible with Mac OS 9, Mac OS X, and all versions of Windows 98 (and later). A number of great programs are available for both Windows and the Mac operating system (OS) that allow you to use your DVD-RAM drive as a 4.7GB floppy (isn't *that* a mind-boggling idea?) except that your DVD recorder is much faster and much more reliable and holds a heck of a lot more.

For DVD packet writing, I use VOB InstantWrite, from VOB Information Systems (www.vob.de). This program provides functionality like Roxio DirectCD for the entire gamut of recordable media, including CD-R, CD-RW, DVD-RAM, DVD-R, and DVD-RW. One thing InstantWrite offers that DirectCD doesn't, however, is the ability to record audio CDs in packet-writing mode. No full-blown mastering software required! (Just in case you need all those fancy controls, though, the company also offers InstantCD/DVD for $69, which is a full mastering program, like Easy CD Creator.)

Let's create a DVD-RAM UDF disc using InstantWrite. Follow these steps:

1. **First, you need to format the DVD-RAM disc for use under VOB. Choose Start⇨Programs⇨VOB⇨InstantWrite⇨InstantWrite Format to display the dialog box shown in Figure 13-1. Click Next to continue.**

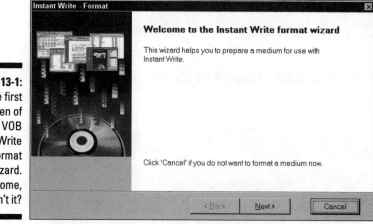

Figure 13-1:
The first screen of the VOB InstantWrite Format Wizard. Awesome, ain't it?

2. **Load the blank disc into your DVD recorder.**

3. **The device selection screen illustrated in Figure 13-2 appears. Click the entry for your DVD recorder and click Next to continue.**

4. **The Volume Name dialog box you see in Figure 13-3 appears. Type a volume name for the disc — a maximum of 11 characters, please. Alternatively, you can format the blank disc without a name by enabling the check box labeled Check this if you do not want a name for the disc. Click Next to continue.**

5. **InstantWrite requests confirmation that you're ready to begin the formatting process. If you want a completion report after the formatting is finished, enable the check box labeled Show a status report after format. Click Next and sit back while the disc is prepared.**

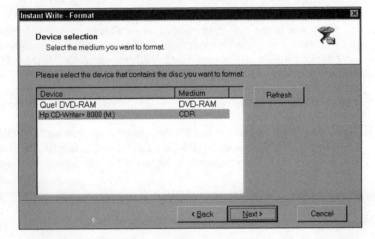

Figure 13-2:
Selecting a
DVD-RAM
disc to
format.

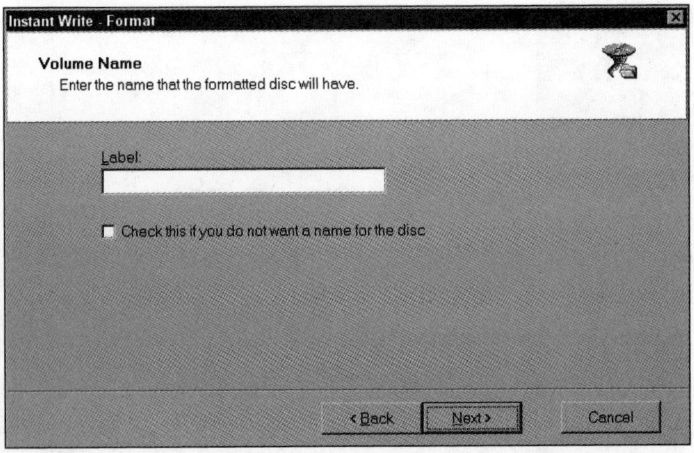

Figure 13-3:
What's in a
volume
name,
anyway?

Now you're ready to begin using your DVD-RAM drive as a removable hard drive. As with a DirectCD disc, you can use your DVD disc with any Windows application, including Windows Explorer. If you want to remove the disc and make it readable on other computers, you have to finalize it first. Follow these steps:

1. **Double-click the My Computer icon on your desktop and right-click your DVD recorder. Choose Finalize from the pop-up menu.**

2. **InstantWrite displays the confirmation dialog box you see in Figure 13-4. If you're really ready to finalize the disc, click Yes. A number of cool progress bars and status dialog boxes flash by your eyes.**

Figure 13-4:
Preparing to finalize a DVD-RAM disc using InstantWrite.

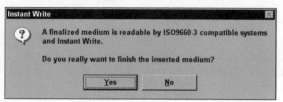

3. **After the disc has been closed, click OK on the success dialog box and eject your new disc.**

To use your InstantWrite DVD disc on another computer with a DVD-ROM drive, you can download the free InstantRead program from the VOB Web site.

Project: Recording a DVD-R with iDVD

Do you have a DVD-R drive in your Macintosh? Then you're a self-contained movie studio, and you probably didn't even know it! (Don't worry — you have plenty of time to hit eBay and bid on a beret, a megaphone, and one of those chalkboards with the clacky thing on top.) On the software end, all you need is iDVD.

In this project, I use iDVD to show you how to create a home video DVD-V disc you can watch in most standard DVD players. You may be amazed at how easy Apple has made the process and how professional your finished DVD will look. The completed disc features

- ✔ An interactive menu system
- ✔ Separate menus for digital video and still photographs
- ✔ An automated slideshow

As a first step, you should convert or export your video in QuickTime format. Both iMovie and Final Cut Pro allow you to export QuickTime movies directly, but you can also use QuickTime Pro to convert video from other formats. If you plan to add digital images, I recommend that they be in PICT or JPEG format.

One cool feature of iDVD is its ability to use a digital photograph as the background for your DVD menu system. If you want to do this, make sure that the image you're using is 640x480. (If necessary, you can resize it with any image editor; I use Photoshop.)

After your source material has been converted to QuickTime, JPEG, and PICT, follow these steps:

1. **Double-click the iDVD icon to launch the program, which displays the iDVD project window you see in Figure 13-5.**

2. **Click Project and choose Project Info to display the dialog box you see in Figure 13-6. Click in the Disc Name field and type the name for your DVD; in this case, I entered** Fun With the Kids. **Click OK to save the change.**

3. **No secret about the next step. Click the huge title that reads "Click to edit title." Man, do I like Apple software! Type the title for your menu and press Return to save it.**

   Next, it's time to choose a theme, which includes preconfigured choices for fonts, button styles, and the background image used in your menu.

Figure 13-5:
The iDVD
project
window,
ready to
receive your
creative
genius.

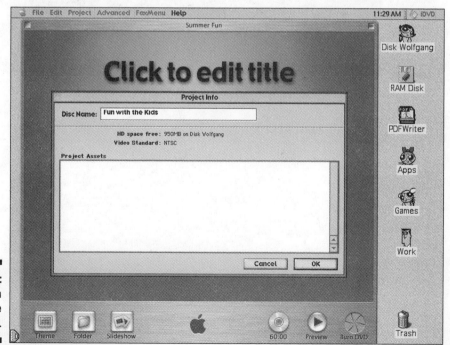

Figure 13-6:
Choosing a
name for the
DVD project.

4. **Click the Theme button at the bottom of the project window and scroll through the choices that appear, as shown in Figure 13-7. For this example, click the Photo Album thumbnail in the list.**

At this point, the blank menu system, illustrated in Figure 13-8, already looks classier than anything I ever did with my VHS camera.

Figure 13-7: Some of the pre-built iDVD themes you can choose from.

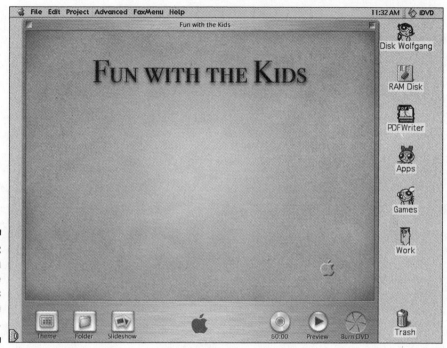

5. Click the Theme button again to hide the Theme strip.

It's time to add a video clip to the menu. That sounds a tad daunting, but there's nothing to fear with iDVD.

6. Open the folder that contains your QuickTime movies and drag one to the iDVD project window.

As you can see in Figure 13-9, the program creates a custom button using a thumbnail image from the video. The button is automatically centered in the screen for you. Definitely not daunting.

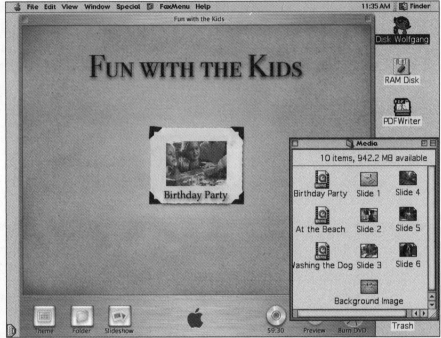

Figure 13-9:
The first video clip appears in the iDVD project.

7. **Because the title under the button is less than descriptive, change it: Click once on the text to display the edit box and type a new name.**

   You can also move the slider that appears above the button to choose the thumbnail image (this is great for clips that begin with darkness or something equally as uninteresting).

8. **Add two more clips by repeating Steps 5 and 6.**

   You can add a maximum of six buttons to a single DVD menu screen; personally, I avoid overcrowding a menu by adding no more than four buttons.

   You may have noticed the Time Remaining indicator, which looks like a DVD disc. The figure above it shows the amount of time remaining on the disc in minutes and seconds. As you add items and submenus, keep an eye on this indicator for a rough estimate of how much room remains.

9. **Add a separate submenu for your "slideshow" display of digital images: Click the Folder button to add a submenu button to the project window and change the button name to whatever you like (I'll type** Slide Show**). Because the generic folder icon doesn't match the theme, drag one of the JPEG images that will make up your slideshow and drop it on top of the folder icon.**

    Voilà! You have a custom submenu button! Figure 13-10 illustrates the completed top menu.

10. **Double-click the Slideshow button to display the submenu screen. Click the title at the top to open the edit box, type your title text (in this example, I'll use** Photos of the Kids**), and press Return.**

11. **It's time to add the slideshow button itself. Click the Slideshow button at the bottom of the iDVD window to add a button to your submenu, which should now look like Figure 13-11.**

Figure 13-10:
The top
menu is
ready to go.

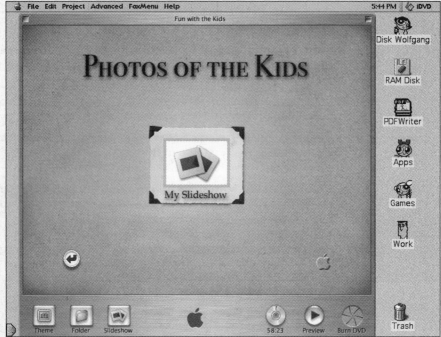

Figure 13-11:
You have
added a
Slideshow
button to the
submenu
screen.

12. **Double-click the button you added to open the My Slideshow panel. Drag the images you want to add from their locations on your hard drive into the window, as shown in Figure 13-12.**

13. **At this point, you need to decide whether you want an automated slideshow or a manual slideshow. If your parents had a slide projector like mine, this step should really interest you:**

   • **Manual:** For a manual slideshow, leave the duration drop-down list box set to Manual. It's a good idea to enable the Display < > on image check box, which superimposes left and right arrows on the image as appropriate. (Although these arrows are optional, they help remind Aunt Harriet how to advance through the photos in a manual slideshow.) The lucky person holding the DVD player remote control presses the right cursor key to move forward through the images and the left cursor key to move backward.

   • **Automatic:** The DVD player displays the images automatically (but you can still move forward and backward using the remote). Click the Duration drop-down list box and choose the number of seconds to delay before switching to the next image. If you like, you can still enable the Display < > on image check box.

Figure 13-12:
Preparing
the contents
of the
slideshow.

14. **If you want to change the order of the slideshow sequence, click and drag the image you want to its new spot on the list. After you've finished designing your slideshow, click the Back button to return to the submenu screen.**

15. **Whoops — now that you have added your images, don't forget to customize the slideshow button itself. Drag the slider to choose one of the images in the slideshow as the button image. To change the button's caption, click it and type your new text; press Return to save it.**

16. **Care to preview your DVD? Click the Preview button at the bottom of the iDVD window, which turns blue to indicate that you're in Preview mode.**

    iDVD displays a most cool-looking "virtual" remote (as shown in Figure 13-13). Note that the slideshow button in the middle of the screen is now highlighted, just as it would be if you were using your DVD player. Use the buttons on the remote to select menu items, and click Enter on the remote to activate the item that's highlighted. When you're done playing with your DVD-to-be, click the Preview button again to return to editing mode (where you can make changes if you like).

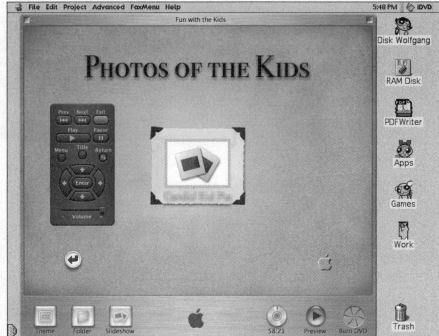

Figure 13-13:
And just
think: You
won't
lose this
remote in
the couch!

17. **You should save your project to your hard drive before you burn it. Click File and choose Save Project As to display a standard Mac OS Save dialog box. Navigate to the destination folder, type a new name for your project, and click Save.**

18. **Okay, you film mogul, you — it's time to record your own DVD! Click the Burn button, which opens to display a glowing fail-safe button.**

    Apple doesn't want you to waste a blank disc with an accidental click of your mouse. (Plus, it's one of the neatest animated controls I have ever used.)

19. **Click the button again to start the recording process, and load a blank DVD-R disc into your DVD recorder when prompted.**

    After the first disc has been burned, you can choose to record additional copies.

I should warn you that iDVD has quite a bit of housekeeping to do to prepare your digital video, so you probably have to wait several minutes before the recording starts. (This preparation time depends on the speed of your Mac, the number of movies you have added, and how long they are.)

The theme is, well, themes!

If you want to import your own image as a menu background — or you want to create your own theme and use it for all your future iDVD projects — click the drop-down list box at the top of the Theme strip and click Custom. As you can see in the following figure, there's much for you to specify here, including the background image, the position and font properties of your title and buttons, and the shape of your buttons. After you have selected what you like from the Custom panel, click Save in Favorites and specify a name for your theme. After it has been saved, you can pick your custom theme for any project. Click the drop-down list box on the Theme strip and choose Favorites to display all your custom themes.

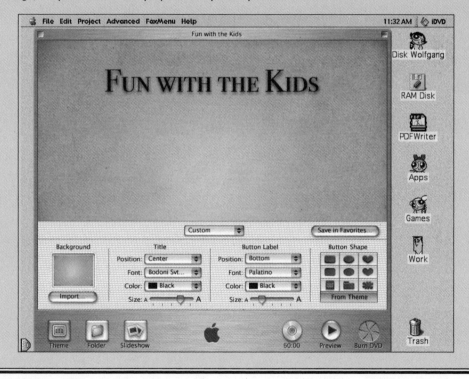

Chapter 14

Adding That Spiffy Touch

. . . .

. . . .

*J*ust how proud are you of your finished discs? I probably should narrow the focus of that question a little: Just how proud are you of the *appearance* of your finished discs?

If you're happy with the sound of an audio CD and your computer can easily read all the information you recorded on a data CD-ROM, you're technically done. If you're distributing your discs to others, though, or you want to include background information on the contents of a CD, I highly recommend that you take the extra step of printing a CD label or jewel case inserts. Heck, for the most professional look, go hog-wild and print a matching set of labels and their accompanying inserts!

In this chapter, I show you how to design and create with CD Label Creator, and you add that spiffy visual touch that separates a ho-hum burning project from a true masterpiece of art.

How Not to Label Your CDs

Before I get down to the business of adding a stylish, professional look to your recorded discs, allow me to make absolutely, *positively* sure that you don't damage them! You can indeed simply write a title on top of the disc — in fact, most blank discs these days are preprinted with straight lines to help you write neatly — but if you would rather label your discs by hand, please make sure that you avoid any of these writing instruments while marking directly on your CDs:

✔ **Ballpoint or sharp-tipped pens:** If your writing instrument has a sharp point and it's metallic, don't even *think* about using it to mark your discs!

Standard ink is hard to see and simply wipes off most discs. That's not the real danger, though: You could scratch the surface of the disc and damage it.

✔ **Soluble markers:** Although I advise you elsewhere in this book to keep liquids away from your discs, soluble (also called *erasable*) markers are also affected by the oil from your fingertips. In other words, if you happen to brush your finger across the disc, *Ella Fitzgerald* may suddenly become *la rald*. That's not enough information to help me determine who's singing — although, in Ella's case, I don't really *need* a label!

✔ **Paint pens:** Kids love these newfangled craft pens — your discs, on the other hand, most definitely do not. The solvents in a typical paint pen can damage the clear protective lacquer layer on top of the disc, and the buildup produced by a paint pen can unbalance the disc if it's heavily used. Also, a disc with any type of buildup may be harder to use in your car audio CD player. Can you imagine what loose flakes of paint could do to that $400 CD deck you bought for your Porsche?

Many manufacturers of recordable DVD discs advise that you shouldn't apply paper labels at all to their media. Check the instructions that accompanied your blank media to see whether you should add a label to that new DVD-Video disc you just burned!

Of course, I may sound overly cautious, but let me be blunt: I have more than a thousand discs in my music collection (some of which are irreplaceable live recordings), and I want each and every disc to last as long as possible! The same goes for data CD-ROMs; any digital camera owner who enjoys the hobby probably would be just as protective of a photo collection archived to CD-ROM.

Hey, You Can Tell a CD By Its Cover

If you're like me, an audio CD isn't really complete with a simple title and an artist name scribbled on top; that works for a road mix with various artists, perhaps, but I would still like to know the name of each track (as a minimum). For my favorite music — and the rarer recordings in my collections — I like to have much more on hand:

✔ The total time for each track in minutes and seconds — good for determining at a glance how long a particular period of musical nostalgia will last. (For me, it's the '70s.)

✔ For live performances, I add the location and date of the gig and who joined in the jam.

✔ For composers, I include the year of their birth and death.

✔ For jazz groups, I like to keep track of who played what instrument.

Naturally, you can't fit all that (or even a significant part of it) on the CD label. Here's where the extra space provided by jewel box inserts comes in so handy: With the two sides of the front insert and a single-sided back insert, I have all the territory I need to satisfy my historical urges.

Easy CD Creator doesn't let you down! As part of the package, Roxio provides a great object-oriented visual editor, CD Label Creator, that's likely to satisfy even the most demanding label and insert fanatic (even those of us who can't produce much more than a stick figure).

The program allows you to

- ✔ Add straight or curved text — with optional justification — using your choice of fonts
- ✔ Include your own graphics and images
- ✔ Use basic shapes like squares and circles in your design
- ✔ Add cut and fold lines to help keep your geometry accurate
- ✔ Choose from a number of preset themes, which apply to all elements of your label and cover set

CD Label Creator can use a huge variety of precut inserts, or you can print to regular paper and use a cutting board to achieve the same results.

If you're using a DVD-R or DVD-RAM drive, check out other label programs that can create inserts for standard plastic DVD cases. New, slimline CD cases that are appearing on the market take inserts somewhat smaller than standard jewel boxes.

"Hmmm, Can I Label with Duct Tape?"

CD labels are big business these days — just visit the software section of your local Maze O' Wires electronics store, and you're likely to see at least three or four different CD labeling packages. Some include only the label design and printing software and some blank labels to get you started; these labels are applied by hand using a template guide, usually while the disc is held tightly in its jewel case. Others include a device to help you precisely align the label with the top of the disc.

I use the NEATO CD labeling system (www.neato.com), which includes the two-piece NEATO label application device shown in Figure 14-1. To use the device, you place your disc upside-down on the spindle (so that the recorded side is facing up) and you put your printed paper label facedown on the base. To apply the label, you simply push the spindle into the base and press down. There's no chance of misalignment, and the finished label is free from bubbles.

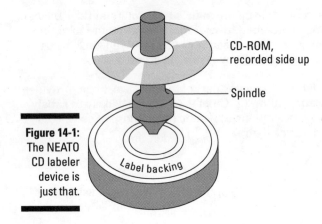

CD-ROM, recorded side up

Spindle

Label backing

Figure 14-1: The NEATO CD labeler device is just that.

After a label is applied to a disc, do not attempt to remove it (unless the labels you're using specifically say that you can do so). Virtually all CD labels are designed to be permanent, and they don't peel off!

I would say that CD labels come in a "rainbow of colors," but that would be cliché — how about "all the colors of the rainbow" instead? You can even get clear labels that allow the color of the disc to show through from underneath — perfect for use with those neon-colored blank discs.

The NEATO system also comes with label design-and-printing software called MediaFACE II (see Figure 14-2), which includes a set of features similar to CD Label Creator. However, MediaFACE II can also add bar codes and import database information directly into fields you set up.

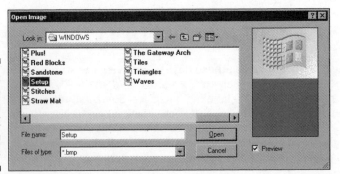

Figure 14-2: Designing a label using MediaFACE II, from NEATO.

Project: Creating Jewel Box Inserts

Ready to dive into CD Label Creator? Let's create a custom set of jewel box inserts for a compendium of classic bluegrass I have just recorded from my

MP3 collection — in this case, it's the legendary Lester Flatt and Earl Scruggs. The inserts should list each track, the time for each song, and the total time for the entire disc. The example uses clip art of a banjo for the graphic.

Follow these steps:

1. **Choose Start⇨Programs⇨Easy CD Creator 5⇨Applications⇨CD Label Creator to display the program's main window, as shown in Figure 14-3.**

   Make sure that the Front Cover icon is selected in the Page display on the left side of the screen.

   You can also choose to launch CD Label Creator as soon as you have successfully burned a disc. Starting the program this way automatically carries the text information from the CD layout into your label project.

   If you like, you can use one of the CD Label Creator standard themes, which provides a common background, entry fields, and a font for you to use. The default theme, Music, works fine; to illustrate how this is done, however, let's use another.

2. **Click Format and choose Change Theme from the menu to open the Change Theme dialog box you see in Figure 14-4.**

   If you hate menus with a passion, you can click the Theme toolbar button instead.

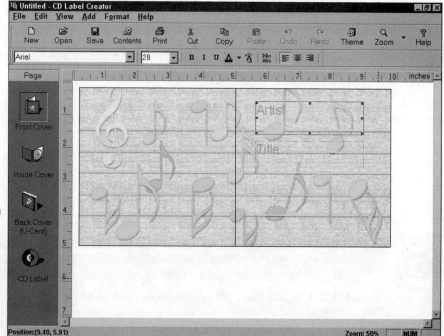

Figure 14-3: Where it all begins — the CD Label Creator main window.

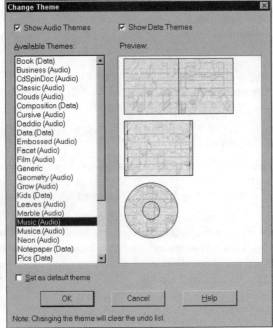

Figure 14-4:
Choosing
another
theme for
your inserts.

Notice that CD Label Creator marks each theme as being either an audio theme or a data theme. Although any theme can be used for any type of disc, these tags indicate which types of fields automatically carry over from a CD layout. (Basically, if you choose to use an audio theme with a data CD-ROM, you have to do more work and create all the fields manually.)

3. **Choose a rustic theme to match bluegrass music: Click Wood to select it and watch as the program updates the Theme preview window. You can continue to check out new themes, but after you're done, choose Wood again and click OK to accept it.**

   If you start CD Label Creator immediately after recording a disc, all the text information is already loaded into the fields. Because you started the program from the Start menu, you need to import the information from the disc.

4. **Load your audio or data CD into the CD recorder.**

   You may remember that I mention earlier in this book that enabling CD-Text is a good thing. This is one of the reasons: CD Label Creator can use CD-Text to import text into a label project at any point in the future.

5. **Click Add and click CD Contents, or click the Contents button on the program's toolbar.**

If you have more than one CD loaded on your system, the program asks you which disc to use — otherwise, it imports the disc information you entered when you burned the disc. As you can see in Figure 14-5, this includes the title, artist name, and track list for an audio CD.

6. **If you want to make a change to any of the fields before you print (for example, to correct a spelling error you may have made when you typed the text the first time), double-click directly on the field. An edit box appears, and you can type the information directly in the field. Press Enter to save your changes.**

If you make a mistake while you're editing your layout, don't forget that old standby: the Undo button on the toolbar.

7. **To add the clip art, click Add and choose Picture from the menu to display a standard File Open dialog box. Navigate to the location of the clip art (which can be in Windows bitmap or JPEG formats), click the filename to highlight it, and click Open.**

8. **The graphic appears in its own resizable window. To change the dimensions of the graphic, move your mouse cursor to any of the square "handles" on the edge of the window and click and drag to resize the edge. To move the entire graphic somewhere else on the layout, click in the middle of the graphic window and drag it to the spot you want.**

Figure 14-6 illustrates the banjo, ready to be resized and relocated.

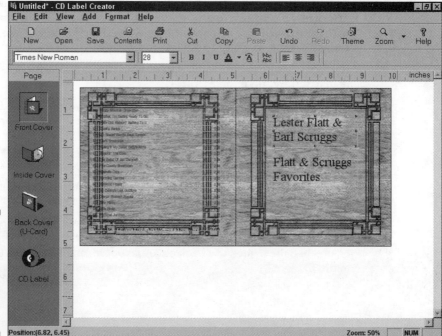

Figure 14-5: It's like magic! All the fields have been typed for you.

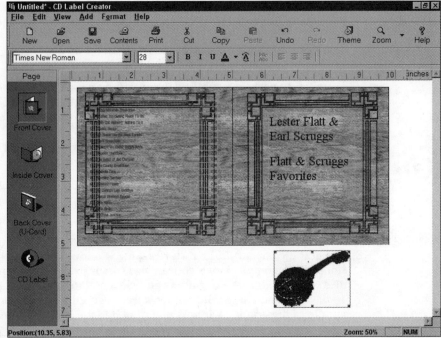

Figure 14-6:
I can do just
about
anything
with this
banjo —
aren't
computers
wonderful?

9. **To add a new block of text, click Add and choose Text or Curved Text. A text block appears, ready for you to resize and relocate, as you did with your graphics. To enter the text, double-click in the box and type something; press Enter to save your changes.**

10. **If you're using precut insert paper, load it into the printer as instructed by the manufacturer.**

11. **When you're ready to print (or you *think* that you're ready to print), use the Print Preview function first — it can save you one or two sheets of paper! Click File and choose Print Preview to display the screen shown in Figure 14-7. If you're satisfied, click Print on the toolbar; if you need to make changes, click Close and return to the layout.**

12. **You can also print a back cover insert by clicking on the Back Cover button in the Page display on the left side of the screen.**

    Because you have already either imported or typed your information, the back cover layout automatically includes all that text. (Whew!) Figure 14-8 illustrates the back cover layout for my Flatt & Scruggs audio CD.

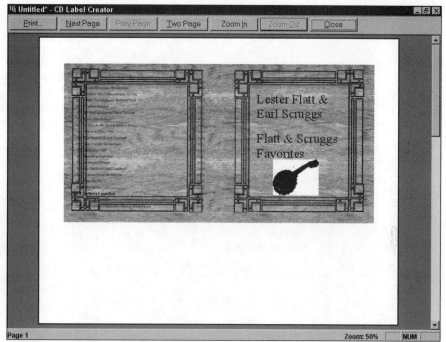

Figure 14-7:
Checking
things out
before
printing
with Print
Preview.

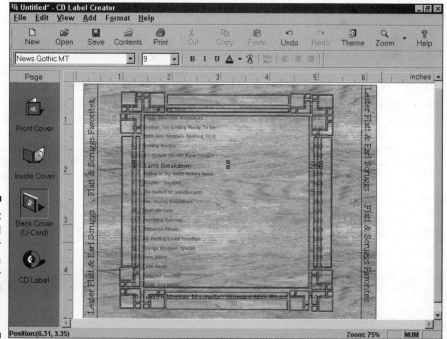

Figure 14-8:
A standard
back cover
layout, with
text already
entered
automati-
cally. Neat!

"Hey, where's my text?"

If nothing shows up when you click the Contents button, CD Label Creator cannot load any text from the disc. Do you give up hope and throw your hands up into the air helplessly? No! You can add that information in two ways:

✔ **Siphon the Internet:** If the disc is a copy of an existing audio CD, CD Label Creator does the Internet thing and tries to download the

information from a CD database automatically. If this doesn't work, make sure that the Enable Audio CD information download check box is enabled; click Edit, choose Preferences, and click the Internet tab to display the field, as shown in the following figure. Enable the check box if necessary and click OK.

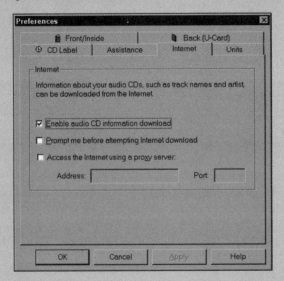

✔ **Start typing:** If CD Label Creator reports that your disc can't be found in the Internet CD database, you have to manually enter any information you want printed on the inserts. Click Add and choose Track to open the Insert New Track dialog box (see the following figure), and enter just the information you want; it can include the track number, title, and the duration. Click Add Track to save the

information to the label layout. Repeat this procedure for each track; after you have finished, click Done. Finally, double-click the words Artist or Title within the main screen to enter the artist name and the disc title. CD Label Creator opens an edit box, and you can type the information directly in the field. Press Enter to save your changes.

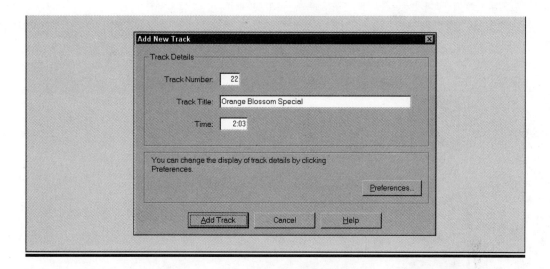

Project: Creating a CD Label

Let's create a CD label for a disc that is a collection of pop tunes for a kid's birthday party. Because I want to give the disc to the guest of honor after the party, it needs to look its best! Follow these steps to create a CD label:

1. **Click Start⇨Programs⇨Easy CD Creator 5⇨Applications⇨CD Label Creator to run CD Label Creator. Click the CD Label icon to select it in the Page display on the left side of the screen, which opens the layout you see in Figure 14-9.**

2. **Import the disc information by clicking the Contents toolbar button.**

   For a standard label, this step fills in the title and artist name.

   You could click the Theme toolbar button and select one of the Roxio themes, but in this case you want to use a background of your own.

3. **Therefore, click Format and choose Change Background to display the dialog box you see in Figure 14-10.**

4. **Click the CD label check box and click Select a Picture to display the File Open dialog box.**

5. **Locate your JPEG or Windows bitmap image file. Click the filename to highlight it and click Open. You see that the background is loaded on the CD label template. Click OK to return to the CD Label Creator main screen.**

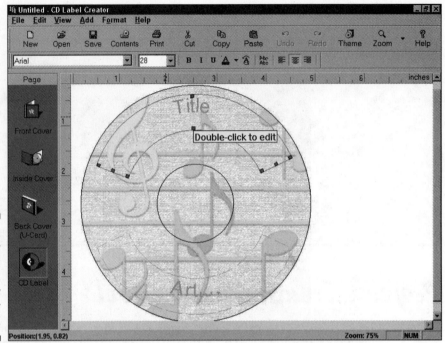

Figure 14-9:
An empty
CD label
layout,
ready
for your
artistic side.

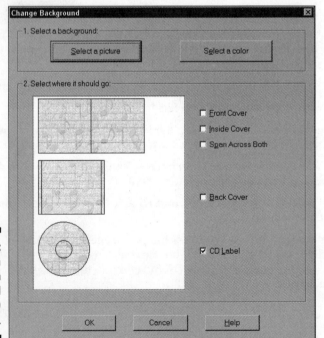

Figure 14-10:
Choosing a
custom
background
for a CD
label.

6. **Choose a festive font — remember that the changes you make to the text format and font affect only the text box that's selected (in this case, the Title box). Click the Font drop-down list box and click a font to select it. (Note the example of the font that appears to the right.) To increase or decrease the font size, click the Points drop-down list box.**

7. **Click the Artist text box to select it and choose the same font and point size.**

8. **Add a Happy Birthday message and the date to the disc. Click Add and choose Text. Resize and relocate the new text block below the spindle hole.**

9. **Double-click in the box and type the text, and then press Enter to save your changes.**

   The completed label is illustrated in Figure 14-11.

10. **Load your CD label blanks into your printer as instructed by the manufacturer.**

11. **Click File and choose Print Preview to check the appearance of the label. If you're satisfied, click Print on the toolbar; if you need to make changes, click Close and return to the layout.**

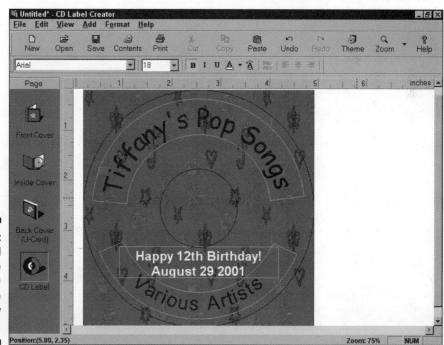

Figure 14-11:
This label turns a mere audio CD into a true birthday present!

Part V
The Part of Tens

The 5th Wave   By Rich Tennant

In this part . . .

You'll find the best of my tips, guidelines, and advice on CD and DVD recording: what to do, what *not* to do, and how to troubleshoot hardware and software problems. I also point out ten programs you'll find invaluable as a part of your personal CD recording studio.

Chapter 15

Ten Hardware Troubleshooting Tips

- -

In This Chapter

▶ Checking jumpers

▶ Turning everything on — correctly

▶ Fixing audio CDs that click

▶ Adding an audio data cable

▶ Fixing driver problems

▶ Updating your recorder's firmware

▶ Using your system's fastest drive

▶ Removing a DVD-RAM disc from its cartridge

▶ Cleaning your drive

▶ Ejecting a stuck disc

- -

*N*othing is worse than a minor hardware problem — except, of course, a major hardware problem. In this Part of Tens chapter, I cover my favorite tips to help you leap over the most common physical troubles with CD and DVD recording: that is, those difficulties that result from your hardware settings, your blank media and — most important — your drive. Some of these items are mentioned earlier in this book, but they're important enough (and crop up enough) that they should be repeated.

"Why, Of Course the Jumper Is Set Correctly!"

Tip: Check and double-check your jumper and DIP switch settings before you replace the cover on your computer.

Let me be honest: Configuring both jumpers and DIP switches is a pain, and both EIDE and SCSI recorder owners are "lucky" enough to have them. Every drive manufacturer seems to use different settings, and if you're installing an older drive (or one you scavenged from a friend or relative), you may find yourself without documentation on what jumpers need to be moved where.

Unfortunately, those settings mean the difference between your drive working and not working; unlike with horseshoes, you don't get points when you're "close" with your jumper settings. Therefore:

- When you're installing an EIDE drive, check any other device on the cable (even if the other device shouldn't have to change its master/slave settings).

- Check your drive's documentation to make sure that the drive is oriented properly so that its pins match the pins in the manual. (After all, a group of eight pins looks the same when viewed upside down.) Most jumper pin sets are marked with identifying numbers on the circuit board to help you determine which pin is Pin 1. DIP switches are easier to "read" than jumper pins because each switch is clearly marked.

- Never use a pencil when setting DIP switches, since the lead from the pencil can result in a shorted switch.

- Save any jumpers you can completely remove; it's amazing just how precious that little chunk of plastic and metal can be. Stick any spares in your parts bin and cherish them.

- If you don't have any documentation for an EIDE or SCSI device and you don't know the settings, visit the manufacturer's Web site and look for manuals in text or Adobe Acrobat PDF format.

It Does Make a Difference How You Turn Things On

Tip: Turn external drives on before you boot your computer.

Most computer owners figure that they can turn on their computers and external toys in any order, but that approach can cause problems — especially with external SCSI drives, which are particularly sensitive to these matters. As a rule, turn on all external peripherals first, like your printer, scanner, and CD or DVD recorder.

You can easily take care of this problem once and for all: Buy a surge suppressor or UPS (uninterruptible power supply) for your system and plug your computer and all your peripherals into it. Just leave everything plugged in and switched on. Then use the switch on the surge suppressor or UPS to turn everything on at one time. (Think of it as that big master switch that Dr. Frankenstein was always pulling to start everything in the laboratory.) Because your external stuff comes on instantly (before your computer even gets started booting up), it's the same thing as turning on everything external by hand.

(This little trick is one of those that separates the novices from the power users, so consider yourself initiated.)

Where Did That Click Come From?

Tip: Always use disc-at-once recording when you're burning audio CDs.

Although this question indicates a hardware problem, it's not a problem you can solve with a setting change on your computer. If you're hearing irritating clicks between tracks when you play an audio CD, the hardware in question is your audio CD player. This happens with many players when you burn audio CDs using the track-at-once recording method; the click is caused by the "gap" your recorder leaves between tracks, which your audio CD player detects. To make things even more frustrating, that same CD plays perfectly in other audio CD players and CD-ROM drives.

To avoid the problem altogether, *always* use the disc-at-once recording method when you're burning audio CDs. Unfortunately, CD recorders older than three or four years may not be able to record using disc-at-once. Because these older drives are as slow as molasses in an Alaskan winter, I strongly recommend that you spend $150 or so and buy a new drive. Not only do you get disc-at-once, but you can also see the progress bar moving when you record a disc.

Your Recorder Wants to Play Too

Tip: Don't forget to connect the audio cable from your sound card to your new drive.

Here's another common problem that I hear all the time: "My recorder works great when I'm burning discs, but if I try to play an audio CD, I get nothing."

If you can hear the audio with headphones connected to your drive's headphone jack, you have pinpointed this problem: You forgot to connect the digital audio output cable from your drive to your sound card. Without this cable, the drive can play an audio CD and you never hear it. You probably received the cable with your sound card — sometimes, drive manufacturers include one, too. If you have already connected a read-only CD-ROM drive to your sound card, use that drive rather than your recorder to listen to audio CDs. Most sound cards have only one of these input connectors.

Driving Miss Data

Tip: Keep up-to-date any hardware drivers required by your drive.

For folks using internal EIDE and SCSI drives, this isn't much of an issue — an internal drive uses the standard hardware drivers that come with Windows or Mac OS. However, external USB and FireWire drives (and yes, even pokey old parallel drives) are a different matter entirely. These recorders typically use drivers supplied by the manufacturer, and it's possible for other hardware installations to overwrite them accidentally, causing your drive to take a dive.

At least, I *think* it's by accident — sometimes, a typical computer system reminds me of a gladiator's arena. Various pieces of hardware and software battle it out with sword and shield to see who works and who fails. (And then, of course, Microsoft releases a new version of Windows, the arena master lets loose the lions, and *everything* fails.)

Your drive's manufacturer may also release new versions of that hardware driver; these updates can solve problems or improve compatibility with your operating system.

Check your drive's manual for the company's Web site and download the latest drivers directly to your computer; if you're not on the Internet at this time, call the company's tech support line and request that someone send you the drivers on a disk.

Keep Your Firmware on the Cutting Edge

Tip: Flash your recorder with the latest firmware.

That advice may sound racy, but in this case the term *flash* means the updating of your drive's internal firmware. Your recorder's firmware stores all the programming for its various functions — much like the BIOS stores settings and configurations for a PC. It's called firmware because it can be updated, just like the hardware drivers I cover in the preceding section. In fact, you update your drive's firmware for many of the same reasons you update hardware drivers: to fix bugs in your drive's operation, improve the performance of the drive, and even add or enhance a feature or two.

Again, the manufacturer's Web site generally offers firmware upgrades, and if you're lucky enough to talk to technical support, you can request that an upgrade be sent to you in the mail.

Speed Does Make a Difference

Tip: Use the fastest drive on your system to store images and temporary files.

With all the sky-high X factors wandering around the countryside — 12x recording, 16x recording, even 20x recording — it's easy to forget that your hard drive's performance also has a direct impact on the success of your CD and DVD burning. (You may remember the defragmenting I mention in Chapter 6.)

If you have more than one hard drive on your system, check your recording software and see whether it has a system test you can run to determine which drive is the fastest. (Easy CD Creator does: To run the system tests, run the program, click Tools, and choose the System Tests menu item.)

If your recording software doesn't offer this feature, use the System Information program that comes with Norton Utilities. You can also download hard drive speed-testing programs from Internet shareware sites.

After you have determined which drive is the fastest, configure your recording software to use that drive for its temporary storage area. Also, choose that drive when you're saving a disc image or when you're collecting files in one place before you add them to your CD layout.

Leave This Cartridge, DVD-RAM, and Seek Your Fortune

Tip: To use a DVD-RAM disc in a DVD player, jettison the cartridge.

I'm a fan of DVD-RAM — I like to use my drive for backups and DV storage. Once in awhile, however, I burn a disc for use in my DVD player (it's a third-generation player, so it can read DVD-RAM discs). Most people who try this technique quickly find out that their DVD players can't accept the huge, clunky cartridge that surrounds a DVD-RAM disc, so they figure that this can't be done.

If you use a DVD-RAM cartridge, you can easily remove the disc from the case for use in tray drives; in fact, the entire front side of the cartridge (by the write-protect switch) is hinged, so it can open. Find the tiny round locking pin at the bottom left of the cartridge; use a pen to punch out the pin and discard it. Locate the release tab on the left front corner of the cartridge — push in the tab with a paper clip, and you can pull the front side of the cartridge toward you.

Keep in mind that the surface of a DVD-R or DVD-RAM disc is much —
and brothers and sisters, I do mean *much* — more sensitive to fingerprints
and dust than a CD-R or CD-RW disc. Take the utmost precaution in handling
a recordable DVD disc: Never set it on a surface (not even label side down),
and leave it outside its cartridge or your drive only long enough to transport
it back and forth.

Take That Cleaning Disc Far, Far Away

Tip: Never, never, never use a "CD-ROM cleaning disc" in your recorder.

They certainly *look* innocent and harmless, hanging on the shelf at your local
discount store. But don't be tempted to try a CD-ROM cleaning disc in your CD
or DVD recorder. These discs typically use a tiny brush on the underside of
the disc, which is supposed to "sweep" dust and dirt from your CD-ROM lens.
Unfortunately, they can damage your recorder's read/write lens system (which,
by the way, is self cleaning anyway). Those tiny bristles can be pulled loose
and stick in your drive, or the brush can scratch the surface of the laser lens.

The best way to keep your recorder clean is to keep the tray closed. Don't
leave it open unless you're loading or unloading a disc. If you have an external recorder, wipe it from time to time with a dry, static-free cloth to remove
surface dust.

When Your Disc Cries "I'm Stuck!"

Tip: Use the emergency eject hole to unload a troublesome disc.

Typically, you use the emergency eject hole on the front of your drive if

- ✔ The disc isn't turning in the drive for some reason (perhaps it was
  loaded off center in the tray).
- ✔ Your computer's operating system has locked up and you can't eject
  the tray.
- ✔ You have a hardware driver problem and the tray doesn't eject.

To manually eject the tray, insert a straightened paper clip into the emergency
eject hole on the front of your drive and push it gently. This technique may
take a few tries because the release button you're trying to press is pretty
small.

Chapter 16

Ten Software Troubleshooting Tips

"It's only software — you can fix it easily, right?" I wish that I had a dime for every time I have heard that question. For some reason, most computer owners seem to feel that a software glitch is automatically easier to solve than a hardware problem. This, dear friends, is about as accurate as Napoleon's assessment of Waterloo. In fact, software incompatibilities can be even harder to track down and solve than hardware problems; both Windows and Mac OS use dozens of drivers and programs (tactlessly spread out over the entire hard drive in locations dark and mysterious) to control the operation of a single CD recorder. They all have to work together as a team, but sometimes some of these files seem to strike out on their own just to generate headaches for you.

I use this Part of Tens chapter to address the software tips I dispense most often to my family, friends, and consulting customers — only the latter have to pay anything, but I eat well during the holidays. I cover three or four of these tips in earlier chapters, but they belong in the Top Ten Tips category, so you also find them here.

Device Manager: Checking Under the Windows Hood

Tip: Use the Windows Device Manager to check for possible software conflicts.

Most Windows owners have used the Device Manager (see Figure 16-1) from time to time to take care of a specific task — for instance, enabling or disabling auto insert notification, which I cover later in this chapter. You may not realize, however, that the Device Manager also makes a doggone good basic software diagnostic tool. With it, you can check

- Whether hardware devices and their software drivers are working correctly
- Whether two hardware devices are "fighting" over the same system resources (which can cause both devices to stop working or your PC to lock up)
- Whether you have hardware devices Windows doesn't recognize

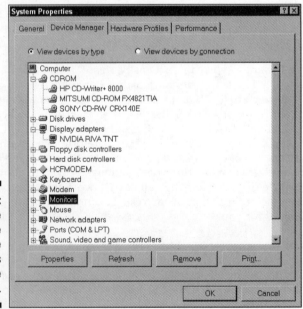

Figure 16-1: The awesome glory of the Windows Device Manager.

You can also use Device Manager to change the settings, configuration, and properties for each piece of hardware on your system. To display the Device Manager in Windows 98 and Windows Me, right-click the My Computer icon on your Windows desktop and choose Properties from the pop-up menu. Then click the Device Manager tab. If a device is causing problems, Windows marks it with either a yellow question mark symbol or a red check symbol. You can display the properties for any hardware device by clicking on it to highlight it and clicking Properties.

If another device is attempting to use the same system resources as your internal recorder, you can display the properties for the offending device and enable the Disable in this Hardware Profile check box at the bottom of the panel. This setting should allow your drive to work (at least you can record while you try to figure out what's wrong). I would also try to remove the conflicting device from your system and allow Windows to reinstall it. To do this, click the device in the Device Manager, click Remove, and reboot your PC.

If you have a copy of Norton Utilities 2001 or Norton SystemWorks 2001, I also heartily recommend the Dynamic Duo of Norton WinDoctor (shown in Figure 16-2) and Norton Disk Doctor — it's a great combination! Disk Doctor can check your drive for file and folder problems (caused by a power failure, for example), and WinDoctor automates repairs for common software problems that crop up over time (like when a program doesn't completely uninstall).

Figure 16-2:
The
WinDoctor
is in the
house.

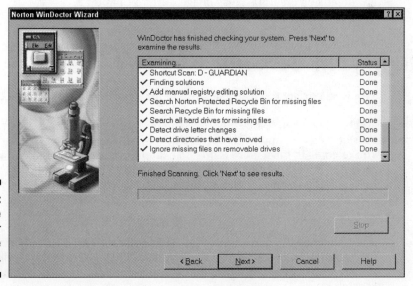

Your Image Can Be Everything

Tip: If your older PC and CD recorder are experiencing buffer underrun errors, record from a disc image.

If you're using an older Pentium and a recorder with a data buffer of less than 1MB, you'll likely still encounter the dreaded Buffer Underrun error. (You may remember from earlier chapters that a Buffer Underrun error indicates that your PC can't transfer data fast enough from your hard drive to your recorder. The recorder aborts the burn.) Although defragmenting helps, it doesn't solve the problem completely; the more files you record and the smaller they are, the more your computer and hard drive have to work to supply your recorder with the ones and zeroes it craves. Buffer underruns don't happen on every disc, but when they do, it's a trip to Coaster City.

What can you do (other than buy a new and faster PC)? Here's a tip that can keep you going while you save up the cash for a new system: Use Easy CD Creator to record the disc as a disc image first, and then record the CD from the disc image. Your computer has an easier time sending a single large file to your recorder than it does sending hundreds or thousands of smaller files, and you're much less likely to encounter recording errors.

For details on creating a disc image, turn to Chapter 8.

"Hey, Your Session's Open!"

Tip: Don't forget to close a session before you're finished with a disc.

You have no need to be embarrassed about this one. If you have written a session to a disc and left it open (either because you forgot to close it or you're going to burn more to the disc later), you can still read it in your recorder. Your computer's CD-ROM drive and a standard audio CD player both spit it back at you, though. To read the disc, you have to use your recorder.

To close an open session using Easy CD Creator, load the disc into your recorder, click CD, and choose the CD Information menu item. From the CD Information dialog box (illustrated beautifully in Figure 16-3), click the drive to display the information for the disc and then click Finalize Session.

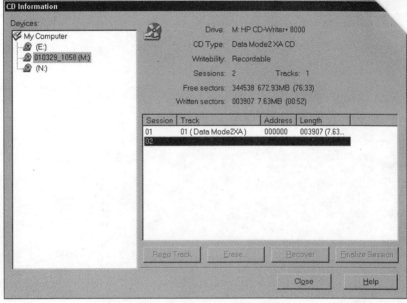

"Captain's Log, Stardate, Uh — Hey, Spock, What Day Is It?"

Tip: Use the recording log to help diagnose recurring problems.

The way I see it, the more information you have — and, in the worst case, the more information your technical support representative has — the easier it is to diagnose what's going wrong with your system. Easy CD Creator can log all error messages to a file in any folder you choose, so you don't have to hover around the monitor with a scratch pad and a pencil to scribble down anything you see.

To enable error logging, click Tools and click the Options menu item to display the Easy CD Creator Options dialog box, as shown in Figure 16-4. Click the Enable error logging check box, and click the Browse button to select the folder where the log will be written. Choose a directory other than the Windows Temp directory (you don't want to lose the log because of a Disk Cleanup operation), enter a filename, like ERROR.LOG, and click Open. Finally, click OK to save your changes and return to Easy CD Creator.

To open the log, you can use Windows Notepad or any text editor — even Microsoft Word will do, in a pinch.

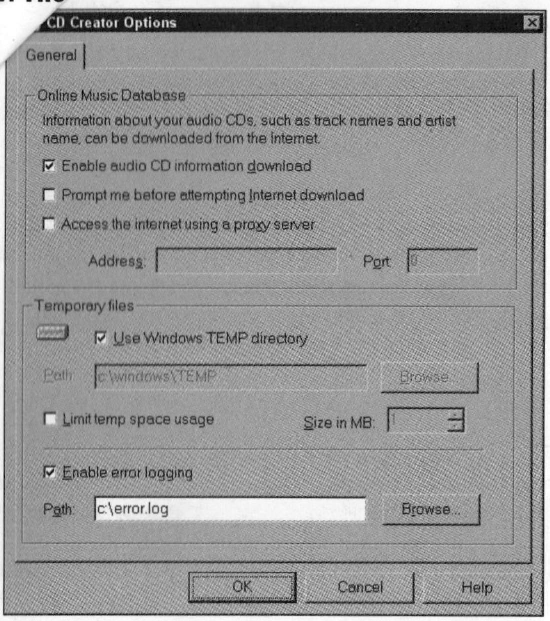

CD Creator Options

General

Online Music Database

Information about your audio CDs, such as track names and artist name, can be downloaded from the Internet.

☑ Enable audio CD information download

☐ Prompt me before attempting Internet download

☐ Access the Internet using a proxy server

Address: _____ Port: 0

Temporary files

☑ Use Windows TEMP directory

Path: c:\windows\TEMP   Browse...

☐ Limit temp space usage   Size in MB: 1

☑ Enable error logging

Path: c:\error.log   Browse...

OK   Cancel   Help

Figure 16-4: It's not a pecan log, it's not a cheese log — it's a recording error log!

Don't Use Dated Software

Tip: Always apply the latest updates and patches to your recording software.

As hardware continues to advance, so must your software! Updates to your recording program can fix bugs, add support for new recorders, enhance the performance of the program, and improve the program's compatibility with your operating system.

However, many folks ask me "Do I need to upgrade to the latest version of the software?" Naturally, that costs you cash — and, not surprisingly, I recommend that you *not* upgrade unless

✔ You specifically need a new feature that has been added to the new version.

✔ The new version performs significantly better on your current system.

✔ The current version doesn't support your brand-new recorder, and your current version will have no future updates. (Some companies have the nasty habit of dropping *all* support for older versions after one or two newer versions have been released.)

Check the software developer's Web site for updates and patches. Also, many programs now have built-in links to the company's Web site, so your recording software can launch your browser for you. Woo-hoo!

Validation Is a Good Thing

Tip: If you're recording an ISO 9660 disc or over the network, validate before you burn.

As you may know, recording an ISO 9660 disc (which doesn't accept long file- and folder names and strictly limits the number of folders you can add to a disc) on a Windows PC usually requires you to rename and move things within your CD layout. Unfortunately, the problems you encounter trying to record a disc are almost never apparent until you're ready to burn — or after you try to read the disc you have burned on a Linux box. Although programs such as Easy CD Creator warn you about these problems, I have used recording software that didn't give you any warning whatsoever and merrily burned a useless disc.

Another common problem occurs while you're recording files over a network from a remote hard drive. If the drive is suddenly taken off the network or the remote user renames a file or folder before you start the recording, the process rewards you with a fat, juicy error and a lovely coaster as a parting gift.

Obviously, what you need in situations like these is a way to verify that

- ✔ The files and folders you have arranged in your layout all conform to the requirements of the file system you have chosen
- ✔ The files and folders that reside on a remote network drive are still available and still bear the same names

Lo and behold, Easy CD Creator delivers with its validation feature, which you can use with any layout type that includes data files. After you're ready to record and you want to verify that everything is Go for launch, click File and choose the Validate Project menu item. You can watch the fun as the program checks each item in your CD layout; if anything fishy turns up, you are alerted (and you can fix it immediately).

In Case of a Disc Loading, Please Notify Windows Immediately

Tip: Know when to enable or disable auto insert notification.

Windows offers a host of small niceties that make your computing life much easier — not the least of which is the ability to automatically run a selected program from a CD as soon as it's loaded. This feature is *auto insert notification,* and many PC owners don't know that they can disable it if they want.

would you want to disable auto insert notification? When you're copying racks or entire discs during a burning session and you load a source CD-ROM, the last thing you want is an installation program automatically starting up! For this reason, many recording programs disable the notification feature automatically. But talk about a Catch-22: If your recording software disables notification, you have to install new CD-ROM software by double-clicking the right program (sometimes figuring out precisely what you're supposed to run from a game's CD-ROM is a little challenging). Plus, when you load an audio CD, you have to run your audio CD player program manually.

Therefore, here's how you can enable or disable auto insert notification as necessary:

1. **Right-click the My Computer icon on your desktop and choose Properties from the pop-up menu.**

2. **Click the Device Manager tab.**

3. **Click the plus sign next to the CD-ROM section to display all the CD-ROM drives and recorders on your system.**

4. **Click the drive you need to configure once to highlight it and click Properties.**

5. **Click the Settings tab to display the panel shown in Figure 16-5.**

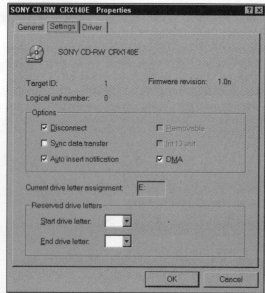

Figure 16-5: There's the culprit — your auto insert notification setting.

6. **Click the Auto insert notification check box to enable on Tips**

7. **Click OK to exit the Properties panel and then click OK to re the Windows desktop.**

Depending on the driver your recorder uses, you may have to reboot imme ately after this process.

Slow It Down, Speed Racer

Tip: Use a slower recording speed when you encounter errors.

This advice is one of those basic truths that should be made into a tattoo. If you're encountering recording errors when your new 16x drive is burning across the landscape at its top velocity, *slow down!* No unwritten law says that you have to record every disc at the maximum speed offered by your drive.

For a number of reasons, your system may not be able to supply data at the top speed supported by your drive. You may be multitasking with a woolly mammoth like Photoshop, or you may be recording a slew of tiny 4K files that are thrashing your hard drive. (Consider writing a disc image first, as I explain earlier in this chapter.) Also, don't forget that most manufacturers "rate" their blank media with a top speed, so if you're trying to write at 12x with discs rated at only 8x, bad things may happen. Your mileage may vary according to your brand of drive and discs.

By the way, this problem disappears with today's burnproof recorders — it's virtually impossible to spoil a disc unless your recording software crashes or locks up.

When All Else Fails, Reinstall!

Tip: In case of massive, horrendous software problems, uninstall and reinstall!

Yes, I know — both you and I have heard that litany countless times, but it's *true. It really works.* If your recording software is continually locking up or crashing, uninstall the program: Click Start and choose Settings⇨Control Panel⇨Add/Remove Programs. After you have wiped the program from your system, reinstall it. Don't forget to reapply any patches or updates (that is, unless all your troubles started immediately after you applied an update).

...is technique work? It's a blanket approach to the problem: When ...all, you erase and replace whatever's causing (or at least contribut- ... the errors. Potential culprits can include missing or corrupted drivers ... shared files, "mulched" configuration files, and — as I said — even updates to your software that have caused things to go haywire.

No, reinstalling doesn't always work, but it is something you should *always* try.

Overdoing Overburning

Tip: Overburn only when you really need the extra space.

As I mention earlier in this book, overburning can squeeze from your blank discs additional megabytes of space (or a minute or two extra for audio CDs) — *if* your recorder can reliably overburn. That's a big *if* because both your recording software and your drive have to support this procedure. However, even if you can overburn, keep these tips in mind:

- Overburned discs are generally unreadable in CD-ROM drives 4 years old or older, and in many audio CD players.
- Switching media brands can suddenly thwart your attempts at overburning — it depends on the manufacturer.
- Check with the manufacturer of your drive to determine the absolute limit in megabytes and minutes and seconds you can overburn. (If necessary, a bit of experimentation can tell you this limit).

I generally recommend that you keep almost all your recordings below the 80-minute/700MB limit and overburn only when it's absolutely necessary.

Chapter 17

Ten Things to Avoid Like the Plague

Mother Nature has ways of telling you to "stay away" from certain plants and animals — you don't want to get involved, usually because of claws, teeth, or poisonous spines. Alternating bands of neon green and orange can't be a good thing, right?

Unfortunately, you can encounter lots of really nasty time-wasting trouble when buying, installing, and using a CD or DVD recorder, and you don't receive any warning beforehand. For example, parallel port drives *sound* like a great idea — until you use them.

In this Part of Tens chapter, I take over as the technoversion of Mother Nature (now *there's* a weird visual image for you) and identify what should be off-limits. Avoid these things like the plague, and you'll thank me!

Antique Parallel Port Drives

Before the arrival of the Big Twosome — USB and FireWire — shopping for an external drive came down to two choices. You could pick SCSI (which was expensive, complex to configure, and quite scary for the average PC owner) or take the easy route and choose a parallel port drive. As I mentioned a second ago, a parallel port drive is easy to install (you simply connect it to the printer port on your computer) and much cheaper than a SCSI adapter card and drive.

Here's what the advertisements for these drives didn't tell you:

- **They're slow.** I mean *really* slow: If Dorothy had used a parallel port drive, she would still be in the Land of Oz. Because the data transfer rate is limited to the top speed of a parallel port, virtually all parallel ports are limited to 2x recording, with a handful of drives capable of a blistering 4x.

- **They often don't play well with others.** There's always a chance that you will encounter problems when both a parallel port recorder and your printer are connected. (Of course, you can't use both at the same time.) What's worse, all parallel port recorders require a hardware driver of some sort, and those drivers sometimes turn out to be incompatible with printers and other parallel port devices. These problems are the same ones that often plague owners of parallel port ZIP drives.

- **They may need special recording software.** You may end up forced to use a strange burning program that doesn't support all the features and formats I cover in this book. (A SCSI, USB, or FireWire external drive can use Easy CD Creator or any other program you choose.)

Unless you have absolutely no recourse — either you use a parallel port drive or you don't burn discs — let these antiques fade away into the hoary pages of history and invest in a USB or FireWire recorder.

"Holy Aqueous Tragedy, Batman!" (Avoiding Liquids)

Not much explanation needed here: *Keep liquids away from both your discs and your recorder!* In a pitched battle, a diet soda always wins. At least you can clean your discs when they have been accidentally dunked — you may have to use a little CD-ROM cleaning solution. However, knock your mug of hot cocoa on your external recorder and you have just created an expensive paperweight.

A Bad Labeling Job Is Worse than No Label

To accurately read a CD-ROM, your drive has to control the speed of the disc's rotation, and — oh, there I go with the engineering-speak again. All you have to remember is that a disc that's badly out of balance is harder to read, so sticking a huge, heavy label on just one side of a CD-ROM you have recorded may render it unusable. This includes large mailing labels, return address labels, and even — gasp — stickers. If a label weighs enough, it throws the disc's balance out of whack. For this reason, many manufacturers of DVD media advise that you never apply a paper label to their discs; check the manufacturer's recommendations before you stick something where it shouldn't go!

The easiest way to avoid this problem is to use CD-ROM labels and a labeling device, like a CD Stomper or NEATO system, which leave your discs in perfect balance after they're applied. Even better, you get quite a bit more space to hang text and graphics.

One note of warning about any label you apply: After it's on your disc, don't try to remove it unless it's specifically designed to come off! Most labels use a permanent adhesive; if you try to peel it off, you will probably rip the label (which can unbalance the disc).

Copy Protection Works

If you're buying a CD or DVD recorder to create backup copies of games or DVD movies, don't expect much success. Most computer CD-ROM games and all DVD-ROM discs are copy protected, and you won't have any luck in duplicating them. (They're also copyrighted, but I don't go into that here.)

One or two recording programs purport to duplicate discs, but a number of different copy-protection schemes are also available (which are continually being updated) — therefore, what works on one disc may not work on the next. 'Nuff said.

Don't Settle for a Tiny Buffer

As I mention earlier in this book, the size of your recorder's data buffer has a direct effect on the performance of your recorder — especially when your system is "under pressure," like when other programs are running in the background or you're recording at 10x or faster speeds. The larger the buffer, the more efficient the recording process, and the less likely you are to encounter errors during the burn.

If you're shopping for a recorder, I recommend a drive with at least 1MB; naturally, 2MB or more would be even better. Most older recorders have a scanty buffer of 512K (or even less), so scavengers beware.

"We Interrupt This Network Recording. . . ."

Let me be straightforward and say that this section is a personal vendetta. I was a hardware technician for a large hospital for several years in my home-town of Columbia, Missouri, and one of the other techs I worked with was continually ruining perfectly good discs trying to record over a network. He was using files from a network hard drive as the source, and because of the constant network broadcast messages and servers going up and down, he produced coaster after coaster. Eventually, I recommended that he try packet writing, which solved most of the problems.

Of course, you may find yourself forced to record over the network if your recorder is installed in a diskless workstation or an older computer with a tiny drive, but if you have the hard drive space on the computer with the recorder, *please* copy those files to the computer's local hard drive and record them from there.

I can't bear to think of any more innocent silver lives being wasted because the network slowed to a crawl.

How Slow Is Too Slow?

This one's for all the scavengers out there: If you have inherited a 2X recorder, consider passing it on to another friend or family member and shopping for a new drive. "Why, that's heresy to a scavenger, Mark! Of all the folks on this planet, *you* should know that!" It's true, I have scavenged more than my share of unwanted 2MB video cards, keyboards, ISA network cards, and SIMM memory from garage sales and basements. However, you have three good reasons to turn your back on 2x (and perhaps even 4x) recorders:

✔ **How much is your time worth?** After you have recorded an entire 680MB disc in 4 minutes with a 10x or 12x drive, you're going to wonder whether your 2x drive is lying dormant in hibernation for 20 minutes (or more) while it's burning a disc.

- ✔ **Older drives don't have the niceties.** With an "antique" 2x drive, you are likely to miss out on most of the features I have been crowing about — packet writing, disc-at-once, burnproof recording, and even CD Extra discs.

- ✔ **Their support has dried up.** Good luck in getting support for a 5- or 6-year-old drive: If you're lucky, the manufacturer may still have a firmware update or two on their Web sites, but it's more likely that support for such an old model has evaporated completely.

Of course, that 2x drive can still burn a mighty nice data CD-ROM of the plain variety. Just have your lunch on hand while you wait.

Give Those Discs a Home!

If you have been burning discs for six months or so, you have followed one of two paths:

- ✔ **The light path:** You have picked up a snazzy CD binder or a jewel box shelf unit, and your discs are resting comfortably in their protected, dust-free environment. Your audio CDs don't skip because of scratches, and your data CD-ROMs never give you a hint of trouble when you read them.

- ✔ **The dark path:** You have two or three stacks of 20 unprotected discs adorning the front of your monitor, and they're picking up scratches and dust right before your eyes. (Also, you knock over a stack from time to time and wake up your significant other with a scream.)

Do yourself — and your discs — a favor and store them the right way.

Putting the Worthless in High-Tech Cleaning

I mention this in Chapter 1, but it bears repeating: You have absolutely no reason to spend $20 or more on a CD cleaning device that looks like a cross between one of da Vinci's flying machines and an automatic bread maker. All you need to clean your shiny round friends is a photographer's lens cloth — any high-density silk material will do in a pinch, too.

If a disc has picked up liquid gunk — remember, I warned you about liquids earlier — then it's a good idea to buy a flask of CD cleaning solution to help clean the toxic waste.

The moral of the story is a simple one: If you carry your discs correctly and store them responsibly, you simply don't need the Rube Goldberg cleaning contraptions now on the market!

Keep 'Em Cool

One thing your CDs share with pets and children: Never, *never*, NEVER keep them trapped in a hot vehicle, especially in direct sunlight. Owners of car CD players know how finicky these beasts can be, and no matter what Aunt Hilda told you, discs can warp. (I haven't seen one melt yet, but I'm only 40 years old. There's still plenty of time.)

How can you fix a warped disc? I guess you could attempt to press it back into shape using a thick, heavy hardbound book — but it's generally a better idea to copy the disc. Most recorders are more tolerant of a warped disc than audio CD players are, so you may get lucky and be able to copy it (or at least create a disc image you can use to record a new disc).

It's best, however, to just keep those discs cool in the first place!

Chapter 18

Ten Nifty Programs You Want

I cover the most popular recording software the world around in this book — Easy CD Creator, Toast, and DirectCD — along with a number of specialized programs, like Adobe Premiere, iDVD, and VOB. With the programs I focus on, you can record just about any type of CD and DVD disc under the sun.

These tools aren't the only ones you can use, of course; you can swear by other recording programs, for example (I don't cover the software you swear *at*), as well as utilities for converting images, creating thumbnails, editing digital audio and video, and much more. I mention classics like iMovie, WinAmp, and Paint Shop Pro elsewhere, and a host of others are available.

In this chapter, I review my favorite programs that I can recommend to everyone with a recorder. I don't present any $5,000 software packages here — most of these programs are shareware, and a few are even free. I think that the programs in this chapter appeal to both novice and experienced drive owners. I've used all these nifty tools on the PC and the Mac, and I would bet that you will find them invaluable too!

CDRWIN

Windows CD recording shareware from Golden Hawk Technology
(www.goldenhawk.com)

CDRWIN has been a shareware favorite of the CD recording community for many years. As you can see in Figure 18-1, the basic interface looks almost comical (pun intended); behind that deceptively simple façade, however, lies a powerful recording engine! (Also, the Golden Hawk Technology Web site is a great place to start when tracking down firmware upgrades for your recorder.)

At the time I type these words, CDRWIN is an absolute steal at $39, and you get versions for Windows 98, Windows Me, Windows NT, and Windows 2000.

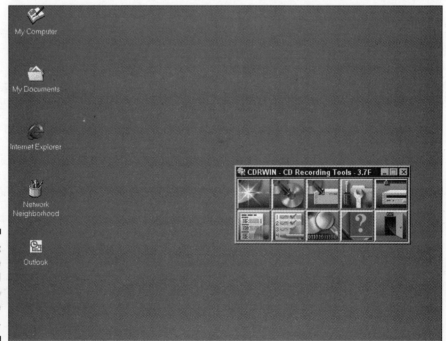

Figure 18-1:
Don't be
fooled
by the
appearance
of CDRWIN.

Along with the basic data and audio CD formats CDRWIN can record, it includes these nifty features:

- ✔ Multiple recorder support, where you can use as many as 32 SCSI and EIDE drives connected to the same computer to burn copies of the same disc *simultaneously*. (Now you understand the attraction of those SCSI device chains.)

- ✔ Extraction of specific sectors on a data or audio CD, which comes in handy when copying just a portion of a mixed-mode or CD Extra disc.

- ✔ Support for advanced CD recorders with the Kodak Disc Transporter, which automates the recording of multiple copies of the same disc.

- ✔ A complete selection of CD-Text fields for each track on an audio CD, including performer, songwriter, composer, arranger, and a custom text description.

- ✔ Extraction of audio files as both WAV and AIFF formats, which makes a difference if you need to send digital audio files to a Macintosh owner.

GraphicConverter

Macintosh image conversion and editing shareware from Lemke Software (`lemkesoft.com/us_index.html`)

For Macintosh owners, GraphicConverter represents the classic shareware success story, and it's now available for both the Classic Mac OS 9.1 and Mac OS X (see Figure 18-2).

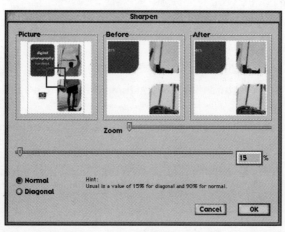

Figure 18-2: Graphic-Converter is a Macintosh image-editing toolbox.

GraphicConverter can import more than 145 different formats of digital images, and it can export almost 50. Although manual and automatic (batch) conversion of image formats is its claim to fame, you can also

- ✔ Browse and view a folder's worth of images from within the program.

- ✔ View images in a slideshow display.

- ✔ Perform basic image-editing chores, like cropping, rotation, reducing and increasing color depth, and adjusting brightness and contrast.

- ✔ Whiz through mundane image-management tasks, like deleting, renaming, and moving images from one folder to another.

For a mere $30, the powerful tool GraphicConverter can't be beat!

PowerDVD

Windows video CD and DVD-ROM player from CyberLink
(www.gocyberlink.com)

In my book, PowerDVD is the best software DVD player available — it demolishes anything from Microsoft (including the Windows XP DVD player) with a lengthy laundry list of features. It can also play video CDs and MPEG digital video you have stored on your hard drive. The most impressive PowerDVD features include

- ✔ Full support for Dolby Digital decoding and Dolby Headphone playback

- ✔ Dual subtitling (which comes in handy if you're studying a new language by watching your favorite movie)

- ✔ Digital 4x and 9x zoom

- ✔ Closed-caption display

- ✔ A screen-capture utility

- ✔ A neat bookmark feature that lets you jump directly to a specific point in a film

- ✔ The neatest and most configurable control panel on the planet (as you can see in Figure 18-3)

You can buy a copy of PowerDVD direct from the CyberLink Web site for $49.50.

Figure 18-3:
PowerDVD
is hands-
down the
best for
watching
DVD movies
on your PC.

Final Cut Pro

Macintosh digital video editor and special effects generator from Apple
(www.apple.com)

If you're serious about DV editing and you're lucky enough to own one of the Apple Power Mac G4 line (including my personal object of lust, the Titanium G4 PowerBook), it's a good bet that you will settle on Final Cut Pro 2.0 as your editor and effects generator of choice (see Figure 18-4).

The program offers blindingly fast performance with these machines, with some of the fastest rendering times available on a personal computer. Features like these are liable to make you faint:

- ✔ Easy drag-and-drop editing with real-time control over multiple sequences
- ✔ Support for direct FireWire DV, Beta SP, and HDTV
- ✔ OMF professional-level audio export
- ✔ Output to monitor, camera, VCR, or NTSC TV
- ✔ Output to streaming Web media (using Cleaner 5 EZ, which is included)
- ✔ Work with as many as 99 layers, including text and still graphics

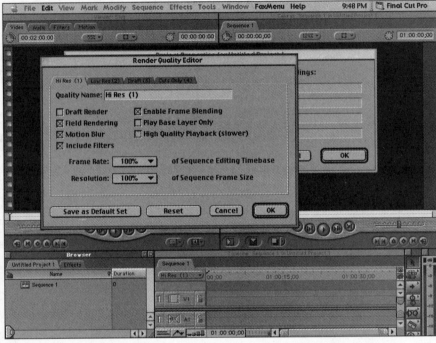

Figure 18-4:
Mac owners rejoice in the power of Final Cut Pro 2.0.

Naturally, a full-blown video editor like this one doesn't come cheap, but the $999 Apple price is a mere fraction of the small fortune you would spend on a professional DV hardware system.

MusicMatch Jukebox Plus

Windows/Macintosh/Linux digital audio freeware/shareware "thing" from MusicMatch
(www.musicmatch.com)

Why do I call MusicMatch Jukebox Plus a digital audio "thing"? Because it does an incredible amount of stuff, all related to digital audio (see Figure 18-5).

Naturally, it's a great player for MP3s, WAVs, and audio CDs, and that's the main function of this program. I also find myself using it at least once or twice a day, however, to take care of other audio chores. With Jukebox Plus version 6.1, you can

✔ Burn audio CDs from within the program

✔ Upload MP3 audio files to your portable MP3 player

✔ Rip songs from existing audio CDs

✔ Convert digital audio files from one format to another

✔ Convert digital audio files from one sampling rate to another

✔ Display cool light shows while your music plays

✔ Print audio CD covers and display album artwork on your desktop

You can register Jukebox Plus with all these features for $19.99, or you can use the free version (Jukebox Basic) that can handle playing, ripping, and 2x burning.

Figure 18-5:
Music-Match Jukebox Plus is a powerful audio thing.

Retrospect Express Backup

Windows/Macintosh backup software from Dantz Development Corporation (www.dantz.com)

I absolutely *promise* that I don't nag you again about backing up your system — I just recommend Retrospect Express Backup, as shown in Figure 18-6, to do it.

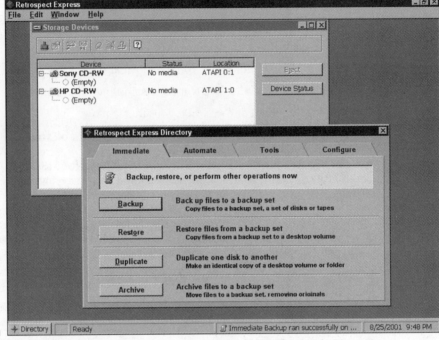

Figure 18-6:
I use
Retrospect
Express
Backup on
both my
Macintosh
and PCs.

This program is easy and fast, and it recognizes internal and external recorders as backup devices, including, I'm happy to say, both CD-RW and DVD-RAM drives. Other features of this excellent program include

- ✔ The ability to create a bootable disaster-recovery disc that can restore your system
- ✔ Efficient software compression to reduce the number of discs you need
- ✔ An easy-to-use source selection wizard to help you specify just what you want backed up
- ✔ Encryption to secure your files
- ✔ Automatic launching of unattended backups
- ✔ Automatic rotation between multiple backup sets

Talk about a bargain — both the Windows and Mac versions are only $49.95 from the Dantz Web site.

Acrobat

Windows and Macintosh document imaging and archiving software from Adobe
(www.adobe.com)

You may be wondering why I chose to add Adobe Acrobat to this chapter. After all, it doesn't have anything directly to do with recording or multimedia (see Figure 18-7). Ah, but what about documents? Many companies use CD and DVD recorders to archive important material, like forms, advertising materials, and even user manuals — and those documents have to be available for use not only on the Web, but also on both Macintosh and PCs.

That's where Acrobat fits in, and that's why it's now one of the most successful document standards. PDF files are very small, which explains their popularity on the Web. You can create in the Acrobat PDF format electronic versions of your documents that look and print exactly the same on PCs, Macs, and even those rabid Linux machines (complete with graphics and special fonts). The reader is free, so anyone can view and print your documents without spending a nickel.

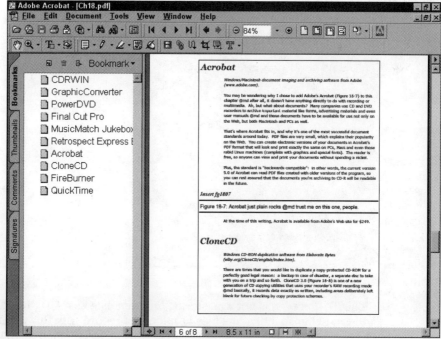

Figure 18-7:
Acrobat just plain rocks — trust me on this one, people.

Plus, the standard is backward compatible. In other words, the current version 5.0 of Acrobat can read PDF files created with older versions of the program, so you can rest assured that the documents you're archiving to CD-R will be readable in the future.

At the time of this writing, Acrobat is available from the Adobe Web site for $249.

CloneCD

Windows CD-ROM duplication software from Elaborate Bytes
(`elby.org/CloneCD/english/index.htm`)

Sometimes, you want to duplicate a copy-protected CD-ROM for a perfectly good legal reason: a backup in case of disaster or a separate disc to take with you on a trip, for example. CloneCD 3.0 is one of a new generation of CD-copying utilities that uses your recorder's RAW recording mode (see Figure 18-8). Basically, it records data exactly as written, including areas deliberately left blank for future checking by copy-protection schemes.

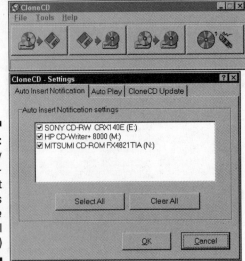

Figure 18-8:
To copy the uncopy-able, get CloneCD. (Is *uncopyable* a real word?)

CloneCD, however, is not a mastering program, like Easy CD Creator or Toast: You can't choose individual files or folders to record with this puppy. Its only purpose is to create exact backups of existing discs, no matter what format they're in. You can also create disc images and save them to your hard drive. Of course, this makes the program easy to use, but it's not automatic by any means. Certain discs require adjustments to the settings that are far beyond the ken of normal human experience. Plus, the program still doesn't work on every type of copy protection, so certain discs just can't be reproduced.

CloneCD can be purchased from the Elaborate Bytes Web site for about $30.

FireBurner

Windows/Linux CD recording shareware from IgD Software
(www.fireburner.com)

Cool name, right? You bet, and this extremely popular shareware CD recording program is just as cool as its name. Compared to the dozens of settings and menu items in Easy CD Creator, FireBurner is a stripped-down hotrod (see Figure 18-9). Yes, that's really the main menu! FireBurner handles data, audio, and mixed-mode CDs with ease. A Linux version is available.

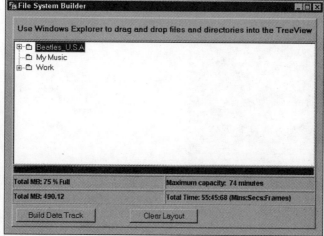

Figure 18-9: The minimalist at work: FireBurner is a popular favorite.

Other features include

- Support for recording from standard BIN and CUE image files
- Burns from digital audio (MP3 and WAV) as well as from PCM audio tracks
- Scanning of disc and track images for errors before you burn
- Burnproof recording support
- Drag-and-drop layout builder

FireBurner version 2.0 sets you back about $30.

QuickTime

Windows/Macintosh digital multimedia player/viewer from Apple
(www.apple.com)

If it's multimedia, Apple QuickTime 5.0 can play it — that includes DV, MPEG and MOV video, digital audio, still images, 360-degree panoramic images, and even Macromedia Flash animations! Plus, as you can see in Figure 18-10, this program looks like a million bucks. (That's important for a multimedia player these days, as the folks in Redmond are finally figuring out.) If your recorded discs carry multimedia content, QuickTime can show it.

Figure 18-10:
QuickTime
is truly a
work of
perform-
ance art.

Along with viewing all these different types of files, I use QuickTime to watch QTV streaming video from my favorite Web sites (everything from BBC World Service to MTV and Nickelodeon).

The basic version of QuickTime is free, and the Pro version — which allows you to perform simple DV editing tasks, convert file formats, create slideshows, and resize images — is only $29.99.

Part VI
Appendixes

The 5th Wave   By Rich Tennant

"Room service? Please send someone up to refresh the mini bar with CD-RW discs."

In this part . . .

These two appendixes include reference information you'll turn to often: a recorder hardware and software manufacturer list and a glossary jam-packed with explanations of those mysterious terms and silly acronyms.

Appendix A

Recorder Hardware and Software Manufacturers

● ●

*I*n this appendix, you find contact information for manufacturers of CD and DVD recorders as well as developers of recording software of all kinds. Whenever possible, I list both the Web site and fax number for each entry; however, note that some companies do not provide direct voice telephone numbers, so you must contact them by e-mail.

Recorder Manufacturers

Addonics Technologies
Phone: (510) 438-6530
www.addonics.com

CenDyne
www.cendyne.com

Compaq
Phone: (800) 888-0220
www.compaq.com

Creative Labs
Phone: (800) 998-5227
Fax: (405) 624-6780
www.creativelabs.com

Hewlett-Packard Company
Phone: (800) 222-5547
Fax: (650) 857-5518
www.hp.com

IBM
Phone: (800) IBM-4YOU
www.ibm.com

Imation Corporation
Phone: (888) 466-3456
Fax: (888) 704-4200
www.imation.com

Iomega Corporation
Phone: (888) 4IOMEGA
www.iomega.com

MicroSolutions
Phone: (800) 890-7227
www.micro-solutions.com

Mitsumi Electronics
Phone: (800)-MITSUMI
www.mitsumi.com

Pacific Digital Corporation
Phone: (800) 486-7800
www.pacificdigital.com

Plextor America
Phone: (800) 886-3935
Fax: (510) 651-9755
www.plextor.com

QPS
Phone: (800) 559-4777
Fax: (714) 692-5516
www.qps-inc.com

Ricoh Corporation
Phone: (800) 63-RICOH
www.ricoh-usa.com

Sony Electronics
Phone: (800) 588-3847
www.sel.sony.com

Teac America
Phone: (323) 726-0303
Fax: (323)727-7652
www.teac.com

Toshiba
Phone: (800) 457-7777
www.toshiba.com

Universal BUSlink Corporation
Phone: (626) 336-1888
Fax: (626) 968-8100
www.buslink.com

VST
Phone: (978) 635-8200
Fax: (978) 263-9876
www.vsttech.com

Yamaha Corporation of America
Phone: (714) 522-9011
www.yamaha.com

Recording Software Developers

Ahead Software AG
www.nero.com

Apple
Phone: (408) 996-1010
www.apple.com

Elaborate Bytes
www.elby.de

Gear Software
Phone: (800) 423-9147
Fax: (561) 575-3026
www.gearsoftware.com

Golden Hawk Technology
Phone: (603) 429-1008
www.goldenhawk.com

HyCD
Phone: (408) 988-8282
Fax: (408) 988-8585
www.hycd.com

IgD Software
www.fireburner.com

NewTech Infosystems
Phone: (714) 259-9700
Fax: (714) 259-9727
www.ntius.com

Padus
Phone: (888) GO-PADUS
Fax: (408) 370-0277
www.padus.com

Roxio, Inc.
Phone: (303) 684-3850
www.roxio.com

Sonic
Phone: (415) 893-8000
Fax: (415) 893-8008
www.sonic.com

VOB Information Systems
www.vob.de

Appendix B

Glossary

● ●

adapter card: A circuit board used to expand the abilities of your computer. The card is plugged directly into the computer's motherboard. For example, you can add FireWire ports to a PC by installing a FireWire adapter card.

AIFF: The standard format for digital audio files for Macintosh computers. Like WAV audio files on the PC side of the fence, AIFF files are used to store CD-quality stereo, usually for transfer to an audio CD.

amorphous crystalline layer: A rather exotic name that describes the layer where pits and lands are created in a CD-RW disc. This layer turns opaque when hit by a recorder's laser beam, resulting in the same effect as a pit on a CD-ROM manufactured in a factory. This layer can be cleared by formatting the CD-RW, allowing the disc to be used again.

backup: A copy of the information stored on your computer's hard drive. In case your hard drive fails or you accidentally delete important files, you can restore valuable programs and data by using your backup. *Back up often — it's the smart power user thing to do.*

binary: The language used by computers to communicate (with hardware, software, and other computers). It's not a particularly subtle language because binary has only two values: 0 and 1.

BIOS: An acronym for Basic Input/Output System. Your PC's BIOS controls basic functions, like the configuration of your hardware and the low-level functions on your motherboard. You can display and change the BIOS settings for your PC by pressing a specific key or key combination during the boot sequence.

bootable CD-ROM: A bootable CD that includes everything necessary to boot a PC or Macintosh without a hard drive: the operating system, support files, and configuration files. In the PC world, bootable CD-ROMs are recorded in El Torito format; your PC's BIOS must support bootable CD-ROMs to use one of these discs.

burnproof drive: A feature that eliminates almost all recording errors caused by multitasking. A burnproof drive can interrupt the recording process whenever you're running another program that can seriously affect the performance of your computer (like Adobe Photoshop or Microsoft Outlook). After your computer is ready to continue recording, the drive automatically resumes burning.

byte: A single character of text stored in your computer's memory or hard drive or on a CD-ROM.

caddy: A thin plastic box (rather than a tray) used to hold the disc on older CD-ROM drives and recorders. These days, drives that use caddies are considered inconvenient, anachronistic dinosaurs.

case: The metal frame that holds all the components. Like jukeboxes, all computer cases can be opened for servicing (some with a separate cover that you can remove and others with a hinged door).

CD Extra: (Also called CD Enhanced.) A mixed-mode CD-ROM with both audio and data tracks. The audio track is recorded first, allowing a CD Extra disc to be played in a standard audio CD player.

CD-R: (Short for Compact Disc-Recordable.) The standard recordable disc, capable of storing both computer data and digital audio. CD-R discs can be recorded only once; unlike a CD-RW disc, a CD-R disc can't be reused.

CD-ROM: (Short for Compact Disc-Read-Only Memory.) A compact disc used on a computer (rather than an audio CD player). CD-ROMs can be commercially manufactured or recorded on your computer using a CD-R or CD-RW drive.

CD-ROM XA: The standard recording format for multisession discs. Note that older CD-ROM drives may not be able to read CD-ROM XA discs.

CD-RW: (Short for Compact Disc-Rewritable.) A reusable recordable CD-ROM that can be erased. CD-RW discs can't be used in most older CD-ROM drives, and they can't be used in audio CD players.

CD-Text: A feature that encodes the disc name, artist name, and each track name when you record an audio CD. If your audio CD player (or your audio CD player program on your computer) supports CD-Text, it displays this information while the disc is playing.

data buffer: Internal memory built into every CD and DVD recorder. This memory temporarily holds data transferred from your hard drive until it's ready to be recorded. The larger the data buffer in your recorder, the more efficient the flow of data (and the less likely you are to encounter buffer underrun errors during recording).

defragment: To order files on your hard drive by rewriting them in contiguous form. After a drive has been defragmented, files take less time to read, and your hard drive's performance is improved.

digital audio extraction: (Also called ripping.) The process of converting a digital audio track (a song, in other words) from an existing audio CD to an MP3, WAV, or AIFF file on your computer's hard drive. Depending on the recording software you're using, you may have to do this before you can record that track to a new audio CD.

DIP switches: A bank of tiny sliding or rocker switches you use to configure devices, like hard drives and recorders. Use the tip of a pencil to set the switches into the correct position.

disc-at-once: The author's favorite recording mode (can you tell?), where the recorder writes the entire disc at once (without turning the recording laser off between tracks). Using disc-at-once may help you avoid "clicks" between tracks when playing recorded audio CDs on some players. Most recorders manufactured in the past three or four years can record in disc-at-once mode.

disc image: A file saved to your hard drive that contains all the data required to record a CD. Disc images are good for creating multiple copies of a disc over a long period. You should record from a disc image if you're experiencing buffer underrun errors while recording.

DVD authoring: The process of designing, creating, and editing an interactive DVD-ROM for personal use or commercial sale. Authoring usually involves building a DVD menu, editing digital video, and adding still images and computer programs.

DVD-A: (Short for DVD-audio.) The DVD recording format due to replace the audio compact disc. A DVD-A disc can store anywhere from two to four hours of high-fidelity music along with video clips.

DVD-R: (Short for DVD-recordable.) A recordable DVD disc that can hold 4.7GB on each side. DVD-R discs can be recorded only once. Most DVD players can use DVD-R discs, so they're popular for folks creating their own DVD-Video discs.

DVD-ROM: (Short for digital video disc and also called a digital versatile disc by those with overactive imaginations.) Rapidly becoming the standard for storing movies and digital video, a type of disc that stores 4.7GB to 17GB in the same physical dimensions as a standard CD-ROM.

DVD-RAM: A reusable recordable DVD disc that can hold 5.2GB on each side. Only the latest DVD players can read DVD-RAM discs, but they're still great for system backups and data storage. Like a CD-RW disc, a DVD-RAM disc must be formatted before you can use it.

DVD-RW: A relatively new DVD format, DVD-RW discs can hold 4.7GB on each side, and they're reusable. However, unlike the unlimited lifespan of DVD-RAM discs, DVD-RW discs can be rewritten only 1,000 times. On the plus side, DVD-RW discs can be read in most DVD players.

DVD-V: (Short for DVD-video.) The DVD recording format used to produce movies on DVD-ROM (using digital video in MPEG format). All home DVD players read DVD-V discs. A DVD-V disc can hold 4.7GB of digital video and data on each side.

dye layer: A layer of light-sensitive dye in a CD-R disc that turns opaque when struck by a recorder's laser beam. The result acts the same as a pit on a factory-made CD-ROM. The dye layer in a CD-R disc can't be turned clear again, so a CD-R disc can be recorded only once.

EIDE: (Short for Enhanced Integrated Drive Electronics.) The interface used by virtually all PCs and new Mac computers for connecting internal devices, like hard drives, CD-ROM drives, and recorders. Most PCs have a primary and secondary EIDE connector; each connector supports two devices.

El Torito format: The somewhat silly name for the format standard used to record bootable CD-ROM discs.

emergency disc eject hole: A hole that allows you to eject the disc manually even if the drive has locked up or isn't working Every recorder and read-only drive has one of these tiny holes. If you can't eject your disc, you can force it out (or force the tray to extend) by pushing a paper clip into the eject hole.

external recorder: A CD or DVD recorder you add outside your computer. It's connected to your computer by a cable and may use a separate power supply. USB and FireWire drives are always external.

FAQ: (Short for Frequently Asked Questions.) A text or Adobe PDF file created by someone who knows the answers to the most common questions posed on a particular subject. The manufacturer of your recorder may post a FAQ on its Web site that answers technical support and installation questions from new drive owners.

FireWire: (Otherwise blessed with the rather cryptic name IEEE-1394.) The most popular type of connection for external devices that require high-speed data transfer, including DV camcorders and CD and DVD recorders. Like USB, FireWire devices can be connected and unplugged without rebooting the computer, but FireWire hardware is generally more expensive. Most new Macintosh computers come with FireWire ports built-in, and you can add a FireWire adapter card to your PC.

formatting: Preparing a blank CD-RW or DVD-RAM disc for use (similar to formatting one of those old-fashioned hard drives). The disc can't be used until it has been successfully formatted.

gigabyte: A unit of data equal to 1,024MB (megabytes), usually abbreviated as GB. DVD discs can hold several gigabytes.

hard drive: A magnetic storage device that provides a permanent home for computer programs and data (at least until it crashes). Most hard drives are internal, but you can also get external SCSI, USB, and FireWire models.

HFS: (Short for Hierarchical File System). The CD-ROM file system used by Macintosh computers.

HTML: (Short for Hypertext Markup Language.) The programming language used to create Web pages. You can also use them to create CD-ROM menus.

HTML Editor: A program used to create or edit Web pages, which are actually HTML files made up of commands. You can edit these commands directly using a character-based editor (like Windows Notepad or Arachnophilia), or you can use a visual HTML editor, like Microsoft FrontPage.

incremental multisession disc: A disc that adds data imported from the previous session to files recorded in a new session (effectively "updating" the data in the previous session).

interface: An extremely fancy engineering-style technical word for *connection* — as in methods of connecting internal and external devices to your computer. Common interfaces for CD and DVD recorders include EIDE, SCSI, USB, and FireWire.

internal drive: A recorder that fits inside your computer's case (like a floppy or ZIP drive).

ISO 9660: The most compatible CD-ROM file system around. Virtually every computer and operating system can read an ISO 9660 disc, which makes it the best choice for recording cross-platform discs. On the downside, ISO 9660 limits the length of filenames and the number of directories and subdirectories you can use in your CD layout.

jewel box: The familiar hinged, plastic storage case that holds a compact disc.

Joliet file system: The CD-ROM file system used for Windows. It allows long filenames with periods and spaces.

jumper: A small wire-and-plastic electrical crossover used to configure a circuit board or internal device in your computer. You can change the settings by moving the jumper to connect different sets of pins.

kilobyte: A unit of data equal to 1,024 bytes, usually abbreviated as KB.

land: A spot under the clear surface of a CD that reflects laser light. If the disc is manufactured, lands are the flat areas between the pits; on recorded CDs and DVDs, pits are the clear areas between the opaque pits.

laser read head: The combination of the CD-ROM's laser lens, prism, and optical pickup. Together, they allow your CD-ROM drive to read a disc.

laser write head: A laser beam on a recorder that can be toggled to high and low power levels.

master: The setting for an EIDE device that designates it as the primary device on that EIDE cable. An EIDE recorder can be set to "single drive, master unit" (if it's the only drive on the cable) or "multiple drive, master unit" (if it's the primary drive with another device on the cable).

megabyte: A unit of data equal to 1,024KB (kilobytes), usually abbreviated as MB.

mixed-mode disc: A CD-ROM disc with both digital audio tracks and a data track. On a standard mixed-mode disc, the first track is computer data, and the following tracks are recorded as digital audio. Mixed-mode discs are often used for storing games. Although a mixed-mode disc can't be played on a standard audio CD player, you can record a CD Extra mixed-mode disc that is compatible with audio CD players.

motherboard: The main circuit board in a computer. The motherboard is where you find the computer's CPU (or processor), the memory modules, and the EIDE or SCSI connectors. You can plug adapter cards into the motherboard to expand your computer's functionality.

MP3: The most popular format for digital audio on the Internet. MP3 files provide CD-quality stereo, and they're often used to record audio CDs.

MPEG: (Short for Moving Pictures Expert Group.) The video format used on commercial DVD-Video movie discs. MPEG is also a popular format for video transmitted over the Web.

multisession: A type of disc that stores multiple separate recording sessions. An incremental multisession disc allows access to only the latest session, and a multivolume multisession disc allows access to all the sessions (one at a time). Audio CD players and older CD-ROM drives can use only multivolume discs.

multitask: To run multiple programs on your computer at one time. If you experience problems recording a CD-ROM while multitasking, consider using packet-writing recording or upgrading to a drive that uses burnproof technology (or just stop recording while using other programs).

multivolume multisession disc: A disc that stores data in separate volumes, each of which can be accessed one at a time. Audio CD players and older CD-ROM drives can read only the last session on a multivolume multisession disc.

network: A system of computers connected to each other to exchange data and share devices, like printers, modems, and recorders.

Orange Book: The international engineering standard that specifies the file structure of recorded CD-ROMs, or CD-R discs.

overburn: To record more data than the rated maximum capacity of a CD-R disc. For instance, your drive might be able to record 76 minutes of music on a standard 74-minute CD-R. The amount you can overburn depends on your recorder and the specific brand of discs you're using.

packet-writing: (Also called UDF.) A recording method that allows you to drag and drop files directly to the recorder's drive icon just as you would copy files to a floppy drive. Most CD and DVD recorders can record discs using packet-writing.

parallel port: A port usually used to connect a printer, although it can be used to connect external devices, like a ZIP drive, scanner, or recorder. Although some CD recorders connect to your parallel port, I don't recommend them: They're much slower and more prone to problems than USB and FireWire drives.

pit: A spot under the clear surface of a CD that scatters light and doesn't reflect it. If the disc is manufactured, pits are actual depressions within the disc. On recorded CDs and DVDs, pits are simply opaque spots within the dye (or crystalline) layer.

RAM: (Short for Random Access Memory.) The temporary storehouse for the data your computer and its programs need to run. As you probably know, however, turning off your computer causes you to lose the data that's stored in RAM (hence the development of the hard drive, which stores that data permanently).

Red Book: The international engineering standard that specifies the file structure of audio CDs. An audio CD you've recorded must comply with Red Book standards to be compatible with your audio CD player.

refurbished: Used or returned hardware that has been "fixed" (hopefully by the manufacturer) and resold at a much lower price. (I would say selling refurbished merchandise is also called a SCAM, but that's also in this glossary.)

restocking fee: (Also called a rip-off.) A fee charged by most online and local computer stores if you return an item — even if it's unopened.

SCAM: (Short for SCSI Configured Automatically.) A feature that allows your SCSI adapter card to automatically allocate SCSI ID numbers to all SCAM-compliant SCSI devices. SCAM makes things easier for both you and your PC.

screen printing: A printing process that adds layers of different-color inks through a series of stencils to create a single multicolored image. Most manufactured CD labels are screen printed.

SCSI: (Short for Small Computer Systems Interface.) A popular adapter choice for high-speed internal and external devices, like hard drives, recorders, and scanners. SCSI adapters are available for both Macs and PCs.

SCSI ID: A unique number assigned to a SCSI device that identifies it. Assigning the same SCSI ID to two SCSI devices will probably result in a locked computer.

secure connection: An encrypted connection between you and a Web site that helps prevent your personal data from being intercepted. Whenever you're buying something on the Web, frequent only online stores that offer a secure connection for your credit card number.

slave: The setting for an EIDE device that designates it as the secondary device on that EIDE cable. An EIDE recorder can be set to "multiple drive, slave unit" (if it's the secondary drive with another device on the cable).

slideshow: Just like the slideshows that Uncle Milton used to bore the entire family during reunions — only now the images are displayed on your computer monitor or your TV. The photographs are files stored on your hard drive or a DVD disc, and your computer or DVD player, rather than a clunky projector, does the work.

static electricity: The archenemy of any computer hardware; a type of electricity that can destroy any circuit board in a flash (pun intended, unfortunately). Always touch the metal chassis of your computer before handling any internal computer device or adapter card to discharge any static electricity on your body.

terminator: Both sides of a SCSI device chain must be terminated using a switch or small resistor pack. Without correct termination, your SCSI devices don't work.

thumbwheel: A rotating wheel you can use to select the SCSI ID on a SCSI recorder.

track: On an audio CD, a single section of audio (typically a single song) you can jump to immediately. On a data CD, a track is simply a section of the CD-ROM that contains data (many CD-ROMs contain only a single data track that holds all the files).

track-at-once: The default recording mode for most recording software. The laser beam writes each track one at a time, and the recording laser is turned off between tracks.

UDF: (Short for Universal Disc Format.) See *packet-writing*.

USB: (Short for Universal Serial Bus.) A type of connection used to add external devices, like recorders and printers, to both PC and Macintosh computers. The USB port offers Plug and Play support, so you can connect a USB device without rebooting your computer.

Video CD: A CD recording format that can store high-quality MPEG video for viewing on a video CD player.

virtual memory: A method that uses hard drive space to "increase" the amount of memory available to your computer. Both Windows and Mac OS use virtual memory to run programs that would normally fail because your computer had insufficient RAM.

WAV: The Windows standard format for digital sound. WAV files can be played directly from your hard drive or recorded as part of an audio CD.

WYSIWYG: An absolutely ridiculous acronym that stands for What You See Is What You Get, now taken to mean a visual or object-oriented computer application. If you know who created this travesty, please let me know so that I can send the culprit a rotten tomato.

X factor: The author's term for the figure used to indicate the speed of CD and DVD recorders (as well as read-only CD-ROM and DVD drives). It represents the multiplier of the data transfer rate for the first single-speed drives (150 kilobytes per second). For example, a 10x drive is ten times faster than an original single-speed CD-ROM drive.

Index

Notes

Notes

Notes

Notes

Notes